Project Zero Frameworks for Early Childhood Education
Volume 3

W9-AEE-006

Project Spectrum:

Preschool Assessment Handbook

Project Zero Frameworks for Early Childhood Education
Volume 3

Howard Gardner
David Henry Feldman
Mara Krechevsky
General Editors

FRANKLIN PIERCE
COLLEGE LIBRARY
RINDGE, N.H. 03461

Project Spectrum:
Preschool Assessment Handbook

Mara Krechevsky

TEACHERS
COLLEGE
PRESS

Teachers College • Columbia University
New York and London

Published by Teachers College Press, 1234 Amsterdam
Avenue, New York, NY 10027

Copyright © 1998 by The President and Fellows of Harvard
College

All rights reserved. No part of this publication may be
reproduced or transmitted in any form or by any means,
electronic or mechanical, including photocopy, or any
information storage and retrieval system, without permission
from the publisher

"Happy Birthday to You" words and music by Mildred J. Hill
and Patty S. Hill. © 1935 (renewed) Summy-Birchard Music.
All rights reserved. Used by permission of Warner Bros.
Publications U.S. Inc., Miami, Florida 33014.

"Up in the Air" words and music by Raymond Abrashkin.
From *Music for Ones and Twos.* © 1983 by Songs Music, Inc. ,
Scarborough, New York, 10510. Used by permission.

ISBN 0-8077-3768-2 (paper)

Printed on acid-free paper

Manufactured in the United States of America

05   04   03   02   01   00   99   98   8   7   6   5   4   3   2   1

CONTENTS

Acknowledgments vii

Introduction 1

   Theoretical Framework 2

   Using This Handbook 6

Chapter 1 Movement Domain 11

   Creative Movement Curriculum
      with Carey Wexler-Sherman 12

   Tables 21

   Obstacle Course
      with Julie Viens 24

   Tables 31

Chapter 2 Language Domain 37

   Storyboard Activity 39

   Tables 43

   Reporter Activities 53

   Tables 58

Chapter 3 Mathematical Domain 69

   Dinosaur Game 70

   Tables 75

   Bus Game 78

   Tables 84

Chapter 4 Science Domain 93

   Discovery Area
      with Jie-Qi Chen and Valerie Ramos-Ford 94

   Tables 101

   Treasure Hunt Game 103

   Tables 107

   Sink and Float Activity
      with Valerie Ramos-Ford 109

   Tables 114

   Assembly Activity 117

   Tables 124

Chapter 5 Social Domain 129

    Classroom Model 130

    Tables 135

    Peer Interaction Checklist
        with Margaret Adams 140

    Tables 144

Chapter 6 Visual Arts Domain 153

    Art Portfolio 154

    Tables 159

Chapter 7 Music Domain 169

    Singing Activity 171

    Tables 175

    Music Perception Activity
        with Jenifer Goldman 184

    Tables 189

Chapter 8 Working Styles 193

    Tables 196

References 201

Appendixes 205

    A.   Spectrum Parent Questionnaire 206

    B.   Sample Calendar for Spectrum Class 208

    C.   Sample Spectrum Profiles 209

    D.   Sample Parent Letter 212

    E.   Spectrum Profile Parent Response Form 213

    F.   Description of Spectrum Activities 214

    G.   Project Spectrum Parent Activities Manual 217

    H.   Related Articles 242

    I.   Other Materials Available from Project Spectrum 243

    J.   Spectrum Network 244

    K.   Handbook Evaluation Form 248

ACKNOWLEDGMENTS

The research described in this handbook was supported from 1984 to 1993 by generous grants from the Spencer Foundation, the William T. Grant Foundation, and the Rockefeller Brothers Fund. I am grateful to the many researchers, teachers, administrators, consultants, parents, and children who have collaborated with us on the various phases of Project Spectrum.

I would like to thank all of the Spectrum research staff who were involved in developing and refining the assessment approach presented here. The project was collaborative from the beginning, with the team members generating ideas, writing up activities, and critiquing one another's work. Certain people were instrumental in initiating the project and conceptualizing many of the assessments in this handbook. The original research group included Ulla Malkus, Janet Stork and myself. Our team gradually expanded to include Lori Grace, Thomas Hatch, Laurie Leibowitz, and Carey Wexler-Sherman, with Margaret Adams, Jenifer Goldman, Valerie Ramos-Ford, and Julie Viens joining us for the final phases. All of these individuals made invaluable contributions to the *Handbook*, either through designing, writing up, or refining the assessment activities.

In particular, the following people contributed major sections to the *Project Spectrum: Preschool Assessment Handbook*: Creative Movement, Carey Wexler-Sherman; Obstacle Course, Julie Viens; Discovery Area, Jie-Qi Chen and Valerie Ramos-Ford; Sink and Float Activity, Valerie Ramos-Ford; Peer Interaction Checklist, Margaret Adams; and Music Perception Activity, Jenifer Goldman. The scoring system for the Visual Arts section was originally developed by Jie-Qi Chen and Sylvia Feinburg for the Spectrum Field Inventory. Valerie Ramos-Ford created the Parent Activities Manual. I am especially grateful to Jie-Qi Chen and Julie Viens for their wisdom and help during the final hours of putting the *Project Spectrum: Preschool Assessment Handbook* together.

Some of the activities in this book were inspired by the previous research of investigators at Project Zero. Specifically, the Storyboard Activity is based on work by Dennis Palmer Wolf, the Bus Game is based on work by Joseph Walters and Matthew Hodges, and some of the music activities are based on work by Lyle Davidson and Larry Scripp. There are probably many other influences that I have not recognized explicitly, but I would like to acknowledge all of my colleagues at Project Zero and the Tufts University Eliot-Pearson Department of Child Study whose work and insights have contributed to this volume.

I would also like to thank the directors, teachers, and graduate students at the Eliot-Pearson Children's School for their support and contributions to the development of the project. Over the years, the following individuals have made important contributions to the research: Betty Allen, Ellen Band, Jinny Chalmers,

Carolee Fucigna, Matthew Goodman, Penny Hauser-Cram, Cynthia Lawrence, Priscilla Little, Sunita Mookerjee, Mark Ogonowski, and Ann Olcott.

I am also grateful to the project consultants, who provided many insights in the early phases of the project: David Alexander, Lyle Davidson, Martha Davis, Sylvia Feinburg, Gerald Lesser, Lynn Meltzer, Roberta Pasternak, Larry Scripp, Joseph Walters, Dean Whitla, Ellen Winner, and Dennis Palmer Wolf.

In the later phases of the project, we benefited from the combined wisdom of a number of researchers, teachers, parents, administrators, and consultants. Among those I would like to thank are Kim Austin, Ann Benjamin, Andrea Bosch, Lonnie Carton, Jill Christiansen, Jackie Cooper, John Davis, MaryAnn DeAngelis, Roger Dempsey, Marta Dennis, Susan Donath, Nathan Finch, Rochelle Frei, Jim Gray, Corinne Greene, Deborah Hicks, Pamela Holmes, Deborah Hurley, Arthur Kempton, Marie Kropiwnicki, Wayne LaGue, Jean McDonagh, Ellen McPherson, Jane Moore, William Moran, Amy Norton, Ellen O'Brien, Mary O'Brien, Miriam Raider-Roth, Deborah Rambo, Ilyse Robbins, Jeri Robinson, Mary Russo, Cheryl Seabrook-Wilson, Gwen Stith, Winifred O'Toole, Lindsay Trementozzi, Ana Vaisenstein, and Roger Weissberg.

I would also like to thank the principal investigators of Project Spectrum, David Feldman and Howard Gardner, without whom this work would not have been possible. They provided the intellectual and spiritual inspiration for the Spectrum framework, as well as much support, guidance, and constructive feedback throughout the project. I owe a special debt to Howard Gardner, whose encouragement, wisdom, friendship, and counsel were instrumental to my completing this book.

A number of individuals made important contributions to the final production of the *Project Spectrum: Preschool Assessment Handbook*. Roger Dempsey created the charming and artful illustrations for the different activities. Emily Isberg's precise and thoughtful editing improved the text immensely. I will always be grateful to her for her clear and careful work. Barry Schuchter provided skill and advice in creating the tables, and with help from Nathan Finch and Julie Viens enabled us to meet our constantly changing deadlines. Shirley Veenema lent her technical and artistic expertise to the manuscript's layout and design, and was instrumental in helping to bring this project to fruition. Throughout the last phase, I turned to her that I might catch a glimpse of the light at the end of the long production tunnel. Finally, Noel White applied his keen proofreading skills to catch last-minute infelicities in the text.

Last, but by no means least, I would like to thank the children and parents of the 1985–1988 Spectrum classrooms at Eliot-Pearson for participating with such enthusiasm and grace in our project. Without them, the *Project Spectrum: Preschool Assessment Handbook* would remain but a gleam in a researcher's eye.

Mara Krechevsky
Cambridge, MA

INTRODUCTION

—A BRIEF OVERVIEW

Project Spectrum is a 9-year research and development project, based on the theories of Howard Gardner of Harvard University and David Feldman of Tufts University. During Phase I of the project (1984–1988), our goal was to develop a new means of assessing the cognitive abilities of preschool children. With support from the Spencer Foundation, we devised a set of curricular and assessment materials to tap a wider range of cognitive and stylistic strengths than typically had been addressed in traditional early childhood education programs. In Phase II (1988–1989), we received support from the William T. Grant Foundation to determine whether the Spectrum approach could be modified to identify relative cognitive strengths in kindergarten and first grade children, particularly those at risk of school failure. The Grant Foundation then provided support for Phase III (1990–1992), during which we investigated whether the academic performance of at-risk children could be improved by identifying and nurturing their areas of strength. We adapted the Spectrum activities for use in first-grade classrooms and implemented them in the Somerville, Massachusetts public schools. We also received support from the Rockefeller Brothers Fund to introduce Spectrum materials in nonschool contexts, such as children's museums and a mentoring program.

Over the past 9 years, the Spectrum approach has been adapted for a variety of purposes by researchers and practitioners. It has provided educators with an alternative assessment tool and a framework for curriculum enrichment. Spectrum is perhaps best viewed as a theory-based approach to assessment and educational practice in the early childhood years, with the explicit goal of identifying and nurturing the distinctive cognitive strengths and interests of young children. By recognizing abilities in music, movement, mechanical science, and other areas that are not usually emphasized, Spectrum provides a way in which to build children's feelings of worth and to identify endeavors in which they can show their competence.

The *Project Spectrum: Preschool Assessment Handbook* provides a comprehensive description of the Spectrum preschool assessment battery developed during Phase I of the project. The assessments include 15 separate measures surveying seven different domains of knowledge (see box on page 3), as well as a list of various working styles that describe a child's approach to a particular task (see p. 196). The assessment criteria are based on our work with 4-year-old children. However, a number of the activities have been used successfully with children as young as 3 and as old as 6, and the scoring criteria can be modified accordingly. The handbook is probably most useful for directors of early childhood education programs, instructors at schools of education, student teachers, researchers, state and city department of education officials, and teachers interested in expanding their resources.

❏ THEORETICAL FRAMEWORK

Over the past decade, a number of cognitive and developmental psychologists, Gardner and Feldman among them, have espoused a broader view of human cognition than traditionally has been put forth. Instead of conceptualizing intelligence as a single or general cognitive structure, they have chosen to explore a more pluralistic view of intelligence, one that takes into account a wider range of skills and understandings.

In 1980, Feldman (1980, 1994) proposed his theory of nonuniversal development in an attempt to move the field of developmental psychology beyond an exclusive consideration of universals in development. In contrast to *universal development*, which is virtually inevitable and will occur in all children regardless of background and experience, *nonuniversal development* is neither spontaneous nor fully achievable by all individuals. Feldman suggests that children progress through a continuum of domains ranging from universal to unique, and that individuals may be highly developed in some domains but not in others (see diagram that follows).

• *Universal* domains refer to developmental experiences that are inherent in human beings, such as object permanence (knowing that an object still exists after it is out of sight).

• *Pancultural* domains, such as language, do not need to be taught formally but develop spontaneously in the presence of other human beings.

• *Cultural* domains are bodies of knowledge and skill that all individuals within a given culture are expected to acquire up to a certain level; reading, writing, and arithmetic are examples in the United States.

• *Discipline-based* domains involve the development of expertise in a particular discipline, such as law or chemistry, whereas *idiosyncratic* domains represent areas of specialization within a discipline. Patent law and organic chemistry are examples of specialties in law and chemistry respectively.

• *Unique* developmental achievements occur when the existing limits of a domain have been transcended. The discovery of the double helix, and the subsequent appreciation of its contribution to our understanding of the nature of life, were unique developmental achievements that transformed biological knowledge.

Both universal and nonuniversal domains can be organized into a broad set of qualitatively distinct stages or levels through which one moves from novice to master (Feldman, 1980, 1986, 1994). In universal domains, developmental progress results from the spontaneous tendencies of the child to learn about the world. In nonuniversal domains, advancement requires specific environmental contributions that must be brought to bear in a sustained and systematic way (Feldman, 1985, 1987). Teachers, schools, peers, materials, competitions, rewards, and the incentives of a domain must all be well orchestrated for development to occur in an optimal fashion.

Like Feldman, Gardner argues that human beings as a species have evolved over the millennia to carry out several distinct, relatively independent forms of competence. In 1983, Gardner set forth his theory of multiple intelligences (MI theory) in the book, *Frames of Mind* (see also Gardner, 1993). Gardner defines intelligence as the ability to solve problems or fashion products that are valued in one or more cultural settings. In contrast to most definitions of intelligence that emphasize linguistic and logical-mathematical abilities, Gardner's definition includes the abilities to compose a symphony, build a bridge, execute a painting, or run a political campaign.

To identify his candidate intelligences, Gardner examined evidence from a wide array of fields, including the nature of cognition in "special" populations, such as idiots savants, prodigies, and autistic children; the breakdown of cognitive capacities under conditions of

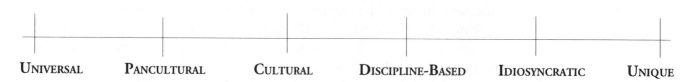

| UNIVERSAL | PANCULTURAL | CULTURAL | DISCIPLINE-BASED | IDIOSYNCRATIC | UNIQUE |

PROJECT SPECTRUM ACTIVITIES

MOVEMENT
- Creative Movement Measure:
    Biweekly Movement Curriculum
- Athletic Movement Measure:
    Obstacle Course

SOCIAL
- Social Analysis Measure:
    Classroom Model
- Social Roles Measure:
    Peer Interaction Checklist

LANGUAGE
- Invented Narrative Measure:
    Storyboard Activity
- Descriptive Narrative Measure:
    Reporter Activities

VISUAL ARTS
- Art Portfolio:
    Yearlong collection of
    children's artwork
    supplemented by
    structured activities

MATHEMATICS
- Counting/Strategy Measure:
    Dinosaur Game
- Calculating/Notation Measure:
    Bus Game

MUSIC
- Production Measures:
    Happy Birthday
    New Songs—"Up in the Air"
                    "Animal Song"
- Perception Measures:
    Pitch-Matching Games
    Song Recognition

SCIENCE
- Naturalist Measure:
    Discovery Area
- Logical Inference Measure:
    Treasure Hunt Game
- Hypothesis-Testing Measure:
    Sink and Float Activity
- Mechanical Measure:
    Assembly Activity

WORKING STYLES
- Working Styles Checklist

brain damage; and the evolution of cognition in different species and different cultures. As a result of this survey, Gardner proposed seven different intelligences: linguistic, logical-mathematical, musical, spatial, bodily-kinesthetic, interpersonal, and intrapersonal. Gardner does not claim that this roster of intelligences is exhaustive; rather, his aim is to establish support for a more pluralistic view of cognition. There may well turn out to be more "intelligences" or even "subintelligences;" in fact, Gardner recently has proposed an eighth intelligence, that of the naturalist, characterized by a fascination with the natural world (Gardner, 1998).

According to Gardner (1987a, 1987b, Gardner & Hatch, 1980), the intelligences can be viewed as psycho-biological potentials or proclivities that may or may not be realized in significant adult activities depending on a variety of cultural and environmental factors. While all humans exhibit the full range of intelligences, individuals differ both for genetic and environmental reasons in the extent to which they display different competencies. The developmental trajectories, information-processing capacities, and problem-solving features of each intelligence are to a large extent independent of one another. However, the intelligences do not work in isolation. Nearly every cultural role or product of any sophistication requires a combination of skills and intelligences.

Project Spectrum is based on the theories of Feldman and Gardner, which share many common features. First, both Feldman and Gardner call attention to the pluralistic nature of human cognition. Second, both theorists recognize the importance of the interaction between biological proclivities and opportunities for learning in a culture. They believe that human culture not only influences, but actively constructs, both the course and degree of an individual's developmental progress. Finally, both Feldman and Gardner maintain that cognitive ability is domain-specific, and that people need to be exposed to materials and information from different domains before their cognitive abilities and potentials can adequately be assessed.

—THE SPECTRUM APPROACH

The Spectrum assessments were designed specifically to identify intellectual *strengths*. (We use the terms *ability*, *strength*, and *intelligence*

interchangeably in the text.) The underlying hypothesis of the project is that because cognitive development is differentiated, each child has areas of relative strength. Many early childhood educators continue to think of children's growth in terms of universal development. Typical informal assessments of preschool children's cognitive ability include such comments as "asks questions," "sees a project through to completion," or "has an age-appropriate attention span." But the Spectrum approach suggests that these processes may vary as a function of the child's ability and interest in a content area.

Rather than offering another test, Spectrum's assessment approach provides opportunities for children to become engaged in a variety of domains. The Spectrum materials ensure exposure to domains that feature social, bodily, musical, mathematical, linguistic, mechanical, artistic, and scientific experiences. We are particularly concerned that children who are strong in areas not traditionally recognized in school be provided with the opportunity to find a meaningful connection with a content area during the course of the Spectrum assessments. Once a child's intellectual profile has emerged, targeted educational experiences can be provided that build on her strengths, foster her self-esteem, and broaden her life experience. (Note: For ease of exposition, the personal pronoun "she" is used throughout the text.) Although we have tried to provide a means for identifying early markers of unusual talents, we cannot yet speak to whether the presence of such markers is predictive of later success, or whether their absence precludes outstanding achievement later in life.

Many teachers have an intuitive sense for what our assessments try to capture; we hope to expand the range of activities on which they can draw to help elicit and document each child's potential. Many classrooms with a full and varied curriculum nonetheless offer only a few of the areas that might tap a child's strengths and interests. Our materials ensure exposure to many domains, including some with which an individual teacher might not have felt comfortable in the past. We hope to give teachers a structure that will help them to think more clearly and systematically about areas they might have skipped over or not known how to approach.

The Spectrum materials can be regarded as useful, even powerful, tools that teachers can select and use as needed. Teachers can adopt the Spectrum philosophy, using its structure to combine learning and assessment and to expand the range of activities available to students. Or, they may use individual activities to support a venture into new educational territory. For example, a teacher more familiar with art than with mathematics might retain her own art curriculum while adopting Spectrum's number tasks.

Teachers also may find that Spectrum's system for identifying children's individual strengths can supplement their current assessment strategies. The teacher mentioned above might use Spectrum's art portfolio approach to document the insights she has gained about a child through personal observation. In addition, she may acquire qualitatively different information in the one-on-one, structured situation of the assessment activity than when working with children as a class or small group. Because teachers have different styles and personalities, they will conduct the activities in different ways. In all cases, the results of the assessments should supplement, not replace, the teachers' own intuitions and observations. Parent interviews and questionnaires can provide even more information about individual children (see Appendix A).

—DISTINCTIVE FEATURES

Using the seven intelligences as a point of departure, we selected for assessment 15 areas of competence, including production and perception in music, invented and descriptive narrative in language, and expressive and athletic movement in the bodily-kinesthetic realm. We then identified a number of core capacities or abilities in each area of competence. For example, in the mathematical domain, we defined as core capacities counting, simple calculation and notation skills, adherence to rules, and strategy formation. We then drew on our observations of 4-year-old children in the classroom to refine further the selection of age-appropriate abilities in a domain.

There are four distinctive features of the Spectrum approach to assessment:

1. *Embedding assessments in meaningful, real-world activities.* We used the concept of adult *end states* to focus on the abilities relevant to achieving significant and rewarding adult roles. Thus, in the language domain, we look at a child's ability to tell stories or provide a descriptive account of an experience, rather than her ability to memorize a set of lines. No matter what the domain, children are almost always given something to manipulate, for example a playdough birthday cake for a singing activity; a board game with dice and small dinosaur figures for a math activity; and a classroom model, with small figures of children and teachers, for a social activity.

Examples of relevant end states include reporter, mathematician, naturalist, mechanic, singer, dancer, and politician. However, as noted above, children's performances on these activities should not be considered predictive of future vocations. Rather, the use of end states helps to insure that the activities involve the application of skills in a context that is both meaningful to the child and recognized as valuable by the culture.

2. *Blurring the line between curriculum and assessment.* We also tried to blur the line dividing curriculum and assessment by rejecting the traditional intelligence test setting of a small room with an unfamiliar test-giver administering timed and standardized instruments. In our view, these provide too limited and skewed a view of the child. The Spectrum games and activities were based on themes that are familiar to and motivating for 4-year-olds; for example, the Treasure Hunt Game and the Classroom Model invite children to get involved in the content area, regardless of their level of skill. The Spectrum assessments are carried out over time in the child's own environment, and resemble other activities in the classroom. Teacher support or scaffolding is supplied as needed to allow the child to put forth her best effort on a task.

Of course, some areas lend themselves better than others to ongoing assessment. For instance, in the visual arts, we use a portfolio approach. But even if a task is presented as a structured activity, the materials can stay in the classroom afterward and yield rich incidental information about what children remember and how they build on what they have learned. Leaving the materials in the room also provides a sense of continuity. Teachers can gain insight into how children teach each other to use the materials and create new ways for using them. We hope that all the Spectrum activities will become part of the regular classroom curriculum.

3. *Attending to the stylistic dimensions of performance.* From our observations of children participating in the Spectrum activities, we soon realized we needed to add

another dimension to our assessment procedures in order to represent more accurately a child's approach to the different domains. We created a Working Styles Checklist that can be filled out for each activity and that describes the child's relationship to the materials or content area (see Chapter 8). Examples of working styles include a child's level of confidence, persistence, and attention to detail. This information can help teachers identify working styles that are content specific versus those that cut across domains.

4. *Using measures that are intelligence-fair.* Finally, the Spectrum measures are designed to tap abilities directly, via the medium of a domain, rather than to use language and logic as the assessment vehicles. Thus, the music assessments are based on singing and playing musical instruments, whereas the mechanical activities entail taking apart and putting together simple mechanical objects. Some materials lend themselves to use in more than one domain; for example, the classroom model can be used for looking at language as well as social skills. However, if a child's proclivity in one domain turns up in another, we make special note of it. Such information can be quite valuable for determining the robustness of a child's particular strength.

☐ USING THIS HANDBOOK

This handbook offers a step-by-step description of the 15 assessment activities as well as an explanation of the theoretical underpinnings, and thus includes all the information you need to perform Spectrum assessments in your classroom. However, few teachers have the time necessary to do the kind of one-on-one evaluation we describe. Therefore, we hope you will adapt our procedures to meet your own classroom needs.

The format of the activities derives from Phase I of the Spectrum study, when we developed most of the activities for a one-on-one research model. Our research site during this period was the Eliot-Pearson Children's School, a laboratory school associated with Tufts University in Medford, Massachusetts. From 1984 to 1986 we designed, piloted, and refined the majority of assessment activities. From 1986 to 1988 we conducted the assessment battery in two classrooms totaling thirty-two 4-year-old children and seven 3-year-old children. The children were primarily white, and from middle- and upper-income families. Unlike many

half-day programs, which are 15 hours a week, or day care and public school programs, which may be even longer, the Eliot-Pearson program was in session only 10 hours a week. This set-up is reflected in our timetable.

We would like to suggest three different models for using this handbook—although there are, no doubt, many more:

• *Research:* This is the model we used in developing the activities. It can be used by other researchers investigating children's cognitive development or by teachers with sufficient resources. Of the three models, it yields the most detailed information about each child, but is the most labor intensive. One adult administers the assessment and another adult serves as observer. If two adults are not available, many of the assessments can be video- or audiotaped and scored later by the task administrator. All children participate in each activity. Alternatively, the Spectrum Field Inventory (Adams, 1993) offers a streamlined version of the full assessment battery. The Inventory consists of assessments from six domains—social understanding, math, music, art, language, and mechanical science—and can be administered in two sessions.

• *Selective Assessment:* Instead of administering all of the activities to all children individually, a teacher might invite selected children to participate in selected activities. The teacher might use this approach because she thinks an individual child exhibits exceptional strength in a domain, or because of a desire to supplement her informal observations with a more structured or comprehensive assessment. Another option is to administer an activity to a small group of children at the same time, perhaps in the context of an activity center.

• *Observational Framework:* Individual Spectrum activities or spin-off ideas can be used to enhance activity centers or lessons already in place. The Spectrum list of domains and abilities provides a framework for organizing informal observations of children as they go about Spectrum and other classroom activities. Anecdotal observations can be recorded daily and saved in children's individual files. The handbook then serves as a vehicle for professional development, offering new ideas for conducting domain-specific observations of children engaged in meaningful tasks.

The teacher can use not only written records, but also audio- and videotapes to record singing, storytelling, conversations, and other classroom activities. The art and discovery areas, block building, group time, and dramatic play all can be videotaped. Children can be encouraged to reflect on their activities by watching videotapes. If resources allow, copies of audio- and videotapes can be made for parents as well.

—HANDBOOK FORMAT

The handbook includes chapters on seven domains, or content areas, as well as a chapter on working styles. Each domain chapter is further divided into sections describing individual assessment activities (e.g., the "Mathematical Domain" chapter includes sections on the Dinosaur Game and the Bus Game). The domain chapters begin with a general introduction to the domain as it is viewed in our culture, including a brief overview of how ability in the domain develops in young children, and some citations of relevant research. The range of abilities exhibited by preschoolers is also described, as well as typical preschool classroom activities and assessment measures. Next, an entry titled "Conceptualizing the [domain] Activities" identifies the end states that guided our creation of the assessment activities, as well as the types of skills that characterize unusual competence in the content area.

The sections on the assessment activities are divided into five subsections: "Purpose and Activity Description," "Materials and Set-Up," "Procedure and Script, Scoring," and "Preliminary Results." All of the activities except for the Obstacle Course and the Discovery Area include preliminary results, the majority of which are from either the 1986–87 and/or 1987–88 class or from both. The results are intended to be illustrative, rather than comprehensive or prescriptive, of the different ways in which our population of children responded to the materials and activities. Most of the domain chapters conclude with a section titled "Further Suggestions for the Domain," which includes additional ideas for domain-related activities generated by the Spectrum research team. These ideas may be used as written, modified, or serve as catalysts to help teachers develop their own sets of domain-related activities.

Many of the "Procedure and Script" sections refer to scaffolding. We define scaffolding as adult assistance designed to support a child's participation in the Spectrum activities (Vygotsky, 1978; cf. Wertsch, 1985). The exact nature of the assistance varies across domains. The assistance is provided in order to determine not only what the child is able to do independently, but also what she is capable of accomplishing with prescribed amounts of help. Both the amount of scaffolding that a child requires and what a child is able to accomplish when supported in this manner vary considerably. Such information would be lost were scaffolding not provided. What a child can do with support has important implications for the types of tasks and guidance a teacher might provide. With regard to scoring, in some activities, points are subtracted for scaffolding (e.g., the Bus Game), whereas others treat scaffolding more as "prompts" to engage a child in the activity, and scoring is not affected (e.g., the Storyboard Activity).

How closely to follow the script and scoring sections depends on the reasons for conducting the activities. For research, the procedures must be consistent across children and activity, and any scaffolding must be systematically administered and recorded. However, if the aim is to introduce children to areas they have not yet explored, or to identify strengths as yet uncovered, then the procedures can be more flexible.

—ONE WAY TO BEGIN

One way to begin using the handbook is to skim all of the sections. Then, start reading carefully in the areas in which you are most interested. It is probably a good idea to practice activities with another teacher, with one or more children while a team member watches, or both. It will probably take at least a year to become comfortable using the Spectrum battery.

If you wish to conduct a structured assessment, we recommend creating short "script" cards to refer to when administering an activity. These cards can include set-up information, diagrams, or both, as well as key words or written-out instructions and scaffolding for the different tasks. If you would like all children to participate, we recommend forming a list of volunteers, and then giving children who do not sign up a choice of taking their turn now or later.

Also, unless compelling reasons exist to the contrary, you should feel free to stop assessing after a certain point and commence other activities as you see fit. For example, if a child is completely unfamiliar with the demands of an activity such as the Dinosaur Game, or has no knowledge of board games in general, you may choose to focus on simply rolling one die. Likewise, if a child is at a loss when presented with the grinder, even after scaffolding, you can abandon the assessment and work with the child just to give her the experience of taking apart and reassembling the object.

—INTERPRETATION OF SCORES

In each domain, we have identified the central or core components of an activity. In reviewing children's scores, it is important for teachers to attend not only to the total score, but also to the points earned in each of the scoring categories. Children who receive the same total score may have different abilities.

For example, in the Dinosaur Game, children can earn points for understanding rules, counting, strategy, and articulation of reasoning. A child might reveal competence in strategic reasoning, but not in counting. Thus, children's overall scores on the activity are often not the most important or relevant piece of information for teachers; rather, they should be considered starting points.

The core components provide teachers with analytic tools that can be used to shape classroom-based observations of children. It is critical to supplement information about children's performances on the activities with information gathered during informal observations. Some of the Spectrum activities include systematic checklists for observing children over time, for example, in the social and natural science domains. The activities can also generate incidental information about a child's ability to understand and follow directions, as well as her general facility with language.

The scores on the Spectrum assessments must be interpreted with caution: They were conducted on a small, relatively homogeneous population, and they have not been normed. Children's performances on the activities should be considered a reflection of ability, interest, and experience in a particular setting at a particular point in time.

In no instance did we give parents actual scores. Findings from the Spectrum activities were reported to parents through narrative profiles and through parent conferences.

—COORDINATING THE YEARLONG BATTERY

The classroom teacher can select which Spectrum activities to perform, and in what order. However, if you wish to plan a yearlong sequence of activities (see the sample calendar in Appendix B), there are a few things to keep in mind:

1. It takes approximately 2 weeks for every child to participate in an activity, although this varies depending on the length of the school day, class size, number of teachers, and nature of the activity.

2. Because the first month of school is typically devoted to becoming acquainted with new surroundings, new people, and the basic classroom routines, the only activities listed on the sample calendar are starting an art portfolio for each child and introducing the Discovery Area. The first structured activity does not take place until October.

3. We recommend introducing the Dinosaur Game in the fall as the first structured activity, since most children find the activity highly engaging. The Dinosaur Game is less challenging than the second math activity, the Bus Game, which is not introduced until mid- to late spring. The fall is also a good time to introduce some of the ongoing activities and to establish them as regular parts of the classroom routine (e.g., the Creative Movement Curriculum and the Weekend News Activity).

4. For a number of activities, such as the Assembly and Storyboard tasks, related materials should be introduced prior to the actual assessment. Also, many of the activities lead to a variety of follow-up activities (e.g., children creating their own storyboards or classroom models to play with at home or in school). The continuity and experience provided by introducing related preparatory and follow-up materials are an important component of the assessment process.

5. To allow children time to settle into their routines and friendships, we recommend conducting the Classroom Model Activity after midyear. This will also give you time to create an accurate "social map" of the classroom, with which children's responses on the activity can be compared.

—SPECTRUM PROFILES

The culmination of all of the information that has been collected on each child is a Spectrum Profile, written at year's end. The profile draws on the formal and informal information gathered in each domain, both from the Spectrum assessments and teachers' regular classroom observations. It is a description of the configuration of a child's intellectual strengths, with recommendations for home, school, and wider community activities.

To make it easier to write profiles, you may find it helpful to create large folders or portfolios for each child. These folders or portfolios might contain scoresheets, observation checklists, anecdotal observations, working style information, the child's written and art work, artifacts, photographs, and video- or audiotapes. Information from parent questionnaires or interviews also can be included.

The focus of the profile is the individual child. The profile begins by identifying a child's relative strengths and interests. Because the Spectrum assessments have not yet been normed, comparisons to a child's age group are made only if the child clearly demonstrates outstanding ability. Although the profiles were originally intended to identify only strengths, responses from the parents of the 1986–1987 Spectrum class indicated that they wanted to hear more about the range of a child's abilities. Thus, subsequent profiles included a broader discussion of children's performances on the Spectrum activities (see sample profiles in Appendix C). The following suggestions provide one model for writing a profile.

In the first part of the profile, we described the most general level of ability in which a child exhibited a strength (e.g., storytelling), supported by specific examples from the child's performance on an activity and reference to core components of the domain (e.g., the child's use of narrative voice or expressive dialogue, along with actual excerpts from the child's story). Wherever possible, we drew substantiating information from classroom observations. As appropriate, we made comparisons across domains (e.g., between the kinds of narrative a child generated when using the storyboard and the classroom model, or between a child's singing and movement ability). Also, we noted whether a child's strengths surfaced in other areas (e.g., if she sang parts of her story, or moved more creatively when storyboard figures were used in the Creative Movement sessions). We also used this first section of the profile to note any changes in a child's strengths, in interests during the course of the year or in both.

The second part of the profile described a child's working styles — in particular, whether her approach to an activity was consistent across domains, or whether it varied depending on the content area. Some children exhibited working styles such as reflectiveness and attention to detail only in their areas of strength (see Krechevsky & Gardner, 1990). This section also addressed issues related to the setting for the activity: Was the child more comfortable with structured or unstructured tasks? Did she prefer to work alone, one-on-one, or in a group?

The third part of the profile included suggestions for activities that could be carried out at home or in the community. We also offered suggestions for ways to link up strengths with areas of difficulty: For example if a child revealed a strength in storytelling, but was struggling socially, we suggested that she tell or act out a story with other children. We believe that it is critical to involve parents in their children's education. However, although nurturing an area of strength may provide a rewarding experience to a child, parents and teachers should not focus only on strengths and pursue them to the exclusion of other experiences.

We mailed the profile home to parents as part of a packet that contained an explanatory letter (see Appendix D), a Profile Response Form (see Appendix E), and resource material. The letter describes how to interpret the Spectrum profile. It cautions parents that the profile reflects the abilities of their child in the context of her current classroom, and should not be interpreted prescriptively. It is also important to make clear that if a child's performance in an area is not discussed, it does not necessarily mean that the child has a weakness in that area, but only that no notable strength was revealed. Because the Spectrum activities were designed to identify strengths, they should not be considered diagnostic of weakness. However, we did comment if a child's difficulty with an activity was particularly noticeable.

To parents of children in the 1987–88 Spectrum class, we also sent a brief description of the Spectrum activities (see Appendix F) and a Parent Activities Manual (see Appendix G). The manual includes suggestions for activities that can be conducted at home, using easily acquired and inexpensive materials. The activities are categorized by domain. For example, math activities include estimating and counting games, science includes seed-growing experiments and assembly activities, and art includes a variety of painting and three-dimensional art projects. We also included a list of local community resources, primarily categorized by domain, at the end of the manual. (The list of sites is intended as a model only, since the information was compiled in 1988 and would need to be revised outside the Boston area.) You can draw on your own curriculum, as well as community resources, to create a document suitable for your own classroom.

—HANDBOOK EVALUATION FORM

For those readers who would like to know more about Project Spectrum or implement the approach themselves, we have included a list of scholarly articles (see Appendix H), a description of additional materials and services (see Appendix I), and a list of teachers, administrators, and researchers who have participated in Spectrum and are willing to discuss their experiences (see Appendix J).

We welcome feedback from readers and users of this handbook to guide us in preparing future editions or other support material. Please use the Handbook Evaluation Form in Appendix K, or send letters to Project Spectrum at

Project Zero
Harvard Graduate School of Education
323 Longfellow Hall
Cambridge, MA 02138.

CHAPTER 1
MOVEMENT DOMAIN

—INTRODUCTION

Physical activity is an important part of the normal development of all young children. Children use their bodies to express emotions and ideas, to explore athletic skills, and to test the limits of their capacities. During the first year of life, the infant's reflexes gradually develop into simple, goal-directed acts as she gains greater control over her movements and articulates intentions. The fine and gross motor skills develop quickly as the child becomes more aware of her own body and starts to explore what she can do. Two-year-olds love to walk and run where they please, relishing the challenge of climbing a new set of stairs or jumping from a low ledge. Three-year-olds enjoy similar activities, but are more physically competent and spend their time riding tricycles, gliding down slides, and improving their climbing skills on a variety of structures. By the age of 4 most children are eager to take some risks. They experiment with jumping from different heights, tumbling, and balancing.

The typical preschool environment emphasizes the acquisition of both large and small muscle skills. On the playground, children can run, swing, balance, climb, and slide. In the classroom, children can manipulate a variety of small objects such as beads and puzzles, improving both fine motor skills and eye-hand coordination. Many preschool programs do not, however, offer a formal movement or dance time for children on a regular basis.

For purposes of assessment, the movement domain traditionally has been defined in terms of a universal, stagelike progression of motor development against which one charts and ranks a child's ability. Testing in this area has often been used in response to concerns about possible lags or irregularities in children's development. Typically, the child is asked to perform a set of standard movements such as hops, skips, or balancing in order to determine her achieved developmental level (see, e.g., Folio & Fewell, 1974; Haines, Ames, & Gillespie, 1980; and McCarthy, 1972). There is little child input or choice, and instances of expressiveness or novel adaptations of movement sequences are not considered. Although experts such as Laban (1960) have developed sophisticated notational and interpretive systems to chart a child's development in creative dance and movement, such systems are often too technical and refined to be used by teachers in the preschool classroom.

The Spectrum approach to the movement domain addresses both children's creative and athletic abilities. We developed a series of movement activities that focuses on children's rhythmic and expressive sensitivities, as well as body control and awareness. This curriculum allows teachers to observe children's abilities over time in a planned setting. In the spring, we introduce an outdoor Obstacle Course to tap children's athletic abilities, including the capacity to execute goal-oriented movements. During the year, children may reveal different movement styles and preferences for aesthetic, athletic, or dramatic movement.

—Conceptualizing the Movement Activities

A variety of end states guided our conceptualization of the movement domain. The range of adult roles includes dancers, athletes, mimes, actresses, craftspeople, and machinists. Whereas dancers master the placement of their bodies through the use of space, balance, timing, and intensity, often with music as an important accompaniment, athletes combine grace, power, timing, speed, and teamwork to perform effectively in different sports. Mimes require keen observational skills in order to imitate and recreate different scenarios successfully. And machinists use both spatial abilities and fine motor skills in working with tools and mechanical equipment. Because the fine motor skills involved in the manipulation of objects can be discerned in some of our other activities (see, for example, the Assembly and Music Perception Activities), we chose to focus the movement curriculum primarily on gross motor skills.

The Obstacle Course requires the types of skills found in almost any sport. It provides children with the opportunity to develop movement strategies and to anticipate the next step in sequences involving complex and combined movements. In order to complete the course successfully, children need to exhibit coordination, agility, speed, balance, and power in adapting to the different kinds of challenges.

The Creative Movement sessions emphasize the more creative, dancelike elements of movement, focusing primarily on the components of rhythm and expressiveness. Children can explore rich imagery and themes with their bodies, often in accompaniment to music, thereby allowing observers to attend to the quality of a child's movement (how she moves) rather than the quantity (how fast or far she moves). Observers also can detect whether a child has a preferred movement style for expressing herself, in terms of tempo (fast or slow), quality (lyrical or staccato), or use of her body (whole body or using primarily one or several body parts).

In the context of assessment, the movement domain presents two main challenges. First, movement is fleeting in nature — when a child has completed a dance or athletic sequence, there are no tangible products to collect. Ideally, the issue of recording a child's performance could be addressed by videotaping the sessions as often as possible; however, we recognize that this is not a viable option in many preschool classrooms. A more realistic procedure is to fill out observation sheets immediately following the movement sessions (see Tables 1 and 2, pp. 21-22).

The second challenge is that many children and adults are sensitive about moving or dancing alone in front of other people. Therefore, the activities probably should not be carried out individually, as they are in other domains. Although a group setting offers a more comfortable context, it also complicates the assessment of a child's competence.

If video equipment is available, the teacher can view the tape several times, focusing on different children. If not, after the initial sessions, teachers can try to identify individual children who exhibit distinctive skills. Then, using the observation sheet and movement scoring criteria as a guide, teachers can conduct more focused observations.

☐ Creative Movement Curriculum

—Purpose and Activity Description

The Creative Movement Curriculum is designed to uncover children's strengths in five main areas of dance and creative movement. *Sensitivity to rhythm* refers both to a child's ability to move in synchrony with stable or changing rhythms, and to her ability to set a rhythm of her own and regulate it to achieve a desired effect. *Expressiveness* refers to a child's ability to evoke moods and images through movement using gestures and postures, and to her ability to respond to the mood or tonal quality of an instrument or music selection, such as lyrical or marching. *Body control* is the ability to place or use one's body to execute planned movements efficiently, for example when asked to freeze or balance. This category also includes the isolation of body parts and the execution of specific movements.

Separate from movement execution, the *generation of movement ideas* is an important component of the choreographer's art. Children who are skilled in this area might offer spontaneous suggestions for movement challenges (e.g., proposing that children in the group try to be a "clock"). These children also might volunteer extensions of or alternatives to a movement idea, like suggesting that classmates raise their arms and make them float like clouds in the sky. Ability in this category is not necessarily linked to skill in execution.

Responsiveness to music combines sensitivity to rhythm and expressiveness. Some children respond more to music than to a verbal idea or image. Moving in response to music is more open-ended than moving in response to a single image. This category identifies children who are particularly able to respond differently to different kinds of music, as opposed to those who repeat one kind of movement regardless of the type of music being played.

Teachers may find it useful to note three more dimensions:
1. *body awareness* (ability to identify and use different body parts and to understand their functions, e.g., shoulders, hips, fingers, etc.);
2. *movement memory* (ability to replicate movements executed by oneself or others);
3. *use of space* (ability to explore all available space, using different levels and areas of the room).

The activities in the curriculum are selected to avoid sex stereotyping and to be enjoyable and nonthreatening to both teacher and child. Use of a game like Simon Says provides an effective vehicle for looking at specific movement components such as body control, isolation of body parts, and responsiveness to expressive themes or images. Concluding every session with a music selection provides continuity and reveals how children synchronize their movements to changing rhythms and respond expressively to different moods.

The movement sessions should include no more than 8 or 10 children and should last approximately 20 minutes. In each session, we recommend that teachers use a balance of semistructured and more open-ended activities, and a mix of teacher- and child-initiated ideas.

—Materials and Set-Up

The movement sessions are most suitably conducted in a large, bounded space where children can move about freely. If such a location is not available, furniture in the classroom can be moved aside to create a space that is clearly delineated and safe for children. To avoid unnecessary confusion and testing of limits, work out any safety rules before the first session. Children's desires to have their own space can be recognized by providing each child with her own carpet square (or square outlined in tape on the floor). This space also

Recommendations for equipment include

1. tape recorder with tapes representing a range of music selections, e.g., Caribbean calypso, rumba, Indian raga, Indonesian gamelan, Appalachian instrumentals;
2. assortment of instruments, e.g., bells, tambourine, drum, rhythm sticks, xylophone;
3. variety of interesting objects for stimulating movement, e.g., miniature figures and strange animals (fluff creature and rubbery dinosaur from the storyboard), dolls (Raggedy Ann, wind-up), dreidels, yo-yos, scarves, and cloth pieces (chiffon, netting, jersey);
4. objects for tossing or for specific games, e.g., balloons, hula hoops, beanbags, and mirror.

Videotape equipment is helpful, but not necessary, for performing the assessment. If video equipment is used, place it above the level where the children are moving to cover as much of the group as possible.

can serve as a distinct and safe spot for children to move on and to which they can return.

—Procedure and Script

The movement sessions are designed to be introduced by the 2nd or 3rd month of school. Earlier in the year, you can use group-meeting, music, or outdoor activity time to introduce and to support basic movement concepts and activities. You can play simple finger and hand games, discuss the movement of mobiles or wind chimes hanging outside, and talk about the meaning of terms such as balance and rhythm. ~~Explaining~~ such concepts to children and encouraging them to think of their own examples of each term are important components of the movement curriculum.

The movement sessions will work best if children are prepared for them and if they see that movement is valued in different contexts. A ploy as simple as paying attention to one's hand brushing a paint stroke across a page can increase a child's awareness of her own gestures and movements.

In the first session, introduce children to the movement area and describe what they can look forward to doing in this "special space" set aside for their exploration of movement. Explain the weekly or biweekly schedule to them as well as any safety rules. Each session will begin with the children sitting on their carpet squares arranged in a large circle. Tell the children that they can choose if and when they want to participate, and that a space will be set aside for those who prefer to watch. Those children can be the "quiet and watchful audience." Finally, tell the children that you will always listen to their ideas, and ask that they in turn listen to yours.

The purpose of the first few sessions is to familiarize children with the space and to help them become comfortable moving in a group. You might also try one or both of the following simple activities:

1. Play a drum, tambourine, or both using different rhythms, and ask that all children wearing blue move to the beat, then all children wearing red, green, and so on.
2. Play a few rounds of Simon Says. Movement ideas include "move your hands very slowly," "make your body round like a ball," "move like a snail," or "move your arms or legs in as many ways as you can." Ask for children's suggestions.

In general, although you can model movement ideas for children to observe in the beginning, only demonstrate a movement once or twice. In this way, you can minimize the role of the adult and reduce the chances that children will rely solely on imitation.

The core activities of the Creative Movement Curriculum include Simon Says; the Mirror, Mirror and Drum and Bell game (see p. 18); moving different parts of the body at the same time; and responding to music, props, and verbal images (e.g., walking a tightrope or moving on ice). Every session ends with free dance to music. This gives children a chance to let go and

teachers the opportunity to sit back and watch. You should try to choose music selections that are culturally and ethnically diverse, rather than focusing solely on traditional Western music. The tempos should be moderate and steady in order to make reasonable rhythmic demands on the children, but some variation is appropriate. The range might include calypso, gamelan, and Peruvian music.

If children become too excited while dancing, you can turn off the music, allow them a minute or 2 to collect themselves, review any important limits, and then turn the music back on. You might also want to make a general rule for children to freeze any time that the music stops or the teacher makes a single drumbeat.

The social dynamics of the group setting may prove distracting for some children and make it hard for them to focus on movement. The individual carpet squares are one way to structure the sessions. The Simon Says game also gives you a means of control, because you can always say, "Simon says 'Stop.'" Some children invariably will suggest "running around" when it comes their turn for an idea. You might try asking for a variation: "What can you do to make it a little different?" "Can you run like a mouse" or "elephant" or "fly like butterflies fly?" The suggestion to "move as slowly as you can" is useful both for slowing children down and for observing them.

Finally, having children freeze when the music stops or when they hear your drumbeat or the word freeze is another effective control device. Using the same signal for each session reduces the need for reminders about what the signal means.

ACTIVITIES CALENDAR

The curriculum presented here represents only one way to implement the ideas we have introduced. You are encouraged to modify the activities to match your own areas of interest, style, and timetable. Also, as with the Discovery Area, some of the activities might not be suitable depending on the part of the country in which you live.

SEPTEMBER

1. Introduce finger, hand, and body movements during singing time. Ask children for their own ideas.

2. Begin to identify major body parts through songs and discussion. Children can discuss and demonstrate the different functions of their bodies and body parts, for example, what are all of the things that hands and fingers can do?

3. Hold an introductory session describing the movement area and its use.

OCTOBER

1. Introduce two basic movement concepts:

Use of space refers to using levels of high, middle, and low space. Ask children for examples of things that live close to the ground or at low levels (e.g., crawling babies, mushrooms, certain animals). Children can explore the different levels using familiar movements such as walking. Suggest that they walk in high and low space.

Directionality refers to moving up, down, over, under, around, and through. You can introduce these terms through such contrasts as high/low and over/under. (Fine-tuning is much easier once children understand the extremes.) Tape squares on the floor to explore directionality. Ask children to move around the squares or to hop in and out of them. You can make a Musical Squares game, asking children to "sit on top of a square" or "outside a square" when the music stops. You also can replace squares with propped-up hoops or chairs to crawl under and over.

2. If you are presenting any classroom activities related to harvesting or Halloween, the end of the movement sessions can be a good time to explore these themes. You can use new songs or select relevant background music for guided creative dances of farmers gathering their corn, Native Americans holding a feast, or the dance of ghosts and pumpkins (with the contrasting light, unearthly movements of ghosts and the round, thumpy movements of pumpkins).

NOVEMBER

1. Introduce the *rhythmic* components of movement. Discuss rhythm as a way of keeping time or expressing a steady beat with your body. Ask children to think of things that move to a set beat like clocks, windshield wipers, and metronomes. It might be useful to bring in some objects to show children.

2. Use a "talking drum" or other percussion instrument to help children keep time. While sitting, children can move their arms, heads, and other parts of their bodies to a steady, moderate beat. Challenge them to freeze whenever the drum stops. Children also

can be invited to close their eyes for part of this exercise to help them concentrate on the sound of the rhythm. This may help children who tend to follow others or to watch the teacher beating the drum.

Focus of Observation: Sensitivity to Rhythm.

3. *Canoe Trip*

Ask children to sit down, leaving plenty of room around themselves. Ask children if they have ever been in a canoe or rowboat. Demonstrate the motions of rowing, explaining that it is very important that a rower has a good, steady rhythm. Tell them that sometimes someone yells, "Stroke, stroke, stroke," so that the oarspeople will stay together, keeping the same rhythm.

When all of the children have their arms ready to begin rowing, start to beat a steady, moderate rhythm on the drum. Watch carefully to see who seems to move with the beat, to time their movements to the rhythm, or both. As you slow down or speed up the rhythm, children's sense of timing will become more apparent. For example, notice whether some children adapt the length of their stroke to allow for the more rapid beats.

Adaptations of this theme include having a canoe race, sawing down a tree, or having two children use opposite sides of an imaginary two-person saw.

Focus of Observation: Sensitivity to Rhythm, Body Control.

4. Introduce *balance.* Give each child a beanbag and have children practice balancing the beanbag on different parts of their bodies: knees, elbows, head, shoulders.

5. *The Tightrope Walker*

Ask children if they have ever seen a tightrope walker. If not, describe or demonstrate how the tightrope walker balances on a thin high wire. Lay down single strips of tape or two parallel lines several inches apart. Ask children to move like a tightrope walker or in any way they like as long as they stay on the line. You might want to add background music.

Focus of Observation: Body Control, Expressiveness.

DECEMBER

1. Introduce *expressive movement* and use of images. Discuss how our bodies help us to show feelings and thoughts. You might model a few moods or images for the children (again, contrasts work best). You also can show a film about the art of mime to demonstrate the use of movement to depict images, mood, and experiences. Or, you can show a dance film and follow up by asking children to describe the image or mood the dancers expressed.

2. Play Simon Says using some of the following examples:

—stiff (robot, tin man)
—floppy (rag doll, scarecrow)
—zig-zaggedy (snakes)
—things that float (balloons, feathers, bubbles)
—stretchy (rubber bands, taffy)
—jumpy (popcorn popping, frogs hopping)

—springy (trampoline, coils popping)

—jerky (marionette)

—smooth (skater)

—things that go around (carousel, spinning top)

—mechanical toy that winds up and goes until it runs down

—candle slowly burning down

You might want to begin the game by asking children to explore some of the more familiar qualities and images. It also will be easier at first if children stay in their own spaces. When possible, use images that children generate themselves.

Focus of Observation: Expressiveness, Generation of Movement Ideas, Body Control.

3. Bring in evocative objects or props that reflect some of the different movements and images you have discussed with the children: stretchy fabric, balloons, scarves, Raggedy Ann doll, tops or dreidels, yo-yos, and storyboard creatures. Use the objects to demonstrate movements and to provide a concrete example of words such as *floppy* and *stretchy*. Note that depending too heavily on the props can be distracting for some of the children.

Focus of Observation: Expressiveness, Generation of Movement Ideas.

JANUARY

1. Continue with expressive movement exploration. Use themes and images that best reflect the experiences of the children. Children may still be talking about the holidays, presents, or winter and outdoor sports, all of which provide rich themes to explore. You also can use suggestions or images based on family trips and outings. For example, a trip to the mountains or a walk through the city park could each be followed up with suggestions for children to "walk like you're in deep, deep snow" or to "move as if you were going across a big frozen pond." A trip to the zoo presents an opportunity for children to try to walk like different animals.

Following children's suggestions may require a certain comfort level on your part. Experiment with how relaxed you feel trying different activities and, as a general rule, be prepared with a few suggestions with which you feel comfortable.

Here are a few examples of images you can propose to the children: (a) Move on different surfaces (walk through deep snow, glide over smooth ice, trudge through gooey mud, walk on hot sand, sled down a hill); (b) pretend to be a balloon slowly getting bigger and bigger . . . float up on a soft breeze . . . and then, losing air, come back down to the ground; and (c) pretend to be a circus performer (juggler, clown, highwire artist, trampoline jumper).

Focus of Observation: Expressiveness, Generation of Movement Ideas.

2. January, often with many indoor days, is a good time to set up a small indoor obstacle course (space providing), or at least to offer some semistructured gross motor activities. You can set up a simple two- or three-step course with hoops to step in and out of, cones to circle around, beams to walk across, and tunnels through which children can crawl.

If you have the proper matting and enough adult coverage, you might try some simple tumbling such as somersaults, back bends, and cartwheels. (See Obstacle Course, p. 24.)

Focus of Observation: Body Control, Movement Memory.

FEBRUARY

1. *Mirror, Mirror*

Explain that you are going to perform certain movements, and that the children are going to be your mirror, doing everything you do. You can try slowly swaying one arm; tilting your head very slightly; bending sideways with a stiff upper body; moving your foot toe-heel-toe; or striking an odd shape or pose, for example, with twisted arms and legs. Observe which children are able to capture the different movements, in both position and quality. If children enjoy the activity, you can extend it by striking a pose and returning to a neutral position, then asking the children to recreate the pose. A more challenging extension is to have pairs of children try to mirror each other.

Focus of Observation: Movement Memory.

2. *Freeze and Melt*

Have all of the children strike a "frozen" pose. When they are ready, explain that they are going to melt *slowly* all the way down. When everyone has melted, encourage the children to recreate slowly their original positions. Notice which children maintain timing, body control, and expressive nuances. Differences also will emerge in children's abilities to remember and assume the earlier pose.

Focus of Observation: Body Control, Movement Memory.

3. *Drum and Bell*

Play a drum and a bell for the children, directing children's attention to their distinct tonal qualities. Ask one child to "be" the bell and one to "be" the drum. Make sure you allow boys to be the bell and girls to be the drum. Ask the children to listen carefully for their sound as you play the instruments alternately several times, varying the tempo. The children should move when you play their instrument, and freeze when you play the other one.

Focus of Observation: Sensitivity to Rhythm, Expressiveness.

MARCH

1. Expose children to different forms of ethnic or tribal dances. Stories, films, or demonstrations are possible activities for a group time. Explain how these dances convey stories that often are connected to real events and that hold great significance for different groups of people. This activity is closer to drama and mime than some of the other activities, and can help children become aware of movement as an important medium for communicating experiences, feelings, and stories.

2. Follow up by encouraging children to invent dances of their own that tell about an important experience. If children have trouble coming up with ideas, you may need to model a three- or four-step sequence in which a story or event is conveyed. You might take a song with which the children are familiar and dance one part of it. This exercise

could be conducted as a guessing game in which children are asked to figure out what part of the song or story you are acting out.

Another suggestion is to prepare short story lines on small pieces of paper. For example: "A child is on a walk one day. All of a sudden, she finds a wonderful toy . . . ." Another plot might begin: "A child is skating over a big ice pond. As she is making a big turn on the ice, it starts to snow . . . ." Children can then act out the sequence.

Focus of Observation: Simple Choreography (Generation of Movement Ideas), Expressiveness, Movement Memory.

3. Teach a simple three- or four-step movement sequence or dance to the group, preferably with a song for supporting cues. After 2 days, invite a child to the movement space or, during playground time, ask her to show you the dance you taught. You may need to take children aside in groups of two or three. Also, you may need to demonstrate the first step or starting position. (Note: This is a fairly advanced activity.)

A possible follow-up is to encourage each child to invent her own three- or four-step dance. You then can try to take a rough notation of the steps. Afterward, ask children if they remember their own dances or the dances of other children.

Focus of Observation: Movement Memory.

4. For a more challenging *rhythm* exercise, end the sessions by playing a tape of music selections with varying rhythmic patterns. Ask children to pay close attention to the rhythms of the different pieces of music. Watch for distinctions in their rhythmic sensitivity.

Focus of Observation: Sensitivity to Rhythm, Responsiveness to Music.

APRIL

This month is oriented around the basic movement skills elicited by the outdoor Obstacle Course (e.g., balance, agility, efficiency of movement, coordination, and timing—see Obstacle Course Activity, p. 24) and children's skills in handling and manipulating objects.

1. On the playground, set up tires or hula hoops into which children can throw balls or bean bags. Ask children to throw the items from different distances. They also can try using one or two hands, and over- and underhand throws. Notice differences in children's eye-hand coordination.

2. Play Simon Says with combined and complex movements such as jumping jacks, alternating arm and leg movements, twisting the upper body while moving one's legs, and so on. Model the movements at the beginning, and then let children try them on their own.

Focus of Observation: Body Control.

3. Blow up two sturdy balloons and ask two children at a time to try to keep the balloons afloat as long as possible. Notice differences in children's eye-hand coordination.

—Scoring

Before beginning the movement sessions, review the scoring categories and definitions (see Table 1). Use the first few movement sessions to become comfortable with the activities. Then start to use the observation sheet (Table 2) in conjunction with the scoring categories. Whenever possible, try to complete the sheets immediately following each session. Table 3 provides a summary sheet for the year.

To use the observation sheet, describe the day's activity sequence in the space provided. Place an asterisk beside the child's name if she exhibits a distinctive example of one of the categories. Mark a double asterisk if her performance constitutes an extraordinary example. Jot down in the comments or anecdotes section the specific observations that led you to check that category. The following are examples of comments and anecdotes identifying movement strengths and styles.

Rhythm: Tina is able to change her movements to match the changes in rhythm, first marching to a steady drum beat, then increasing her pace when the drum beat quickens.

Expressiveness: Sam responds mostly to narrative themes and images, especially when storyboard figures are used. To represent the rubber dinosaur stalking his food, he walked purposefully around on all fours, sniffing and turning his head in different directions.

Body Control: Shannon froze completely when the music stopped and carefully held her pose.

Generation of Movement Ideas: Juan suggested that children be a clock, and that they walk as if they had no knees.

Responsiveness to Music: Benjy's movements become more daring and diverse when music is being played. He makes effective use of high, middle, and low space, swinging and twirling his arms above his head and low on the ground.

When scoring, remember that the category of "responsiveness to music" is intended to describe children who are unusually expressive and rhythmic when music is being played. Thus, it may overlap in part with the "expressiveness" and "sensitivity to rhythm" categories.

—Preliminary Results: 1986–1987

Children's movement profiles from the 1986–1987 year reveal varying levels and combinations of ability. Three of the 19 children stood out in several areas; 5 exhibited strength in a single area. A major distinguishing characteristic was whether children generated their own ways of moving, or whether they waited until other children started moving, relying primarily on imitation. Other differences emerged in children's abilities to articulate movement ideas. Whereas some children only repeated the suggestions of the teacher, others generated a variety of movement challenges, for example, "Move as if you don't have any elbows."

Some children indicated a preference for focusing on one kind of movement such as tumbling, or imitating familiar balletic poses and walks. One child displayed the strongest response to those activities involving recorded music or instruments, apparently requiring the rhythmic component in order to become engaged. Other children differed in their preferences for fast or slow movement. One girl tried especially hard to anticipate the end of a piece of music in order to complete her dance in a particular position. She was also sensitive to differences in the tempo and mood of musical selections.

One boy offered immediate and original responses to the movement ideas proposed in the Simon Says game, although his body control was awkward and he could not regulate his timing to match rhythmic changes. Other children showed effective control and were confident and agile in their movements, but did not try to vary their responses and were reluctant to explore different kinds of movement. The open-ended nature of some of the activities inhibited these children's expressiveness more than the structured formats. One child found it easier to move rhythmically when he vocalized or sang along with the music.

It became clear from our observations in the classroom that, for some children, movement was the primary means of expression. For instance, one child who did not feel comfortable or confident in classroom activities such as blocks or dramatic play gained a sense of competence and mastery in the movement sessions that often carried over into other activities.

TABLE 1: CREATIVE MOVEMENT SCORING CRITERIA

SENSITIVITY TO RHYTHM:

Ability to synchronize movements to stable and changing rhythms (generated by an instrument or recorded music) or to set one's own rhythm.

Child attempts to move with the rhythm as opposed to being unaware of or disregarding rhythmic changes. Child can set a rhythm of her own through movement and regulate it for desired effects. Take note whether she uses one part of the body, for example, swinging an arm, or whether she moves the whole body in synchrony.

Target Activities: Canoe Trip, moving to percussion instruments, Drum and Bell, free dance to music.

EXPRESSIVENESS:

Ability to evoke moods or images through movement. Stimulus can be verbal image, prop, or music.

Child is comfortable using gestures and body postures to express herself. She responds vividly to different verbal images, to moods and tonal qualities of different instruments, or to both, for example drum and bell. Child also varies response to music selections, interpreting the quality of music in her movements.

Target Activities: Tightrope Walker; Simon Says; movement based on verbal themes, images, and props; Drum and Bell; simple choreography; free dance to music.

BODY CONTROL:

Ability to place body, and to isolate and use body parts effectively, to achieve desired effects, for example to freeze, balance, melt, and the like.

Child can plan, sequence, and execute movements efficiently. Movements do not seem random or disjointed. She accurately executes movement ideas proposed by adults or other children. Look for whether child can freeze her body when asked. Also notice *body awareness* (ability to identify and use different body parts such as hips and shoulders, and to understand their functions) and *movement memory* (ability to replicate her own movements and those of others).

Target Activities: Obstacle Course; Canoe Trip; Freeze and Melt; Simon Says; Mirror, Mirror; using balls, beanbags, balloons.

GENERATION OF MOVEMENT IDEAS:

Ability to invent novel movement ideas or to offer extensions of ideas, for example, suggesting that classmates make their raised arms float like clouds in the sky. Execution of movement is not necessary to excel in this category.

Child responds immediately to ideas and images with original interpretation.

Target Activities: Simon Says; simple choreography.

RESPONSIVENESS TO MUSIC:

Ability to respond in different ways to different kinds of music (combines sensitivity to rhythm and expressiveness).

Notice if child responds to rhythm or to mood of music, or to both. Also notice *use of space:* the ability to explore available space comfortably using different levels and to move easily and fluidly. Look for whether child anticipates others in shared space or experiments with body in space, for example turning and spinning.

Target Activities: Free dance to music, moving to instruments.

TABLE 2: CREATIVE MOVEMENT OBSERVATION SHEET

Activity Sequence _____ Date _____ Observer _____

Child (age)	Sensitivity to Rhythm	Expressiveness	Body Control	Generation of Movement Ideas	Responsiveness to Music	Comments and Observations

* = distinctive example
** = extraordinary example

TABLE 3: CREATIVE MOVEMENT SUMMARY SHEET

Child _____   Age ___   Observer _____   Time Period _____

Date	Activity Sequence	Sensitivity to Rhythm	Expressiveness	Body Control	Generation of Movement Ideas	Responsiveness to Music	Comments and Observations

* = distinctive example
** = extraordinary example

23

❏ Obstacle Course

—Purpose and Activity Description

The outdoor Obstacle Course features activities that elicit children's athletic movement abilities. The course enables teachers to assess a child's "motor fitness," or the quality of the child's performance during various movement tasks.

The skill areas targeted for observation include *power, agility, speed,* and *balance.* The definitions of the target skill areas are based largely on Gallahue's (1982) *Developmental Movement Experiences for Children.*

Power refers to the child's "ability to perform one maximum explosive force" (Gallahue, p. 33). Power is a combination of strength and speed, and is assessed in the long jump and hurdle jump stations of the Obstacle Course.

Agility is defined as "the ability to move from point to point as rapidly as possible while making successive movements in different directions" (p. 33). It involves "the ability to make quick and accurate shifts in body position and direction of movement" (p. 34). Both the obstacle run and the hurdle jump stations assess agility.

Speed is "the ability to move from one point to another in the shortest time possible over a short distance" (p. 32). This measure includes both reaction time and movement time. The final sprint, the last station of the course, assesses speed.

Balance refers to the "ability to maintain one's equilibrium in relationship to the force of gravity in both static and dynamic movement situations" (p. 33). It includes the ability to make small changes in body position. *Static* balance involves moving the body in a fixed position; *dynamic* balance refers to balance while the body is in motion. The child's walking on the balance beam and on the ramp jump allows one to assess the child's dynamic balance.

This is not an exhaustive list of motor skills. A more comprehensive course, however, would likely be awkward and difficult to implement and score, especially when working with a large group of children. We also wanted the course to be fun and engaging for the children. Therefore, we organized the four target skill areas and their respective stations into a streamlined Obstacle Course that incorporates the basic elements of movement, but does not require elaborate equipment. The course takes approximately 10 minutes for each child to complete.

For each Obstacle Course station, we chose an activity that we felt would accurately represent one of the target skill areas. However, teachers also should feel free to set up their own course with a different set of stations for the different skills. Although each station involves more than one skill, to facilitate scoring we focused on no more than one or two skill areas per station. Additional observations can be noted in narrative form in the comments section of the observation sheet.

Optimally, the assessment of children's athletic movement abilities would occur over time and in a meaningful context. Many skills (e.g., balance, agility, coordination, gracefulness) can be observed in either the creative or athletic movement domains; however, children may feel more comfortable or able to perform in one domain than another.

The Spectrum Obstacle Course provides a context for observing how children respond to various kinds of challenges, such as adapting to the transitions between stations. We also recommend, in addition to the Obstacle Course, observing children at play in less structured settings, such as at the playground, on recreational equipment, or while playing games. (See Table 7, p. 36, for a sample observation sheet.)

SPECTRUM OBSTACLE COURSE

LONG JUMP ⟶ BALANCE BEAM ⟶ OBSTACLE RUN ⟶

FINAL SPRINT ⟵ HURDLE JUMP ⟵ JUMP FROM HEIGHT ⟵

—Materials and Set-Up

The Spectrum Obstacle Course is a basic six-station course. The course is designed to be simple, yet challenging for preschool- and kindergarten-age children. Feel free to supplement or substitute stations, equipment, or both.

The Obstacle Course is best administered in a playground setting. If you do not have access to a playground, you can use a gym or a room set aside for movement activities. For safety reasons, it is preferable to administer the course with two adults present. One adult can spot the children while the other observes and scores. Having two or more adults present speeds up the activity and ensures that all children receive the appropriate modeling. You can either administer the course to a few children at a time over a period of days or weeks, or you can combine classes with another teacher, sharing duties of spotting, scoring, and playing games with waiting groups of children. Safety tips include outlining any safety rules for the children before they begin the course, ensuring that there is sufficient space between stations, and checking the equipment periodically to make sure it is stable and secure.

If you have access to video equipment, videotaping the children as they proceed through the course will be extremely useful for scoring purposes, particularly if only one adult is present. (The camera can be set up on a tripod.)

You may choose to implement the Spectrum course as diagrammed below and on the preceding page, or to change it to suit your equipment and space needs. To avoid confusion and collisions, it is probably best to arrange your course in the shape of a circle, square, or horseshoe. Figure-eight courses may confuse children whereas straight-line courses leave room for children to wander off. The simplest shape for constructing a course is the circle, with each station leading directly to the next, and ultimately back to the first. A horseshoe shape such as the one presented here is probably most efficient if the final station is a sprint.

It may take some trial and error before you arrive at the optimal layout for your setting. The course should be set up with adequate space between each station, yet not so much that children miss or confuse the order of stations.

In terms of equipment, the long jump can be represented by a measuring tape secured to the ground or floor. The balance beam can be delineated by tape, ribbon, a line chalked on the ground, or a narrow piece of scrap lumber. Pylons can be created from any safe, agreed-upon markers. Children may run around stacked-up blocks, tires, or chairs. The jump ramp can be a wide board that is well secured at the base and raised and secured on the opposite end. Hurdles can be made of blocks, ribbon, or bamboo sticks.

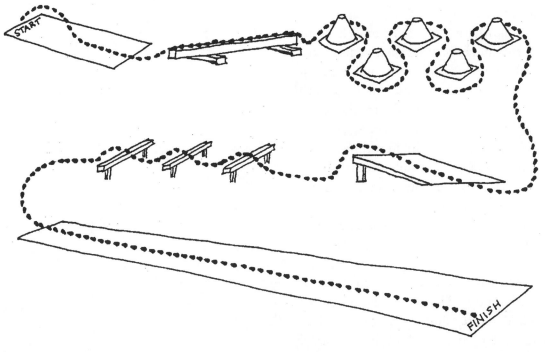

—Procedure and Script

The Obstacle Course is introduced in the spring, ideally in a playground setting. Waiting until spring gives children ample time to become comfortable with the set-up of the playground and the equipment, and to practice the skills targeted in the assessment. You can begin to conduct informal playground observations as soon as children seem comfortable in the setting.

Like the Creative Movement Curriculum, the Obstacle Course works best if children feel that movement activities are valued. The course can be supplemented with outdoor movement games or other organized activities; it also can be enriched through work with children on the movement challenges presented by the different playground equipment.

Before you introduce the Obstacle Course as a whole to children, we recommend that you introduce the separate components or related activities. This will give the children some experience and confidence in the relevant skill areas before they are assessed. For the assessment, take children in groups of six or less, and give an introduction such as the following: "Today we're going to do something called an Obstacle Course. This is what our Obstacle Course looks like. When we go through our Obstacle Course, we move in different ways. We'll be running, jumping, and balancing on the beam. The most important thing to remember is that this is not a race. In some parts, you can try to go as fast as you can, but you can go as slow as you want in other parts. So be careful and have fun."

Start to move through the Obstacle Course as the children watch, slowly and carefully modeling the desired movements and explaining what to do at each station. To check comprehension, have children repeat back to you what they are being asked to do at each station. If there is only one adult, it is best to model the entire course once or twice, depending on the level of the group, and then take the children through the course, one station at a time. If a child needs a station to be modeled again, make a note of the additional scaffolding on your observation sheet.

If you are conducting a more formal assessment, you will need to take into account the fact that some children will go through the course immediately after you model it, whereas others will have to wait. Of course, the latter group will also get the benefit of watching the children preceding them. It may be best to take no larger than groups of three for the formal assessment. You can also have all of the children run through the course twice, scoring them only during the second round or using their better score.

Clear and accurate modeling at each station is critical. Young children will want to find their own ways of using materials and equipment, for example, some children might prefer to crawl under or step over hurdles, rather than jump over them. Outside the actual assessment, children can and should be encouraged to use the course as they choose (as long as safety is maintained). However, for accuracy of assessment and safety, it is very important to model the correct movements. If a child does transform an activity, physically or verbally, make note of it on the observation sheet.

THE STATIONS

The Spectrum Obstacle Course, described below, is based on the work of Gallahue (1982). The six stations were set up as a horseshoe, although you may substitute other configurations.

Station 1 LONG JUMP

The Obstacle Course starts with the long jump because it requires the most extensive explanation and modeling. Have children stand still at the start of the jump.

Explain and demonstrate how to crouch before jumping, showing how your feet should stay together before and after jumping, and using your arms and torso to propel the body forward. Knees should be bent at the start of the jump, and then extended during takeoff.

Demonstrate how to swing your arms back to create the momentum to jump, then swing your arms forward. Emphasize that horizontal, not vertical, movement is the goal of the long jump.

Primary Focus: Power.

Station 2 BALANCE BEAM

We selected the balance beam as the second station because children will not yet be so tired or excited from one of the running stations that they will be unable to concentrate on balancing.

Modeling the desired technique, tell children to walk slowly across the beam heel-and-toe. Behaviors to be stressed and modeled are alternating feet, looking ahead while walking, and using different parts of your body to maintain balance. When using a raised beam, spotting is necessary.

Primary Focus: Balance.

Station 3 OBSTACLE RUN

By this point, children should be ready to run. Set up this station by placing five obstacles (we used pylons) in a row.

Ask children to run as quickly as they can, while weaving as closely as possible around the pylons without touching them. First, model a successful run: face forward, run lightly, and weave closely around the pylons, using a good arm swing (neither too inhibited nor too exaggerated). Attend to lifting your knees and pushing off the balls of your feet. Stress that the goal is to get as close to the pylons as possible while running as fast as you can.

After the careful, deliberate movement of the balance beam activity, running around the obstacles will give children the chance to loosen up a bit.

Primary Focus: Agility.

Station 4 JUMP FROM HEIGHT

The ramp jump provides a transition between the obstacle run and the hurdle jump. Because most children find a high jump exciting, and can execute the jump successfully, this station is well placed in the middle of a course. By this point, you should also be able to note each child's approach to the Obstacle Course as a whole, including how she responds to the challenges presented by each station.

If necessary, place a mattress on the ground onto which children can land. Have children run up a wide ramp (a flat board raised approximately two feet off the ground at its farthest end), and jump, with feet together and knees bent, to the ground or mattress. Stress that the goal of this activity is to land on both feet at once, without wobbling or falling. Model the use of arms to maintain balance.

Primary Focus: Balance.

Station 5 HURDLE JUMP

The ramp jump naturally leads into the hurdle jump. The hurdle jump consists of three or four hurdles, which can be constructed from plastic or bamboo rods. The hurdles should be approximately one half to one foot off the ground. The rods should be loosely secured so that they will easily give way should children hit them when completing their jump.

Explain to children that this station involves running and jumping over the hurdles without touching them. Place the hurdles about three feet apart, to leave children enough room to land, take a few steps, and prepare for the next hurdle.

Appropriate modeling is especially important for this station, since children may invent their own ways of getting past the hurdles. To model this activity, demonstrate a run as in Station 3, as well as a running jump over each of the hurdles. If a child is hesitant or unwilling to jump, you can ask if she would like to cross the hurdles in a different way.

Primary Foci: Power and Agility.

Station 6 FINAL SPRINT

As the last station, a relatively long sprint gives children a sense of completion of the course. Have children run as fast as they can over a distance of approximately 20 yards to a fence or finish line. Make sure that the children will not be running into unsafe areas, perhaps by making it impossible for them to overrun the course. Model a fast run with long, even strides. Run lightly, leaning slightly into your run, synchronizing your arms and legs, lifting your knees, and pushing off from the balls of your feet.

Primary Focus: Speed.

ADDITIONAL STATIONS

An optional second session consists of three stations: another balance beam walk, hopscotch, and a beanbag toss. The second session can proceed as follows:

Station 1 BALANCE BEAM II

Ask children to cross a balance beam (or a line drawn on the ground) moving backward or sideways. To model crossing the beam sideways, demonstrate instep-to-instep shuffling; to model crossing the beam backward, model alternating your feet backward heel-and-toe. If children are crossing the beam backward, tell them not to look backward in the direction they are going, but to face the direction from which they began. Crossing the beam backward or sideways is much more difficult than crossing forward; hence it will require closely spotting the child, offering your hand as needed.

Primary Focus: Balance.

Station 2 HOPSCOTCH

Sketch a hopscotch board on the sidewalk or playground. Draw outlines of one or two feet in the squares to help children understand how many feet they are allowed in a box. When modeling, stress the use of arms and torso to control balance, and the importance of remaining within the lines of the boxes. Feel free to substitute other hopping games as desired.

Primary Focus: Agility.

Station 3 BEANBAG TOSS

Give children three beanbags, and ask them to toss them one at a time toward two buckets or lines. You can model two different goals: distance and accuracy. Place the targets at different distances to provide different degrees of challenge.

Primary Foci: Power and Eye-Hand Coordination.

—Scoring

Appropriate modeling at each station is essential for ensuring accurate scoring. Refer to the Obstacle Course Scoring Criteria (Table 4), to familiarize yourself with the scoring criteria before conducting the actual assessment.

Use the Obstacle Course Observation Sheet (Table 5) to assess the children as they run through the course. Narrative comments for each station can be made on the far right of the sheet. Use an asterisk to indicate exceptional ability. Comments in the General Notes section might include descriptions of the child's transitions from station to station, as well as her overall approach and quality of movement. Were the child's movements fluid and efficient? Was she hesitant or confident? Did the movements seem deliberate and planned out, or were they randomly executed? If possible, jot down a summary impression of the child's overall execution of the course.

Use the Obstacle Course Summary Sheet (Table 6) to summarize information for the entire class. This sheet also can be formatted to reflect the specific skills targeted in the course, such as balance and speed, rather than the individual stations.

For the playground observations, begin by observing children at play, noting which activities they are naturally drawn to and which skills are exhibited. A sample observation sheet for informal playground observations is provided in Table 7. You also can organize your observations around the equipment or individual activities, specifying the particular motor skills elicited by each activity.

Other, more general categories for observation might include activities that involve *locomotion* (such as hopping, leaping, sliding); *stability* (such as twisting, swinging, stretching); and *manipulation* (such as throwing, catching, kicking) (see Gallahue, 1982). Additional skill areas to be considered include eye-hand or eye-foot coordination, timing, movement memory, and the generation of movement strategies.

—Further Suggestions for the Domain

The Spectrum Obstacle Course addresses a limited number of motor skills. As noted above, other abilities that teachers may want to consider include body awareness and control, flexibility, use of space, coordination (bodily, eye-hand, eye-foot), gracefulness, and timing. Teachers can either integrate activities that elicit these skills into other obstacle courses, or provide the relevant activities on the playground. Many movement games and activities—especially those using balls—draw upon a combination of these skills.

Teachers also can rotate variations of the Obstacle Course throughout the year. Children can be included in the design process. Some of the simpler variations include changing or reordering the stations, or adding music in the background. A tumbling mat is a useful addition; children can be asked to perform somersaults and leaps, or to perform a movement of their choice. Children also can be asked to crawl through various structures such as hula hoops, tires, or wooden barrels. On the balance beam, children can be presented with various challenges such as walking on tiptoe or dipping their foot down next to the beam before taking the next step. Ascending and descending ramps are alternatives for demonstrating balance.

On the playground, swings and jungle gym play provide good opportunities for children to demonstrate power and coordination (e.g., pumping and coordinating arms and legs to swing higher on the swings, and lifting themselves up and maneuvering around on the jungle gym). Other common playground movements include climbing, pulling, pushing, sliding, throwing, kicking, dodging, hanging, hopping, galloping, and somersaulting. A mattress or some other thick, soft surface can be provided for children to jump onto from a short distance or height. Finally, balancing activities are many and varied: standing on tiptoe, lying on one side with one's eyes closed, bouncing on a trampoline (with close supervision), and balancing objects while moving (rolling a tire or balancing a beanbag on an arm while walking).

TABLE 4: OBSTACLE COURSE SCORING CRITERIA

1 LONG JUMP

1 = does not prepare body for jumping movement; does not use arms to propel body forward; extension of lower body at takeoff is limited; does not keep feet together; may end up stepping instead of jumping; length of jump is short

2 = completes the jump, but does not prepare fully for jumping movement; exaggerated or insufficient crouch before jumping; loses balance when jumping, lands with legs splayed, or both; insufficient use of arms to propel body forward; jump is medium length

3 = jumps successfully with strength; propels body with arms and torso; keeps feet together before and after jump; jump is long, with emphasis on horizontal distance

2 BALANCE BEAM

1 = has difficulty maintaining balance; frequently slips or steps off beam; needs to hold adult's hand; seems hesitant and tentative; may only shuffle feet; body tends to be rigid

2 = has some trouble balancing; approach is tentative, but uses strategies to regain balance; may step off beam to prevent falling; wobbles; alternates or shuffles feet, or both

3 = moves forward while maintaining balance; walks straight across without hesitating; looks ahead; alternates feet; body is relatively relaxed

3 OBSTACLE RUN

1 = hesitates before running around obstacles; is not able to maneuver close to obstacle or touches and knocks obstacles over, or both; poor control of limbs; change of direction is awkward and slow

2 = runs at a moderate speed around obstacles with some hesitation; tries to stay close to obstacles, but may touch or knock them over; some lack of control of limbs

3 = runs quickly around obstacles without hesitation; stays close to obstacles without touching them or knocking them over; keeps limbs close to body; makes quick and accurate shifts in body position and direction of movement

4 JUMP FROM HEIGHT

1 = cannot jump from ramp successfully; does not push off with or land on both feet; hesitates or stumbles; exaggerated use of arms for balance; upon landing, loses balance, squats, places hands on ground to steady or does some or all of these

2 = jumps from ramp successfully, but legs may be splayed; little hesitation before jumping; one foot may trail the other; may lose balance upon landing

3 = jumps from ramp successfully, with feet together at beginning and end; no hesitation before jumping; uses arms to control balance; lands with no wobbling or falling

5 Hurdle Jump

1 =   cannot jump over hurdles successfully; trips or stumbles; squats or places hands on ground to steady herself, or does both; great hesitation; might complete station by stepping over hurdles

2 =   jumps over majority of hurdles successfully, but with sloppy form; sometimes long hesitation before jumping

3 =   jumps over hurdles successfully; little hesitation before each jump; runs and jumps with good form; body preparation and timing are well coordinated

6 Final Sprint

1 =   lacks control of arms, feet, or both while running; body parts not in synchrony; short, uneven strides

2 =   strides are of moderate length, moderate speed; some flailing of arms, feet, or both while running; body parts somewhat asynchronous

3 =   runs with lengthy, even strides; speed of stride is fast; good control of arms and feet; synchrony of alternating body parts

ADDITIONAL STATIONS (OPTIONAL)

1 Balance Beam II

A. Sideways

1 =   has difficulty maintaining balance; constantly falls; needs to hold adult's hand; very hesitant; shuffles across beam with very small steps

2 =   has some trouble balancing and makes frequent attempts to regain balance; approach is tentative and wobbly; shuffles across beam with medium-sized steps

3 =   is able to move sideways without losing balance and with minimal hesitation; shuffles across with wide, confident steps

B. Backward Heel-and-Toe

1 =   cannot walk backwards heel-and-toe — resorts to shuffling; cannot stay on beam without total reliance on adult for balance; extremely tentative and wobbly

2 =   often stumbles and loses balance; wobbles, frequently relying on adult's hand for balance; constantly needs to check behind

3 =   can walk backwards, heel-and-toe, with little stumbling and looking behind; generally stays steady and does not hesitate

2 HOPSCOTCH

1 =   cannot coordinate hops and jumps; cannot stay within boxes; resorts to stepping instead of hopping or jumping

2 =   sometimes hops when should jump and vice versa; sometimes steps outside boxes; some stumbling or tripping

3 =   hops and jumps appropriately; does not stumble or trip; stays within boxes

3 BEANBAG TOSS

1 =   cannot throw the beanbags to the first target

2 =   cannot reach farther target, but exhibits enough power to throw most of beanbags between the two targets or into first

3 =   throws two or three beanbags past or into farther target

TABLE 5: OBSTACLE COURSE OBSERVATION SHEET

Child _____

Age _____

Date _____

Observer _____

Station: **Focus:**   **Skill Level:**   **Comments:**

1 Long Jump   Power   _____

2 Balance Beam   Balance   _____

3 Obstacle Run   Agility   _____

4 Jump from Height   Balance   _____

5 Hurdle Jump   Power/Agility _____

6 Final Sprint   Speed   _____

General Notes:

* =Demonstrates exceptional ability

TABLE 6: OBSTACLE COURSE SUMMARY SHEET

Child (age)	Long Jump	Balance Beam	Obstacle Run	Jump from Height	Hurdle Jump	Final Sprint	TOTAL	Comments and Observations

* = Demonstrates exceptional ability

TABLE 7: PLAYGROUND OBSERVATION SHEET

Date _____   Observer _____

Child (age)	Activity	Balance	Power	Agility	Speed	TOTAL	Comments and Observations

* = Demonstrates exceptional ability

CHAPTER 2
LANGUAGE DOMAIN

—INTRODUCTION

In every known society, language ranks among the most highly valued cognitive and social capacities, important in its own right and as an adjunct to performance in almost any domain. Most children learn to talk within a few years, beginning with the baby's babbling and progressing to the one-year-old's first spoken words. Toward the end of the 2nd year, children start combining words into simple phrases, and by age 3, most children have acquired a substantial vocabulary and the basic rules of grammar and syntax. The language of 4- and 5-year-olds increasingly resembles adult models. Relatively early in language development, individual differences in children's vocabulary begin to emerge. Some children learn words for labeling objects and describing their properties, whereas others are more concerned with expressing feelings or wishes, and tend to focus more on social interactions (Nelson, 1973, 1975). We have observed some children at the preschool level who appear interested in describing materials and explaining how things work, whereas others are more focused on engaging adults and peers in conversations about people and their activities.

Most 4-year-olds exhibit a wide range of linguistic abilities, from using figurative language and inventing rhymes to relating short tales describing their own experiences. They can also adjust their language to address audiences of different ages (Shatz & Gelman, 1973). The typical preschool classroom affords children the opportunity to use their language skills in a variety of ways (Heath, 1982). In group meetings, children have a chance to talk about themselves and the different classroom materials and activities. The writing table, dramatic play area, and reading corner also provide children with a forum for exploring their language skills. Of course, children talk all the time in their classroom, regardless of the curriculum area. Language development is a central component of every preschool agenda.

Linguists traditionally have divided the language domain into four components: *semantics* (word meaning), *phonology* (the sound system), *syntax* (the rules governing word order), and *pragmatics* (the uses to which language can be put). In the past, researchers typically have examined sentence grammar in isolation, rather than looking at language abilities in rich social contexts. But recently, many educationally oriented researchers have begun to assert that examining language at the level of discourse may be more revealing than simply focusing on sentence-level structure (Snow, 1991; Wolf, 1985; Wolf & Hicks, 1989). We, too, are interested in exploring discourse-related features of children's language. In our assessments, we use specific measures such as richness of vocabulary and variety of sentence structure, as well as broader measures such as attention to narrative structure and thematic coherence.

Many standardized tests for preschool children take a traditional approach to assessing language skills. The verbal components of tests like the Wechsler Preschool and Primary Scale of Intelligence (Wechsler, 1967) and McCarthy's Scales of Children's Abilities (McCarthy, 1972) include vocabulary questions asking children to identify common objects and define words; verbal memory items involving repetitions of word series and sentences, or the retelling of a short story; and verbal fluency sections that entail naming as many items as possible in a given category within a 20-second period. There is also a large verbal component in related sections such as "comprehension," "similarities," and "information" (see Wechsler, 1967; McCarthy, 1972).

In contrast, the Spectrum activities are directed toward assessing discourse, rather than isolated linguistic components such as grammar and vocabulary. Telling a story or explaining a procedure requires the use of linguistic devices in service of a specific, applied, and meaningful task.

—CONCEPTUALIZING THE LANGUAGE ACTIVITIES

The adult end states that we used to guide the development of our assessments in the language domain include the role of author in such capacities as storyteller, poet, and orator, as well as the roles of those who use language prominently in their work, such as reporter, announcer, and historian. At one extreme, the poet plays with word meanings and sounds, focusing attention on each word and phrase, whereas at the other end of the spectrum, the historian emphasizes the communication of ideas (Mukarovsky, 1964). In the latter example, the exact language used is important only to the extent that the message is conveyed as desired. In the short term, the goals for young children are to be able to use language effectively in different school-related tasks such as working on a science problem, constructing a story, or talking about a math or art project to a teacher.

We devised two sets of language activities, the Storyboard and the Reporter Activities, to represent both the more expressive and aesthetic aspects of the domain as well as the more pragmatic, factual, and descriptive components. The Storyboard Activity was developed to pick out the child who brings strength in invented narrative to any task she undertakes, making up stories on the spot and using language suggestive of typical storytelling formats. Another, possibly independent, strength in this domain is the ability to give an accurate and coherent account of an event that one has experienced. Supplemented by informal in-class observations, the Reporter Activities are designed to tap the child's capacity to describe an experience in correct sequence, the appropriateness and level of detail she provides, and other skills related to presenting a realistic narrative account.

Our activities look only at abilities involved in spoken language; written language may involve a different set of skills (Olson, 1977). It is generally assumed that writing is more decontextualized than speaking. Although the abilities tapped by a relatively spontaneous activity such as the Storyboard may indeed indicate a budding novelist or playwright, we have not yet gathered the necessary longitudinal data to confirm such a connection. It is quite possible that the abilities of a more planful and reflective child may not emerge until later, when the child will have at her disposal the resources to think through and organize her thoughts in a more careful fashion.

Informal classroom observations supplement the language activities and have tended to support the findings of our assessments. Some children exhibit a special interest in playing with words as evidenced by an appreciation of puns or an interest in rhyming. Others may engage in logical argument and inquiry, or ask for the meanings of words and offer explanations of what a new word means. These spontaneous demonstrations of language skill are just as important as performance in the more structured setting of the activities.

☐ STORYBOARD ACTIVITY

—Purpose and Activity Description

The Storyboard Activity is designed to provide a concrete but open-ended framework in which children can produce invented tales. After listening to examples of storytelling, children are asked to tell a story using a *storyboard*, a board or box top outfitted with figures and a setting. The activity serves as a variation on dramatic play. With the storyboard, the child becomes narrator as well as participant (Britton, 1982). The activity differs from telling a story on one's own without any props in that children need not rely on short-term memory for their discourse: The figures remind the children what is happening. The opportunity for the emergence of creative and unique tales is greater than that tied to the pictures of wordless books.

If the teacher is able to hold more than one session with the child, the activity also allows a view of development over time. The gifted storyteller may well show growth over time in the form and cohesiveness of her tales, demonstrating a distinctive style and approach to the materials.

To be sure, few children are able to tell a story that embodies the structure most adults are used to, with a beginning, middle, and end; nevertheless, they are quite capable of producing smaller narrative vignettes that can be examined for different linguistic skills. We can assess how children tie together successive events, or further elaborate on characters, places, or objects once mentioned, or adhere to the same script continuously. Such familiar elements of storytelling as characterization, dialogue, and dramatic ploys can be examined as well as the capacity to denote place, time, and causal sequence.

Individual differences emerge with regard to the introduction of new elements into the story that go beyond the immediate actions of the characters and description of the landscape and props. Some children include the thoughts of the characters or create relationships for them. The story language can merely reflect the child's response to items on the storyboard or events in the classroom ("now he's standing up" or "the pail fell over") or it can venture further into providing a framework for the action, including individual motivation and contrasting moods and scenes. Examples include "The next morning . . ." or "A little boy lived on the other side of the rainbow."

Some children may bring a performance element to the activity, supplying expressive voices and sound effects and displaying an effective sense of timing, but such flair is by no means a prerequisite. When the storyboard is left alone in the classroom, children can use it to tell stories in groups of two or three, or to finish stories the teacher has begun for them. Children also can be encouraged to create their own storyboards with materials similar to those used in the activity.

—Materials and Set-Up

The materials for the assessment include a small tape recorder with a high-quality microphone, a storyboard with an ambiguous landscape that can be interpreted a number of ways, and an assortment of figures and props. (See illustration, p. 40.) Our storyboard is made of a 21" by 28" rectangular board covered with a soft, black vinyl material. The landscape consists of a cave and arch made out of DAZ, a molding clay that hardens without baking. The items are large enough that at least some of the figures on the board can stand inside them. The cave also has steps carved out of its side. An irregularly shaped, green vinyl patch is glued onto the center of the board. Several lavender felt pieces and a circular, blue vinyl patch are scattered in the surrounding areas for the child to rearrange. The green patch suggests grass to many children, and the blue patch is reminiscent of water. Three trees made of small branches from pine trees or bushes stand in balls of plasticine. A set of 10 purple wooden columns about 2" in height are arranged in a semicircle in one corner of the board, and a wooden triangle sits at the other end. A large hollow shell, which can serve as a dwelling or a vehicle, among other possibilities, is also on the board.

The figures include a small, rubber king with a spear painted onto his robe, positioned inside the cave; a large, purple dragon with an open mouth, positioned in front of the arch; one or two Playmobile figures, to be used as either girls or boys; a turtle positioned by the blue patch; a small fluff creature with two antennae; a black, rubber, octopus-like creature with a single diamond eye; and a black pipe cleaner curled into the shape of a snake. The props include a small treasure box with a catch that the child can press to open, revealing three or four jewels inside (small, colored, plastic beads); a small, red metal bucket; and several tiny shells. The treasure box is placed inside the semi-circle formed by the purple columns, and the bucket and shells are positioned by the blue patch.

You can keep a box with extra figures and props near the storyboard. The contents of the box should be concealed from the child's view to avoid overwhelming her with the variety of materials available. If the child needs help telling a story or seems capable of introducing more characters, you can offer the use of additional pieces. The box we used contains a selection of farm animals—goat, cow, pig, and hen; a second fluff creature of a different color; a mother bear with a baby bear clinging to her back; a small plastic suitcase; some plasticine berries; and a small lump of plasticine for the child to shape as she pleases.

The quality of the materials that you choose for this activity is important. They should be sturdy, colorful, and attractive, with some more fanciful and ambiguous in nature than others. If you wish to use different characters and props than we did, be sure to include a dwelling (large enough to fit the figures); an assortment of people, animals, and ambiguous creatures; clearly demarcated areas on the board; and a variety of landscape items (trees, shells, arch). Try to provide props such as a treasure box that suggest story ideas. Avoid superheroes and other familiar characters that might prompt well-known scripts that are too often rehearsed. You might select a few figures that look similar to each other, because sometimes the suggestion of an implicit family relationship helps to elicit a story. The pipe cleaner snake is especially evocative, since it can be transformed into smoke, rope, or other story elements. We do not recommend using the lump of clay all the time. While it lends itself to many creative uses—snow, quicksand, a shawl, pancakes—it also can be distracting.

It is very important to limit the number of things on the board so that the children are not intimidated or distracted by the wealth of materials. Of course, you also could create different figures for children from different cultural backgrounds.

Place the storyboard in a quiet corner of the room, preferably far enough away from other classroom activities that classmates' voices will not interfere with your ability to hear the child's story. Ask the child to sit on the floor in front of the storyboard, but facing away from the class, with the tape recorder as close to her as possible. If time allows, conduct the activity several times with each child to see how different story schemas evolve.

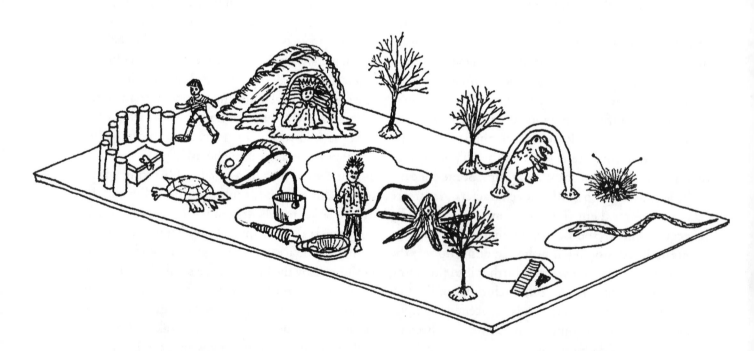

—Procedure and Script

A few weeks prior to the assessment, introduce the idea of storytelling to the children in a more formal way than they may be used to. You can read stories to them at group times, modeling the use of different voices for different characters as well as the use of narrative. You can also give them a very simple storyboard with just a few figures, which they can use for storytelling. Then, when the formal activity is introduced at group time, tell children: "A special storytelling board is in the classroom for you to use to tell stories, one at a time." (Have the storyboard out for children to see.) "You can tell stories using characters like this." (Hold up the dragon or some other creature.)

Once the child is seated in front of the storyboard, introduce the activity to her as follows: "This is a storytelling board. You can tell your own story using any of these creatures, and you can use your voice in different ways. You can be the storyteller and tell what the people and animals are doing, and you can give them voices and make them talk . . . like this:

"One day, Peter decided to go for a walk. Suddenly, he saw a strange creature. [*low voice*] 'What are you doing here? This is *my* home,' said the creature. [*normal voice*] 'I didn't know that,' said Peter, 'I guess I'll go visit Mr. Turtle. He likes to have visitors.' So off went Peter to see Mr. Turtle.

"Think of which things you want to use for your story. If there are some things you don't want to use, we can take them away." Allow the child time to look around and figure out which materials she would like to use, and turn on the tape recorder.

If the child is hesitant to begin, you can look at the materials with her. You can point out the king and treasure box filled with jewels and suggest that she might want to use them in her story, or you can ask her directly, "Which character do you want to start your story with?" If the child is not using her voice, you can tell her to use her storytelling voice: "For telling a story, you need to use your voice." Or, you can say that she needs to use words so that you can hear. You also can suggest that in order to save her story on the tape recorder, she needs to use her voice. If the child continues to speak softly, then whispered suggestions, in a collaborator's role, might help her sustain the storytelling role.

If the child still requires further help, you can show her some of the extra materials in the box, and ask if she would prefer to use some of those characters. You also can give her a list of story ideas from which she can choose the one she likes best. Suggestions based on the box of extra materials include "You could tell a story about a mother and baby bear looking for some berries, and here are the berries." (Pick up the figures and props as you refer to them.) "Or you could talk about a girl or boy feeding the animals on the farm; or about Susan, Spikey, and Fluff all searching for a lost treasure; or about Peter who meets the magic wizard on Planet Erp. Here is Peter, and here's the wizard, and here are the things that live on Planet Erp." Just mention three of the four possibilities for a story, and vary the order in which you list the scenarios for each child. Most children will not require this much scaffolding.

Once the child starts her story, stay in the background as much as possible, indicating interest only through eye contact and short exclamations. When she is finished, ask her if she would like to hear part of her story on the tape. After each session, use the Storyboard Observation Sheet (Table 11, p. 51) to record any relevant visual information, such as the child's expressions or physical manipulation of props, or any other comments.

If there is time for more than one session, introduce the storyboard for the second time as follows: "Now remember, you can use different voices, and also tell what the people and animals are doing. Look and see if there are some props you want for your story, and we can take away those you don't want." This procedure serves to refocus the child on the activity. Further story modeling is probably not necessary at this point.

—Scoring

The scoring system developed for this activity is based on written transcripts of the children's stories. It includes instructions for transcribers who were not necessarily present for the storytelling (Table 8), transcription sheets (Table 9), scoring instructions (Table 10), and an observation sheet and summary sheet (Tables 11 and 12). The transcriber guidelines also should be given to scorers who do not administer the activity themselves to provide them with a sense of context.

To score the transcribed narratives, first read through the scoring instructions and examples (Table 10). Then score the transcripts for each of the children using the categories on the observation sheet (Table 11). Scoring should be based primarily on the main segments of the child's narrative, although still in the context of the entire production. For example, you do not need to start from the first line when judging "nature of narrative structure" if a child is having a difficult time beginning her story. Rather, begin scoring only after the child begins the narrative proper. The category of "expressiveness" should be scored either by the adult administering the task or by the transcriber. The "primary language function" category is not scored. There are a total of 24 possible points.

—Preliminary Results: 1986–1987

Children's stories reflected a wide range of narrative ability. On one end of the spectrum, children were unable to put a story into words, and relied on moving around the figures and props. Some were able to explain what was happening only when questioned by the adult:

Adult (A): What's the spider doing now?

Child (C): The guy's getting him.

A: Uh oh. Now what's happening?

C: He's taking the treasure to his land, to his house.

A: What happened then?

C: He punched the dinosaur because he couldn't put him in jail.

At the other end of the spectrum, several children created coherent narratives using descriptive language, expressive dialogue, and complex sentence structure:

C: Once upon a time, there was a lonely monster behind a cave named Exor Cave. There was a king that lived in that cave. And a little boy lived on the other side of the rainbow. One day, he sat under his favorite tree and a turtle was walking by, and suddenly that turtle went through the rainbow, under it, I mean. And he went back and he was a person. "Hello." [*higher voice*] "Hey, let's go and run through the rainbow." [*lower voice*] "Let's even jump over it. Jump on." [*high voice*] "I'm gonna bring this pail with me. I might find little treasures over in your land."

In most of the narratives, the children described their manipulation of the props. There was little thematic coherence and the links between characters, props, and action were tenuous:

C: Peter and the king went for a walk, and they bring the dinosaur where the goat was, and the goat runned it over. This is made of the same stuff as the other. It is 'cause it's hard. So the goat kicked it. See,

it's rubber. So they bring back home, and so they went for a walk what saw these things. And one was a heart and one was a shell. They bring this big shell back home—they couldn't even carry it. What's that inside there? So they bring this big shell home. And they bring it in the big wall. And so when they did that, they bring all the ones home. So they went inside the fuzzy (_____) and so they went to step on the big wall, so they jumped to the other, and jumped to the other. And the goat is standing right in the middle. So the turtle went on the side and the furry thing was right behind the wall.

However, several children were able to invent a narrative problem and construct a story line that combined characters, props, and action in a common enterprise. Most children employed both dialogue and narration, and some were able to use distinctive voices for the different characters:

C: The next morning . . . [*high, child voice*] "Eh, my treasure's gone, oh, Daddy, my treasure's gone!" [*low voice*] "I think I know the dragon's place. Ooh! Come here son, look." [*child voice*] "Oh yeah, how do we get it out?" [*father voice*] "It's sealed on. He won't be waking up until a half hour." [*child voice*] "OK, come on." (sound effect and *child voice*) "Ooh. We got—I got it. Your old diamonds. Now, I want you to, and now let's open it and see the jewels. Oops. (_____) Are you sure this isn't magic, that you got from the thing?" [*father voice*] "I am positive." (sound effect and *child voice*) "I'm gonna sleep here." [*father voice*] "Oh no. Sleep where you do." [*child voice*] "But it's so comfy." [*father voice*] "OK., sleep right here."

Regardless of the level of language ability, most of the children were interested in exploring the storyboard scene and enjoyed playing with the characters and props. While the fantasy component appealed to some, others used mainly real-life themes.

TABLE 8: STORYBOARD TRANSCRIPTION GUIDELINES

SET-UP

The following materials are available to the children for the storyboard activity:

1. Landscape

> Clay cave with steps
> Clay arch
> Trees
> Colored felt and vinyl pieces—one green (like grass) and one blue (like water)
> Triangular wooden napkin holder with small carved heart inside
> Small movable purple wood columns arranged in semicircle
> Large shell which can be used as dwelling

2. Characters

> King, open-bellied dragon, turtle, 1–2 Playmobile people (gender ambiguous), small fuzzy creature, black spiderlike creature with diamond eye, black pipe cleaner snake.

3. Props

> Treasure box with jewels inside, red bucket, clay berries (optional)

4. Box of extra pieces

> Goat, cow, fuzzy creature, pig, hen, mother and baby bears, suitcase, lump of clay

INTRODUCTION

The adult introduces the activity to the child as follows:

This is a storytelling board. You can tell a story using any of the creatures on the board and you can use your voice in different ways. You can be the storyteller and tell what the characters are doing, and you can give them voices and make them talk . . . like this: "One day Peter decided to go for a walk. Suddenly he saw a strange creature. [*low voice*] 'What are you doing here? This is *my* home,' said the creature. [*normal voice*] 'I didn't know that,' said Peter. 'I guess I'll go visit Mr. Turtle. He likes to have visitors.' So off went Peter to see Mr. Turtle." Think of which things you want to use for your story. If there are some things you don't want to use, we can take them away.

SUGGESTIONS FOR TRANSCRIPTION

Try to include all words that are audible, even if the child misspeaks or edits her own story. You do not need to transcribe the set-up discussion between the adult and the child. Begin your transcription when the child starts telling the story. Use your best judgment in determining what constitutes a sentence. This will be obvious at times, such as when characters in the story change voices, or when there is a drop in intonation or a pause. Do not spend too much time worrying about whether an utterance is a complete sentence. Insert a solid line (_____) to indicate those parts of the story that are difficult to understand. If there is a particular word in the story about which you are unsure, indicate your uncertainty by placing a question mark directly after the word. "Scrambled off" (?) is an example.

TABLE 9: STORYBOARD ACTIVITY TRANSCRIPTION SHEET

Child _____

Date _____

Session # _____

Observer _____

Story Length _____

Transcriber _____

Transcription Time _____

STORY

TABLE 10: STORYBOARD SCORING CRITERIA

CHILD'S PRIMARY LANGUAGE FUNCTION(S) DURING ACTIVITY

_____ storytelling:

> "But one day the boy was grown up and he went to the king. And he looked at these dead people, and he looked at his daddy. . . ."

_____ interacting with adult:

> "You know what, I have one of these at home."

_____ investigating:

> "What's this stuff? Why is this clay soft?"

_____ describing:

> "The dragon has a big rip in his stomach. . . . And this guy only has one eye."

_____ labeling or categorizing:

> "This is a spider."

> "I'm gonna put all the animals together."

NATURE OF NARRATIVE STRUCTURE

1 = child's story only describes manipulation/action of props; child refers to events, objects, characters in the most general terms (e.g., does not name or assign roles to or establish relations among figures):

> "They jump over the trap . . . and then they go, they come in here . . . and then the turtle knocks these over and these things come out of it . . . and they throw this all the was. . . ."

2 = story's action predominantly arises out of props; however, child assigns names, roles, or both to some props; relations between characters are mentioned but not developed; child occasionally inserts characters' thoughts or motivations:

> "He's gonna walk . . . to the king and queen's castle 'cause he wants to get the treasure. Oh, this cave over here will be these two little fluffy things. They found a jewelry monster over here . . . the king's sleeping so they gotta walk quietly."

3 = child invents narrative problem—something occurs that provides impetus for a story line (e.g., good vs. bad characters or forces); identifies one or more characters and develops relations between them; includes detail about characters' cognitive, emotional, or physical states:

> [_child uses different voices to represent King, Andrew, and Kevin_]
>
> King: Good evening, Andrew and Kevin—I see my knights couldn't fight that evil dragon.
> Andrew: Yeah, majesty, but we could.
> King: . . . [He's been] bothering us for ten hundred years. I think you better kill him sometime.
> Andrew: OK We'll try to kill him right now!
> Kevin: But I'm scared, Andrew. I'm scared of that mean dragon.
> Andrew: Don't worry, Kevin—leave it to me.
>
> [_child uses own voice_] "And so Andrew and Kevin left the castle to go find the evil dragon who was sleeping in his cave somewhere."

THEMATIC COHERENCE

(see Examples of Scoring Levels at the end of the table)

1 = transitions from one thought to the next are unclear; child gets distracted (usually by materials on the storyboard); story line is interrupted and then not resumed

2 = story line is tenuous and sustained for only brief periods (e.g., a few consecutive sentences); child briefly develops portions of stories with inconsistent story lines

3 = child maintains a coherent and relatively consistent story line for more than four consecutive sentences; connects events to sustain a story line and achieve resolution; seldom departs from development of story

* add asterisk if story is exceptionally long

USE OF NARRATIVE VOICE

1 = child seldom assumes a narrative voice to provide the audience with elaborative or explanatory information about her story:

> "And then he went over here. And he got this box and he took it over here."

2 = child assumes narrative voice with occasional elaboration or explanation of the action of her story:

> "Then the monster came along—he walks like this 'cause he has no legs . . . he thought it was a stream so he swam."

3 = child frequently assumes narrative voice to provide descriptions, explanations and extra information about her story to the audience; offers evaluative or comparative comments, metaphors or similes, or commentary about the story, or a combination of all of these:

> "The two huntsmens are just resting in the night. They're not sound asleep—but they're so still that they look like statues. They're making sure everything is OK. . . . They're gonna take care of the bad person and train the dragon."

USE OF DIALOGUE

1 = child includes little or no dialogue in her story

2 = child includes dialogue in her story; however, conversations between characters are perfunctory and brief

> "Hello, Mr. Turtle." "Hello, Mr. Snake. How are you today?" "I'm fine—aren't you cute today."

3 = child includes much dialogue in her story and sustains it for several sentences; conversations between characters are meaningful and include thoughts, feelings, and information:

> [*child uses different voices to represent Kevin and Andrew*]
>
> Kevin: I'm scared, Andrew, I'm scared.
> Andrew: Don't worry, Kevin—leave it to me.

Kevin: But you're not strong enough to do it yet. Here—
take one of these cans of spinach and broccoli and eat it so
you'll be stronger than he is.
Andrew: Good idea, Kevin. You eat one too and then we'll
both be stronger than that dragon 'cause all he eats is slime.
Kevin: OK Now we're ready to get the powerful heart-to-
heart laser so we can destroy that bad dragon.
Andrew: Yeah! Let's go!

USE OF TEMPORAL MARKERS

1 =   child uses only simple, sequential connectives to denote the course of her
       story (then, and then, so now)

2 =   child sometimes includes more complex temporal markers, such as logical
       conectives that indicate time relations between events (before, after, until,
       while, next) and time adverbs that indicate the time of occurrence of
       events (nighttime, the next morning, hundreds of years ago)

3 =   child consistently uses the more complex temporal markers listed in
       level 2

EXPRESSIVENESS

(This category refers only to sound effects used to *support* story; not sound effects that
comprise the story.)

1 =   child uses little or no emphasis in her story; story is presented in a mono-
       tone and child does not use different character voices or sound effects:

       . . . "And then he finds the flowers but then he sneaks into the
       cave and then he finds the jewelry . . . and then he takes it away
       and he gets home and so he puts it into the case."

2 =   child occasionally uses sound effects, other forms of expressiveness
       (character voices, emphasis, singing), or both when telling her story:

       "And the king came along again then he fell in the quicksand.
       AAAARRRGH! . . .Then they're screaming along AAAAYYYY!
       AAAAYYYY!"

3 =   child consistently uses sound effects, lively character voices, and highly
       expressive narration:

       "And then the snake came over, Sssssssssss. And then the giant
       spiders came over, Bow bow wow wow wow! And I shouted: [*high
       voice*] Kevin! Yes, Andrew. . .? [*high voice*] *Go and get this guy!*
       [*lower voice*] Kakagoogoo! Kakagoogoo! Ha ha ha ha. [*very soft
       voice*] OK, Kevin, let's go.' " [*sings a song*]

LEVEL OF VOCABULARY

1 =   child predominantly uses simple language with little use of adjectives:

       "He went over to there."

       "She ate these things."

2 = child uses Level 1 vocabulary but sometimes includes more descriptive and expressive language; some use of adjectives

> "Then the king ran to his little cave."

> "The turtle ate three berries."

3 = child uses a variety of vocabulary; includes adverbs as well as adjectives in her story; uses highly descriptive, mood-setting vocabulary

> "The king crept into the dark and scary cave."

> "And then the magical turtle gobbled up the berries."

SENTENCE STRUCTURE

1 = child uses simple, choppy, parallel sentences or sentence fragments when telling story

> "They're gonna eat this and then they're gonna eat the flowers and then they go away. And then they're walking."

> "He's walking along. He sees a tree. The tree falls down."

2 = child uses Level 1 sentences but also includes prepositional phrases and compound sentences in storytelling

> "The man saw a fuzzy thing and brought it home."

> "The king sent him back in his cave with the jewelry box."

3 = child uses a variety of sentence structures, including Level 1 and 2 sentences, as well as adverbial clauses, relative clauses, participial phrases, or a combination or all of these.

adverbial clauses:

> "Kevin has a can of broccoli in here and I have a can of spinach so we can both get stronger than him *because all he eats is slime*."

> "*If you're good,* I'll let you stay here."

relative clauses:

> "This is supposed to be the trap *that the king set for the dinosaur*."

> "The dragon's power will never get through the brick wall *that I'm building*."

participial phrases:

> "He saw this creature, *looking very hungry*, with his mouth wide open."

> "There was the bead, *falling down his tail*."

EXAMPLES OF SCORING LEVELS FOR THEMATIC COHERENCE

Level 1
(C = Child; A = Adult)

C: I don't know what to start with.

A: The first thing that you can start with is whatever you want. . . .

C: [*Very soft voice*] "Hello." "Who are you?" "I'm the octopus."

A: That's good. Just a little bit louder. He said, "Who are you?" and he said, "I'm the octopus." And then what did he say?

C: I don't know what I want to say.

A: OK Do you want to think about it for a little while?

C: [*Indistinguishable. Much of what child said was difficult to hear.*] OK I'd like to start out with this. "Wow, look at this gold. . . . How did it get here. . . ." "Hi, King." "Hi, turtle." "Hey, turtle (?)." "Wow, it is gold. Hmmm. Let's close it up . . . See you later, turtle." "Who are you?" "I'm a (_____) and I'm going to eat you up." [*to adult*] What are these little funny things? They look like, like creatures from outer space [*referring to white and green furry figures*].

A: Uh huh.

C: They fall (?) from outer space. So . . . "Where is he? Oh, there he is. Hi, King." "Hi, hi, hi, Mars people." I don't know what I have to do.

A: You don't know what you have to do? [*Suggests three story ideas.*]

C: I think that would be a good idea.

A: Which one?

C: The one where people want to find the gold.

A: [*Points out figures and narrates beginning of a story.*]

C: "There's a octopus over there." He . . . stand for black (?). "I found it." "What?" "Oh boy, he found it." Mr. Fox . . . and then Mr. Octopus. [*low voice*] "They found the gold." [*to adult*] I don't know what to do next.

Level 2

A: Can you tell me what's happening? . . .

C: He's taking this and (_____) in here. . . And then he took his suitcase, so he put it down, and now he's gonna get the bucket. Then he's gonna go fill it up with water and then he's gonna put it in the cave and then the dragon's gonna put flowers in it so that fire can get out. And the king got, and then got (?) the treasure and then he tried to open it . . . But he couldn't so he put it back. And then he saw the creature and the creature said, "Who are you?" and he said, "I'm a little creature," and he make out (_____) and hopped over to the turtle pond and went into the (_____), so the king saw a snake and he went here. So the king went to the river and saw a person there so, and the turtle was in the river and the turtle comed out and the play (?) went in and went, whoopsie daisy, and the king (_____) went right in . . . Also, the little girl went to help the king up. So the king went up to his house and into the cave. The monster used to live (and then another monster lived here [?]) outside. So the little girl saw the treasure so she picked it up and she was carrying it and she saw, saw a friend of hers and she was standing (?) and the friend went away right over to here, and the snake comed off and over here and this and it (?) out. And that was (_____) and he took his suitcase and he went over to in here and that's where he standed with his suitcase but put his hand up and he put that sidewards, so, and then he went under here to stand up until the friend comed back [*moves figures around*].

Level 3

C: . . . And then the guards dropped into their hobby car and drove away without the king following them and he said, [*high voice*] Wait, wait, stop, wait." So they stopped and the king hopped into the car and they all drove away. "Rrrrmm" [*sound effect for car*]. And they stopped to pick up some treasures. The king picked up one and dropped it on his crown and put the treasure in the car and dropped some more treasures in the car and dropped them on the crown and they left them there swinging. . . . (?) The king said, [*high voice*] "Wait, wait for me." Then he jumped! "Now the gold(?)." They put all the gold in a suitcase and decided to pack all out (?) clothes and go on a trip.

A: Uh huh.

C: But that's not the end! The monster dropped into the castle by mistake and the guards were looking out the window and said, and closed his mouth and then he scrubbled away, and then everyone came out. . . . Now pretend all the treasures were belonged to the king, so the king put all the stuff, the treasures away in the cave and brought them home. . . . He picked up all the treasures that he had dropped on the ground and put them into his, the cave, he left some out for the bears and dropped them into the forest for the bears to find because he loved them so much, very, very much. . . . He closed up the suitcase and walked home to the castle, but then the wicked monster moved out and started chasing everyone away and he left footprints in the blooming snow. Hey, I got it—this could be some falling snow [*holding up clay*].

TABLE 11: STORYBOARD OBSERVATION SHEET

Child _____   Date _____

Age _____   Observer _____

Please comment as much as possible on the following:

physical manipulation of props   –   for example, child seems overwhelmed by props or seems more interested in setting up scene than in telling story

transformation of materials/activity –   for example, child uses clay arch as rainbow or uses extra-props box as a ship

skills from different domains   –   for example, child sings her story or counts the objects on the storyboard

Be specific and detailed in your account of these and any other visual cues so that the scorer has a more complete sense of the physical dynamics of the child's storytelling.

Primary Language Function: Language Skills: Comments:

_____ storytelling   Nature of Narrative Structure ☐

_____ interacting with adult   Thematic Coherence ☐

_____ investigating   Use of Narrative Voice ☐

_____ describing   Use of Dialogue ☐

_____ labeling or categorizing   Use of Temporal Markers ☐

                Expressiveness ☐

                Level of Vocabulary ☐

                Sentence Structure ☐

                TOTAL ☐

Scorer_____

Date_____

TABLE 12: STORYBOARD SUMMARY SHEET

Child (age)	Nature of Narrative Structure	Thematic Coherence	Use of Narrative Voice	Use of Dialogue	Use of Temporal Markers	Expressiveness	Level of Vocabulary	Sentence Structure	TOTAL	Comments and Observations

Date _____

❏ REPORTER ACTIVITIES

—Purpose and Activities Description

The purpose of the Reporter Activities is to identify and assess language skills not elicited by the Storyboard Activity. Although both activities assess narrative abilities, each taps a different genre of narrative: storytelling and reporting, respectively. The Reporter Activities focus on the child's ability (a) to report content accurately, (b) to be selective in reporting detail, and (c) to recognize and articulate sequential or causal relations or both. The activities also address a child's level of focus: Does she recount main events and provide a sense of the broad picture, or does she concentrate more narrowly on the specifics of one or two episodes? Finally, measures similar to those examined in the Storyboard Activity, such as complexity of vocabulary and sentence structure, are also taken.

Like the Storyboard, the Reporter Activities are designed to examine children's linguistic abilities applied in a meaningful context. The assessment consists of two separate activities, the Movie Report and Weekend News. For the Movie Report, children watch a short movie or video. Then they are asked to recount everything that happened in the movie from start to finish.

The movie presents a strong stimulus for eliciting reporting language in the past tense as well as summarization skills. It is important that the movie contain little or no oral narration so that the interviewer can learn how a child invents and represents what is happening, rather than what she repeats from the soundtrack.

Showing all the children the same movie provides a single, controlled stimulus to which the interviewer can refer when assessing accuracy of content. In addition to looking at the child's use of past tense and ability to summarize the material, the interviewer can also determine whether the child takes into account that the adult has not seen the movie (applicable only in some versions of this activity). Finally, the interviewer can look at whether the child's language is appropriate to the content of the film (e.g., using words such as *hatched, chick,* and *beak,* rather than *came out, bird,* and *mouth*).

The second activity, Weekend News, is intended to become part of the ongoing classroom curriculum. Every 1 or 2 Mondays, children are asked to tell what happened over the weekend. They may relate personal interactions or focus on describing events and activities. Children's accounts most likely will include a variety of reality-based and fantasy events. The news format was chosen because it gives teachers a deliberate context and structure in which to collect and document over time numerous samples of children's reporting language.

The Weekend News Activity gives children an opportunity to practice recall and to reflect on what they have done. This activity also may give them a better understanding of time (e.g., which day was *yesterday,* which day was *Saturday*). Teachers can increase their awareness of children's discourse by becoming familiar with the type of analysis reflected in the scoring criteria. They can look at which events a child decides to highlight, the number of events that she is able to report, the accuracy of the time sequences of the account, and her ability to introduce new topics while maintaining a consistent point of reference.

Teachers may discover that some children are more comfortable reporting in a one-on-one context than during group times (or vice versa). Although weekends provide a rich source of information, other possible topics include describing special events in school, holidays, vacations, and field trips.

1. MOVIE REPORT

—Materials and Set-Up

Select the movie or video for this activity carefully. Although the content may vary, choose the film with the following criteria in mind:

1. it should be unfamiliar to the children;
2. it should not be narrated, though background music is a welcome feature;
3. it should be short, preferably no longer than eight minutes;
4. if possible, the development or plot of the film should contain a clearly defined sequence of events.

Possible subjects include natural events, such as a beaver building a dam. Fictional content is not desirable, for you should avoid eliciting the fantasy component already embedded in the Storyboard Activity. Movies such as *Chick, Chick, Chick; Smile for Auntie;* and *The Red Balloon* meet some, but not all, of the above criteria. If time and resources allow, you may want to create your own video, tailoring it to the above features.

In the weeks preceding the movie, discuss the notion

of reporting. In such preparation, you can talk with children about what they are doing when they "share their news" at group time. Stress that reporting means telling the *important* things that happened. If children are familiar with *Sesame Street,* you can ask them to describe what Kermit, the News Reporter does.

The movie can be shown in the classroom or, if available, in an audiovisual room. Children enjoy receiving tickets and small cups of popcorn as they enter the "theater." If possible, show the movie to small enough groups of children that you will be able to interview them all on the same day. Interview each child separately in a relatively private and quiet corner of the room, recording the child's account on tape for scoring later.

—Procedure and Script

Introduce the movie to the class as follows: "Today we will be seeing a movie about _____. After it is over, we will pretend to be reporters (like Kermit), so let's try to remember what happens." You may not want to tell children the title of the movie so that you can see if they are able come up with a title of their own. Writing down the sequence of events in the movie will assist you in the interviewing and scoring parts of the activity. (See Table 13, p. 58, for a list of scenes in *Chick, Chick, Chick* [Churchill Films, 1975], the movie used in the development of this activity. It is now available on videocassette from SVE in Chicago.)

After the movie, interview the children individually. A list of the questions used for *Chick, Chick, Chick* is included in Table 14. Each child receives the same introduction: "Now we are going to be news reporters and tell the important things that happened in the movie. I'll start and you can continue. The first thing I saw happen was _____ [e.g., "a rooster went 'cock-a-doodle-doo' " in *Chick, Chick, Chick,* or "a little boy found a balloon" in *The Red Balloon*]. Now you be the reporter, and tell me the things you saw happen after that. What did you see next?"

If children are reluctant to talk, additional prompts include "Tell me everything that happened to _____ from start to finish." "Tell me the other things that happened." "What else happened?" and "What happened next?" To end the report, ask the child to think of a good name to call the movie. Children may also enjoy hearing their voices played back on the tape recorder.

Because some children will be interviewed sooner than others, you may want to give a second chance to children who seem adversely affected by having their report delayed. You can either show them a new movie on which they can report, or you can show the same movie a second time.

—Scoring

If time allows, transcribe the tapes of the children's reports. Otherwise, score the narratives directly from the tapes. Use the criteria in Table 15 to record individual children's scores on the observation sheet in Table 16. Use the summary sheet in Table 17 for compiling the results for the class as a whole.

—Preliminary Results: 1985–1987

Children watched and reported on the film *Chick, Chick, Chick.* The type and sophistication of their reporting varied greatly. There was an especially wide range in the following areas: accuracy of content, ability to identify main events and to distinguish "general" from "particular," richness and abundance of detail, and the degree to which the report was free from fanciful ornamentation. Children also varied in their ease of entry into the activity and the degree of prompting needed.

At least two factors influenced children's abilities to report the content effectively. One was the degree to which children let their imaginations color their reports. One child described with great enthusiasm a dog who chased a cat and a kitty-cat who climbed a tree. He also saw a bald eagle, a runaway bull, an ostrich, a puppy dog that barked, and pigs that were killed for bacon. None of this was in the film. While the detail in his report was rich and abundant, it was not accurate. The second factor was children's hesitancy to report beyond the scope of the interviewer's question. Another child reported very little spontaneously and included almost no detail. He depended on the adult's prompts to trigger recollections and reported only in broad strokes. In his account, the film contained a pussycat, chickens, and pigs: "They were all playing around together." The movie was about "animals running around." In contrast to the first child's report, this report was accurate, but lacking in depth and richness of detail.

Children's language also differed in color and precision. One boy relied heavily on sound effects and gestures, letting them substitute for words. All of the children became most detailed and precise in the descriptions of the baby chick—the most remarkable, perhaps even exotic, part of the film. Children's specificity of word choice varied greatly: At the most general level, one boy referred to animals as "stuff" on the farm; on a more specific level, one boy described the chick as follows: "It looked like it had hair when it came out. It didn't look like the mom, it didn't look like the little babies who were already hatched, it had fuzz on it." Another child said, "It was sweaty and wet, with no feathers." Other children commented that it looked like "a gross slug," "a little tadpole," "a spider," "hairy and fuzzy," and "disgusting."

Only a few children indicated a sense of the general framework of the movie (i.e., flashbacks to a chick hatching from an egg). One child said, "They keep showing him coming out." Another reported, "Every once in a while they showed it hatching, and then at the end, the chicken was squeaking." Another volunteered, "We saw a baby chick coming out of a shell. They took different times showing it." But most children did not refer to the sequence of shots revealing the chick's birth.

One child artificially imposed an order on the content of the film. He said at the beginning of his report that he had "four things to tell." His report did not clearly articulate each thing, but he clung to his stated structure. At the end of the interview, he made several efforts to recall the "fourth thing" he wanted to tell. (His structure may have reflected what he has perceived as an "adult style" of reporting.)

Several children drew inferences about the content of the movie, although such speculation often was colored by fanciful digressions. One child was especially able and willing to speculate about the reasons behind different events: "I didn't see the farmer's head, I only saw his legs. I thought he came to feed the animals." When she reported that the chicks "rolled in the pig's mud" (an invented detail), she commented, "Their mom, I guess, didn't like that when she saw them." Another child said, "It was about a farm . . . you know what was missing? A sheep." Inviting children to come up with a title for the film proved difficult for some. One child could suggest only *A Book*. Other titles included *Farmyard Fun*, *The Majestic Farm*, *Farm Animals*, and *Chicken Movie*.

A few children transformed the task to suit their particular interest or strength. For instance, one boy used the farm scene to create his own jokes and humorous

scenarios. Another spun a fanciful tale about an earring that frightened a chick. Finally, one child was interested primarily in how the movie projector ran.

2. WEEKEND NEWS

—Materials and Set-Up

Weekend News supplements the Movie Report and can be conducted in a number of ways. Teachers can set aside the writing table every Monday for children to tell their news, or the class can be divided into small groups, with each group placed in a different activity area of the room. While one child gives her news, the others can play with blocks, art materials, or playdough until every child has had a turn. This set-up allows you to work with one child at a time, while keeping an eye on the rest of the group.

You can write the child's name and date on notebook paper, and then post the children's news for parental viewing at the end of the day. The collection of news then becomes part of a large notebook that serves as the classroom newspaper. Children usually enjoy choosing different-colored markers for teachers to use in recording their news. Children also can make drawings to accompany their news reports. A back-up tape recording may come in handy if children talk too quickly for you to transcribe their news accurately.

—Procedure and Script

Before beginning Weekend News, discuss the meaning of the term *weekend* with children. At group time, talk about what children and teachers have done on their weekends. Send a note home to parents informing them of the Weekend News Activity and asking them to help children gather their news. On Fridays, remind children to collect their news for the Monday reports. You also can set aside a group time to choose a title for the newspaper.

The format of the activity will vary depending on teacher preferences and classroom set-ups. News can be collected on a weekly or biweekly basis, with all or part of the class. You may want to start children off with a relatively open-ended, initial prompt: "Tell me about your weekend." This can be followed up with such prompts as: "After you went home from school on Friday and went to bed, what did you do when you got up on Saturday morning?" If you wish to keep track of the number of prompts provided, indicate with an asterisk prompts such as "What else?" or "What did you do/see there?" If children seem interested, you can play tapes of the children's news at group time.

—Scoring

In light of issues of transcription and time, this activity is perhaps best scored informally and holistically. If time allows, you can choose several days during the year when the children's reports will be taped or transcribed or both for more structured scoring. The purpose of the criteria and definitions listed in Table 18 is to provide a framework for thinking about and analyzing children's reporting abilities. If you desire a more structured assessment, you can use the scoring sheet provided in Table 19.

To score this activity, choose a set of 6 to 10 reports for each child. If a child has not given 6 reports, do not include her in the assessment. If a child has more than 10 reports, choose the best ten for scoring purposes. Record children's scores in the summary sheet provided in Table 20.

—Preliminary Results: 1987–1988

The Weekend News reports reflected a wide range of reporting ability. Some children were able to give a detailed and coherent account of their activities with little or no prompting from the adult:

C: I went to the museum with knights and I saw a lot of knights and flags and my dad was interested in the helmets and the knights too. My dad took pictures of them, but then there was some more left and the camera didn't work so my dad didn't use it. It had one more picture, but it didn't work. . . . So then he wanted to go in the place where the rest of the knights were and there was Greek armor and Roman armor. They used to be real, but they're not real anymore. They're dead, but they put the pieces together. . . . Then he went back down the stairs to look at the castle and then he went upstairs to see the other knights. And they had, like, gauntlets. And there are things that move so you can pinch the guy. And I saw one with pointy feet armor.

Many children were able to provide details only when prompted by the adult. The sentence structure and complexity of vocabulary varied from simple sentences and sentence fragments to more complex sentences, featuring relative and adverbial clauses. A typical sequence:

A: What did you do this weekend?

C: Yesterday I stayed home because I was sick.

A: Did you do anything special while you were home?

C: We played a monster game. It wasn't really scary.

A: What is that?

C: There's a little rectangle you put them on. The one that gets to the board first wins. Me and my mommy did it! Daddy was working. Actually, daddy worked all day.

A: Anything else?

C: We went to my friend's school and brought two friends home.

A: What did you and your friends do?

C: We played, we watched *Sesame Street.* Last night, it was "Christmas on Sesame." Did you watch it? Big Bird was some place and somebody couldn't find him . . . and Cookie Monster ate the leaves on the Christmas tree!

A number of children offered only brief accounts of their weekend activities, even when prompted by an adult. They used mainly simple sentences with basic vocabulary and connectors:

C: I goed swimming, goed at the park, goed on the swings, go to my grandma—my grandma came to my house.

A: What did you do with your grandma?

C: We played Chutes and Ladders. That's it for today.

Occasionally, some children seemed to invent or combine activities, or they reported experiences that likely took place at another point in time:

C: I went to Disney World two times! After that day, I went to California. I see Mickey Mouse and Minnie . . . I caught a black bear.

A: What else did you do?

C: I went on upside-down roller coaster. It had seat belts. You had to hold on tight, real tight!

Sometimes, children revealed in their reports strengths or interests in other areas. For example, one child, in the middle of her description of the play *H.M.S. Pinafore,* decided to sing "Little Buttercup" in falsetto. Another boy with an interest in science explained in detail how to play a sophisticated video game.

All 20 children in the group participated in the activity at least once during the year. Four children were eager participants, sharing their news regularly every week or two. Some of the children were either unable or unwilling to report their weekend news. When asked for their news, these children would usually respond that they did not do anything or that they could not remember. Three children reported on their weekends no more than once or twice during the year. Finally, for some, group time proved a more comfortable format for reporting their news.

—Further Suggestions for the Domain

You can conduct the following activities to enrich children's experience in the language domain:

• A storytelling area with different activities that allow you to look at language skills across various types of narrative tasks. For example, individual differences are likely to appear when children are asked to tell a story that stands on its own, as opposed to telling one based on pictures in a book or figures on a terrain. Some children will be able to move easily across the various options.

You also can set up a listening library/recording studio in one area of the classroom with a large tape recorder, blank tapes, and wordless books. Children can record themselves telling stories they have invented or with which they are familiar. Other children then can listen to the tapes.

• Play rhyming and metaphor games with the children. For example, tell a story about a little girl who, whenever she hears certain words, finds a rhyming word to go with them. To elicit metaphors, ask children to make up pretend names for a range of real and ambiguous-looking objects or shapes.

• Give children richly illustrated magazines and a pair of scissors and ask them to find a picture about which they would like to tell a story. Have children cut out the picture and paste it on a big piece of construction paper. Write children's stories underneath the pictures they choose. Magazines such as *National Geographic* offer a variety of colorful and intriguing photographs, or you can use children's own artwork for this activity.

• Set up a small puppet theater with a set of provocative characters such as a pirate, a baby, and a clown. Use of the puppets serves as a stimulus for *present tense* dialogue. Demonstrate a first scene for the children that they can continue.

• When conducting some of the activities above, you might ask yourself these questions:

1. Can you identify who is doing what to whom? Is there a plot—something that happens to somebody? Can you identify each character?
2. Is the content novel, fully elaborated, or both? Are the events recounted "thick" (full blown, fleshed out) or "thin" (simple, without much embellishment)?
3. Does the child convey a sense of mood? Does she vary her speed and tone of voice, for example slowing down for the suspenseful parts?
4. Does the order of mention correspond to the order of occurrence, or can the child tell things out of order? Does she use temporal and causal sequencing? Is her timeline clear?
5. Does the child use a single tense or is she able to use additional tenses (past, present, progressive) to create contrasts?
6. Is the child able to select appropriate vocabulary for her script (e.g., using the word *grabbed* instead of *took*)? Does she use figurative language?
7. How many voices does the child use? Does she use narrative, dialogue, or stage management (e.g., setting up the scene for the viewer/listener)?

TABLE 13: SEQUENCE OF EVENTS IN *CHICK, CHICK, CHICK*

[** = shots of birth of baby chick, which are interspersed throughout the film]

I. WAKE-UP

    we hear rooster's "cock-a-doodle-doo"
    everyone stretches: chick, horse, cow

II. FEEDING

    farmer's feet enter chicken coop
    we hear him call, "Here chick, chick, chick"
    we see farmer's hand throw corn onto ground
    mother hen gets off her nest
** we see eggs in the nest for the first time
** one egg has a tiny crack
    chickens are feeding on the scattered corn
    horse saunters over to where the chickens are feeding
    horse starts eating the corn
    a red-and-black bug crawls past the chicks
    two chicks have a fight over the bug
    one chick wins and gobbles the bug up, swallowing it with a loud gulp
** back to the nest with the egg: the shell is partly broken off now and we can see something wet and hairy throbbing inside

III. ADVENTURES

    chick wanders through corn rows—field looks like a forest of dried corn plants
    chick leaves the corn rows and finds itself among cows
    the cows sniff the chick
    chick wanders away from the cows and enters a pigpen
    big, muddy pigs are eating
    the pigs see the chick and start sniffing it
    the chick runs off madly until it takes cover under its mother's wing
    we see the hens at the mud puddles
    the movement of the chickens' feet in the mud is coordinated with the music and sound effects
    we see the chickens drinking and again hear sound effects
** back to the nest with the egg: the egg is throbbing heavily and opening more and more
    danger: a kitten sits watching the chickens and a hawk circles overhead
    the mother hen scurries to round up the chicks
    rooster scares kitten off
    the kitten runs off howling

IV. BIRTH

** frequency of shots cutting from chicken family to egg increases
** we see baby chick trying to pull itself out of the egg
** finally, baby chick is outside the egg
** baby chick is wet, breathing heavily, with big eyes
** baby chick cheeps over and over again and the movie ends

TABLE 14: THE MOVIE REPORT INTERVIEW: QUESTIONS ABOUT *CHICK, CHICK, CHICK*

1. Now we are going to be news reporters and tell the important things that happened in the movie. I'll start and you can continue. The first thing I saw happen was a rooster went "cock-a-doodle-doo." Now you be the reporter and tell me the things you saw happen after that. What did you see next?

2. What different [other] kinds of animals did you see on the farm?

3. What were the animals doing?

4. Tell me what the newborn baby chick looked like. How was it the same as the other chicks? How was it different from them?

5. What do you want this story to be called?

TABLE 15: MOVIE REPORT SCORING CRITERIA

ENTRY INTO ACTIVITY/LEVEL OF SCAFFOLDING

0 =   very little or no reporting; rarely reports when questioned or prompted; often responds with "I can't remember" or "I don't know," or does not wish to participate in the activity at all*

1 =   child reports, but only with prompting

2 =   child reports, in response to questions and prompts *and also spontaneously*

3 =   child reports on events in the movie with little or no prompting

* The rest of the scoring may not apply; proceed only if there is enough reporting to score

ACCURACY OF CONTENT

0 =   not applicable because child transforms activity by telling a story of her own or recounting events that were not in the movie

> "There was a peacock . . . and a bald eagle . . . and a rooster who said, "I'm the king of the barnyard!"

> "When I went to the farm with my dad and mom . . . my father said to the pig . . . 'Hey pig, how's the slop?' "

1 =   child identifies very few main events or characters from the movie

> "I remember seeing a pussycat and a chicken."

> "There was a horse and some pigs and some chicks."

2 =   child identifies several main events, characters, or both from the movie

> "The thing I hated the most . . . was the mud. And I saw a baby chick in there too. . . . And I saw a rooster cock-a-doodle-doo. . . . And the next little thing was the regular chicken that was laying the egg."

3 =   child identifies many or all of the main events, characters, or both from the movie

> "The pig was in the pigpen and then the chick flew over, and then the pig found the chicken and the chicken started running. . . . I also saw a chick hatching . . . and every once in a while they showed it hatching and then at the end the chicken was squeaking."

☆ =   child is able to identify several main events, characters, or both from the movie in correct sequence

SENSE OF STRUCTURE/THEME

0 =   not applicable because child transforms activity by telling a story of her own or recounting events that were not in the movie

> "There was parrots, different color parrots, little birds, baby goats . . . little kittens . . . and other like bobcats, tigers, lions. . . ."

> "The pigs were writing pictures . . . and then the cow said to the pig, 'I gotta drink some milk—I'm getting fat!'"

1 =   child reveals minimal awareness of the movie's theme; focus is narrow and child is not able to generalize from the specific isolated events to the theme of the movie

> "I remember seeing a chick . . . and I remember seeing, but I might not have, I remember seeing a cow."

> "I know there was . . . a duck . . . just a duck."

2 = child reveals a limited perspective of the movie's framework; child is somewhat able to develop the theme of the movie, but the account is sparse

> "[There were] cows running around. . . . The farmer came in to feed the animals."

3 = child reveals a broader focus by generalizing from specific, isolated events in the movie to a general or recurrent theme; child appears to have some sense of movie's framework

> " And the next thing is we saw the baby chick coming out of the shell . . . they took different times showing it."

> "I also saw a chick hatching and . . . every once in a while they showed it hatching and then at the end the chicken was squeaking."

COMPLEXITY OF VOCABULARY/LEVEL OF DETAIL

1 = child's descriptions of events in the movie are sparse and undetailed; child uses simple language with little use of adjectives

> "There was a farm."

> "There was a chicken and some cows."

2 = child's descriptions of events in the movie are sometimes detailed; child recounts some specifics about certain events in the movie, but not others; child includes some specific and expressive vocabulary

> "[There were] cows running around."

> "[The newborn chick] looks like a different color and it makes a littler noise."

3 = child's descriptions of events in the movie are often detailed; child uses a variety of vocabulary; language is frequently specific and expressive

> "And we also saw the farmer's shoes. He was walking. We didn't see his whole body."

> "In the egg there's a liquid that you can't see and the little chickie gets the liquid on it."

> "[The newborn chick] was all sweaty and wet with no feathers."

SENTENCE STRUCTURE

1 = child uses simple sentences or sentence fragments

> "The chickie was wet."

> "Chickens running around."

2 = child uses Level 1 sentences but also includes prepositional phrases, compound sentences, or both

> "The dog was chasing the cat, *but* the cat climbed *up the tree*."

3 = child uses a variety of sentence structures, including Level 1 and 2 sentences, as well as adverbial clauses, relative clauses, participial phrases, or a combination or all of these

> adverbial clause: "It looked like it had hair on it *when it came out*."

> relative clause: "In the egg there's a liquid *that you can't see*."

> "It didn't look like the little babies *who were already hatched*."

> participial phrase: "We saw a baby chick *coming out of the shell*."

> "There was a red ant *crawling across the chicken place*."

TABLE 16: MOVIE REPORT OBSERVATION SHEET

Child _____ Age _____ Date _____ Observer _____

Categories of Skill	Score	Comments & Observations
Entry into Activity/Level of Scaffolding		
Accuracy of Content		
Sense of Structure/Theme		
Complexity of Vocabulary/Level of Detail		
Sentence Structure		
TOTAL		

Child (age)	Entry Into Activity/ Level of Scaffolding	Accuracy of Content	Sense of Structure/Theme	Complexity of Vocabulary/ Level of Detail	Sentence Structure	TOTAL	Comments and Observations

TABLE 17: MOVIE REPORT SUMMARY SHEET

TABLE 18: WEEKEND NEWS SCORING CRITERIA

ENTRY INTO ACTIVITY/LEVEL OF SCAFFOLDING

0 = very little or no reporting; rarely responds to questions and prompts; often responds with "I can't remember" or "I don't know"; does not wish to participate in the activity at all*

1 = child reports, but only with prompting

2 = child reports, in response to questions and prompts *and also spontaneously*

3 = child reports on events or experiences with little or no prompting

* Proceed only if there is enough reporting to score

NARRATIVE COHERENCE

(see Examples of Scoring Levels at the end of this table)

1 = very little linkage between sentences; transitions from one thought to the next are unclear; child's report mainly consists of different, unrelated items

2 = some relation between sentences, but often thoughts are not directly connected

3 = child presents a coherent and well-connected report

EXPANSION OF MAIN EVENTS

1 = child's descriptions are sparse and undetailed

"I went out with my dad."

"I went to the circus."

2 = child's descriptions are sometimes embellished; child recounts some specifics about certain experiences

"I went to the playground and I went on the slide. I went on the bars and I even went on the slide, and the trees were different colors."

3 = child's descriptions are often detailed; important events are elaborated on

"I went to a play one day and it was called *H.M.S. Pinafore Ship* and it was fun. And there was a lady and she was called their Little Buttercup. And my sister knows how to play it on the piano and I know how to sing it. . . . She went like this [*sings 'Little Buttercup'*]."

COMPLEXITY OF VOCABULARY/LEVEL OF DETAIL

1 = child speaks in very general terms and uses simple language with little use of adjectives

"I go swimming, go at the park, go on the swings, go to my grandma."

2 = child uses level 1 language, but also includes more specific and expressive vocabulary

"My grandmother and her best friend came. And we had so much fun. And they let me go along with them when they went to outings . . . outings mean going on trips and buying things in stores."

3 = child uses a variety of vocabulary; language is often specific and expressive

"They had knights with different kinds of helmets. They were real knights. I got a belt, I got a sword, a shield, and a plume. A plume is a feather. A real knight . . . touched me like this [*on head*] and this [*on shoulder*]."

Event Relationships /Use of Connectors

1 =   child uses mainly simple, sequential connectors (sequential connectors indicate the sequential structure of the report, e.g., *and, then, so*)

2 =   child uses mostly Level 1 connectors and also includes a few differentiated (sequential and temporal) connectors (temporal connectors indicate time relations between events, e.g., but, *until, first, in the end*)

3 =   child uses a variety of connectors (sequential, temporal, and causal/logical) ranging from simple to highly differentiated, but not necessarily repeatedly or consistently (e.g., *because, since, except, even, when, while, before, after, finally, the next day*)

Sentence Structure

1 =   child uses simple sentences or sentence fragments

"I had a cold."

"They jumping through the fire."

2 =   child uses Level 1 sentences but also includes prepositional phrase, compound sentences, or both:

"Donny came over my house *and played knights*."

"I went over my daddy's and we sitted *by the fire*."

3 =   child uses a variety of sentence structures, including Level 1 and 2 sentences, as well as adverbial clauses, relative clauses, participial phrases, or a combination or all of these:

adverbial clause:

"*When we went home*, my sister made us apple sauce."

"*Over the weekend*, I went to Vermont."

relative clause:

"I saw a man *who was dressed up to be a wolfman*."

"They have a merry-go-round and a Ferris wheel *that goes upside-down*."

participial phrase:

"There was a man *jumping up and down*."

"We were in a train *going really fast*."

EXAMPLES OF SCORING LEVELS FOR "NARRATIVE COHERENCE"

Level 1

"When I trick or treated, my mom had to hold the bag because it got so heavy. In the summer, I goed to my papa's pool. That's it."

"I stayed home all day because I was sick. I had some pills before school. After I ride my bike, I go inside and come home. I saw the Michael Jackson movie and then I came and I was dancin' all around. Then I went to Copley Center. Then I knocked my chair down. Then I saw little polka dots at the Michael Jackson movie and then I came right home."

"I went to the circus. And I made some leafmen. And I . . . watched television."

Level 2

"I went to New York, to Disney World, North Carolina. I saw Christina there. It was boring in New York because there were no rides there."

"Over the weekend, I went to Vermont. And I stayed at my condo. When we went home, my sister made us applesauce. When I went home from Vermont and before I came home, I brushed my teeth. I didn't do anything else."

Level 3

"One of my big crickets died. I kept him in my house. I think he jumped way up and then came way down so that's why he died. I have a little cricket too."

"This weekend I'm going to a new beach. It's filled with toys and playthings. And they have lots of cotton candy and I think it's free. And I think they have food and drinks, of course. They have a merry-go-round and a ferris wheel that goes upside-down. I can't wait 'cause I didn't do anything at home the last days. I been on a Ferris wheel before, you know."

TABLE 19: WEEKEND NEWS OBSERVATION SHEET

Child _____   Age _____   Date _____   Observer _____   Number of Reports _____

Categories of Skill	Score	Comments and Observations
Entry Into Activity/Level of Scaffolding		
Narrative Coherence		
Expansion of Main Events		
Complexity of Vocabulary/Level of Detail		
Event Relationships/Use of Connectors		
Sentence Structure		
TOTAL		

										Child (age)
										Number of Reports
										Entry Into Activity/ Level of Scaffolding
										Narrative Coherence
										Expansion of Main Events
										Complexity of Vocabulary/ Level of Detail
										Event Relationships/ Use of Connectors
										Sentence Structure
										TOTAL

TABLE 20: WEEKEND NEWS SUMMARY SHEET

Date _____

CHAPTER 3
MATHEMATICAL DOMAIN

—INTRODUCTION

The mathematical domain is highly valued in Western culture: Numerical operations are taught and modeled in every part of our society. Mathematical understanding begins with the world of objects and actions performed on those objects, later becoming increasingly abstract and removed from real-world referents. For the preschool child, logical-mathematical competence ranges from early counting and incrementing skills (the ability to increase or decrease a quantity by 1) to the ability to record and organize number information in a notational system. Nearly every preschool child is familiar with numbers in such forms as ages, telephone numbers, and the number of cookies available for snack. A vast amount of literature building on the important and influential work of Jean Piaget (1952) provides a description of the universal and stage-like development of mathematical ability (Case, 1985; Gelman & Gallistel, 1986), yet relatively little has been written about what distinguishes one child's ability from that of another. The Spectrum number activities attempt to capture the range of individual differences seen every day in the preschool classroom.

Preschool assessment in this area typically has been closely tied to the traditional measures of IQ. Mathematical problems have answers which are finite, universal, and clearly delineated as right or wrong. A typical question in the arithmetic section of the Wechsler Preschool and Primary Scale of Intelligence (WPPSI) asks: "If one apple costs 2 cents, how much will two apples cost?" (Wechsler, 1967.) Although such measures are relatively easy to administer and have been shown to predict academic success, they also have many disadvantages. As noted in the Introduction to this handbook, the tests typically are administered in a single meeting outside the familiarity of the classroom environment by a person the child has never met. They involve a large language component (even when the area being tested is mathematics), and often include hypothetical situations without concrete objects for the child to manipulate.

In any attempt to conceptualize the number domain, it is important to bear two issues in mind. First, logical-mathematical ability in 4-year-olds may or may not be related to learning to count. Counting is a special skill, limited in scope. The bulk of early number research, focusing on counting and early arithmetic skills, is not especially useful for designing assessment tools that are in accordance with the guidelines set forth in the Introduction. Second, the differences between logic and mathematics, or logic and language, are not completely clear. Are these abilities related on one continuum or are they discontinuous? Children may show insight into logical structures and causal principles without drawing on any verbal skill. Research has shown that children gifted in mathematics are quite capable of solving problems through intuition without understanding why the answer is correct (Consuegra, 1986). The potential interrelationships of such competencies have yet to be clearly delineated.

Counting begins in a social context where children learn to recognize small quantities while playing with objects and numbers. By age 4 1/2, most children have acquired one-to-one correspondence (the principle of successively assigning a single, distinct number name to each and every item to be counted), but are not yet troubled if they make a mistake or do not know the next number word. Of course, poor performance on a counting task also may reflect lack of effort or inaccurate execution rather than lack of understanding. Children at 4, then, although not always reliable counters, do have some knowledge about how the number system works and can make inferences that are *not* based on specific experiences with counting. For example, one child, in a Spectrum classroom, held six markers in his hand, with his thumb dividing them in half. He said, "I know I have six markers because there are three here, and three there, and 3 and 3 make 6." Such inferencing is not merely rote skill; however, the reasoning involved may apply only to the number system, rather than indicating a more general logical ability.

Most children can adjust small quantities by increments of one or two units. However, incrementing ability is not the same as the ability to recite the next number word. Indeed, there are data to suggest that incrementing skill serves to organize the development of a child's counting skills. Evidence also suggests that number conservation is independent of counting ability (Walters, 1982). Since the ability to explain one's reasoning develops after the reasoning skills themselves, any task that is aimed at assessing number concepts must restrict the verbal component.

—CONCEPTUALIZING THE MATHEMATICAL ACTIVITIES

To elicit the variety of ways in which children think about numbers, we developed two mathematical activities: the Dinosaur Game and the Bus Game. In developing these games, we drew on the above-mentioned research on early mathematical skills as well as our own observations of children in the on

classroom. The child who is particularly strong in the math domain takes special delight in numbers and is alert to almost any reference to them. When asked how many children are at school, she makes calculations such as: "Well, if there are usually 24 kids, and 2 are absent, easy—22 kids are here today." Such a child enjoys thinking in terms of numbers, spontaneously challenging herself to count in her head, or spending 20 minutes playing a number card game. The Dinosaur Game is especially intriguing for such children, giving them a chance to figure out strategies that can help them win.

In designing the number assessments, we also focused on those abilities that are relevant to the achievement of significant and rewarding adult roles in our society. Meaningful end states include accountant, bookkeeper, computer programmer, and mathematician. Skills relevant to this domain include finding shortcuts for calculations, problem solving, making reasonable estimates, noticing relationships between numbers, rapid comprehension and generalization, and inventing and using notation. A 4-year-old we observed correctly estimated the age of an experimenter by drawing on his own relevant information—the age of his mother. Some children also demonstrate a sensitivity to the aesthetics of mathematics, such as noticing symmetry and patterns. Teachers should record observations of math-related performances such as these in a number notebook.

❑ DINOSAUR GAME

—Purpose and Activity Description

The purpose of the Dinosaur Game is to assess children's understanding of number concepts, counting skills, ability to adhere to rules, and use of strategy. The game also assesses children's understanding of the significance of symbols and their ability to translate symbol into action. The assessment is based on playing a board game in which two plastic dinosaurs race against each other in an effort to escape from the dinosaur pictured on the board. The players use dice to determine the direction and number of spaces that their dinosaurs can move. Children also are given the opportunity to articulate in their own words their understanding of both rules and strategy.

By embedding the measure for understanding numbers, rules, and strategy in a board game with movable pieces, we were able to make the concepts concrete and give children an active part in the game. The language used in administering the task is simple and familiar to 4-year-olds, revolving around the two dinosaurs fleeing from the hungry mouth of the diplodocus pictured on the board. We sought to avoid the phrasing of formal arithmetic to prevent unnecessary confusion. We took our lesson from Martin Hughes's (1981) study of preschool children's arithmetic abilities. A 4-year-old, when asked what 1 and 2 makes, replied that she could not answer because "she didn't go to school yet"—revealing unusual insight into the kind of language being used. The problem solving in the Dinosaur Game, in contrast, is concrete, active, and relatively independent of verbal skill.

After all of the children have had an opportunity to play, the Dinosaur Game becomes a part of regular classroom activities. This serves a number of purposes, including promoting discussions among the players concerning numbers and number rules. The teacher notes which children come back to the game repeatedly and how children play the game on their own: Do they remember the rules, create their own, or teach other children? A game-making area can be provided later in the year with dice and paper to enable children to invent their own games.

—Materials and Set-Up

The game board consists of a cut-out dinosaur (shaped like a diplodocus) glued onto a 27" by 31" foamcore board. (See illustration below.) A path with 35 spaces along the top of the dinosaur leads from the dinosaur's head, down its back, to the tip of its tail. START is written in the 14th space from the head. Four 1/2" wooden cubes are used as dice. One cube has two sides with one dot, two sides with two dots, and two sides with three dots. This is the number die. The second cube has three sides with plus signs and three sides with minus signs (the minus signs should look like the letter I turned horizontally (⊢⊣) so they will not be mistaken for the number 1). This is the 3+/3- or directional die. The third cube has five pluses and one minus (5+/1-) whereas the fourth cube has one plus and five minuses (1+/5-). Two different small plastic dinosaurs are used as the pieces that the players move on the board.

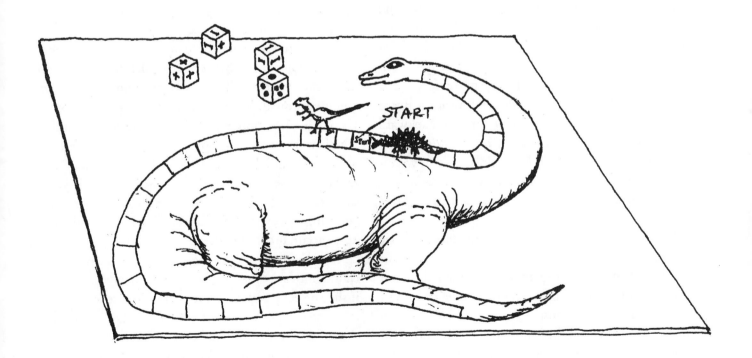

The assessment is conducted with one child at a time. Either an observer or the adult playing the game with the child can record the child's responses on the observation sheet. (See Tables 21 and 22, pp. 75–77, to record observations of individual children and of the class as a whole.)

—Procedure and Script

Introduce the Dinosaur Game as follows: "Today we have a new game in the classroom. It's called the Dinosaur Game. One child at a time can play it with _____ [*adult's name*]. Your dinosaur will race against _____'s [*adult's name*] dinosaur while they try to escape from the big dinosaur called Diplodocus. You will roll dice to find out how to move your dinosaur." Children can then choose the game as one of their activities. This gives children who are eager to play a turn early on, and serves as a further indication of the child's interest in this area. A waiting list helps children keep track of when they will have a turn.

Have the child sit next to you in front of the board. Ask her to choose one of the plastic dinosaurs and take the other one for yourself. Place both dinosaurs on the START space. Say to the child:

"The dinosaurs will be racing against each other while they're trying to escape from Diplodocus. [*Emphasize that escape means getting away from the head.*] Let's see which dinosaur gets closer to the end. [*Point to the end of the diplodocus's tail.*] These two dice tell us what our dinosaurs will do. This die [*show number die*] tells how many spaces they can move. This die [*show 3+/3- die*] tells if they move forward or backward. This sign [*show plus sign*] means forward, and this sign [*show minus sign*] means backward. [*Reinforce that forward means towards the tail, to escape from the mouth.*] You roll both dice to see how your dinosaur will move. So if you roll this [*put dice on +3*], you'll move your dinosaur forward three spaces, like this."

Demonstrate, emphasizing movement of the dinosaur one space at a time while saying "one, two, three." Then model a -3 move with your dinosaur, again counting the steps out loud. Ask the child what she would do if her dinosaur got a +2, and allow her to make the move for her dinosaur. If she does not understand what to do, show her the correct move and count the steps out loud. Repeat this sequence with the dice on -2 for the child's dinosaur. (Note: Do not count

your moves out loud after you start playing the game.) Remember to make the moves pronounced and face the dinosaur toward the tail, even when moving backward.

Since many children will not know the words *plus* and *minus*, you might describe the signs as a "cross" or "X" for the plus, and a "line" or "I" for the minus. You also can ask children what the signs look like to them so you can use their own terminology. The important thing is for children to know that the symbols stand for forward and backward motion. If a child asks about the meaning of the signs during the game, give one reminder that the plus means forward and the minus means backward.

If an observer is present, she should sit behind the child so as to not create any distraction. You take the first turn so that the child can observe as you use the dice. For the child's turn, suggest that she hold one die in each hand and throw them at the same time. Record the accuracy of her move on the observation sheet in terms of *directionality* (forward/backward) and *counting* (see Table 21). When recording accuracy of the direction of the move, enter the directional symbol (plus or minus) rolled by the child in the "correct" or "incorrect" column. When recording accuracy of counting, enter the number that the child rolled in the "correct" or "incorrect" column.

If the child's counting is incorrect, when possible also note the number of spaces that she actually moved. Some children are reluctant to move their full roll when the direction of the move is backward. If it appears that inaccuracy in counting is intentional, note this in the comments and disregard this turn for scoring purposes. Using this notation makes it possible to determine whether or not there are patterns in the child's errors (e.g., the child has more difficulty with backward moves). If the child passes the space on which your dinosaur has landed or the START space without counting it as a space, give her credit if she nevertheless keeps accurate count of the spaces she does touch. If the child's dinosaur is near the end of the tail and she cannot move the full number of her roll, give her credit if she correctly counts the remaining spaces.

Continue playing, alternating turns. Do *not* correct the child's errors. You might want to remind the child of the goal of the game if she seems to be having trouble remembering which way the dinosaurs are headed. Comments such as "Look, now your dinosaur is ahead of mine," made during your turn, help to reinforce the significance of moving *forward*. Record any reminders that you give children in the comments section of the observation sheet.

For assessment purposes, continue playing the game with these two dice until the child has had 11 turns. If the child has no concept of the game, for example, she merely floats her dinosaur around the board, it is not necessary to complete the 11 turns. If the child's dinosaur piece reaches the diplodocus's mouth (the last square on the board behind the START space) before you have finished playing, move it back to START. If your dinosaur reaches the mouth, it stays there until a + is rolled. If a dinosaur reaches the tip of the tail, you can move the piece back 10 spaces, to the beginning of the tail.

After turn 11, introduce the 5+/1- and 1+/5- dice and say, "Here are two new dice. If you would rather use one of these for your dinosaur instead of the one you are using, you may do that. Look very carefully at all the different sides before deciding." Record which die the child chooses in the spaces provided on the observation sheet. Ask her why she chose that die and record her response. If the child answers ,"because I like it" or "because it has a lot of crosses," you can use neutral probes such as "why do you like it?" or "what does that mean?" to elicit a fuller response. You each take three more turns, with the child using the die she has chosen and you using the 1+/5- die, whether or not that is the die the child has chosen. Your use of the 1+/5-die helps to insure that the child wins. Record her moves on the observation sheet in the spaces for turns 12, 13, and 14.

After turn 14, put aside the 5+/1- and 1+/5- dice and give the child the 3+/3- die and the number die. Say: "This time, instead of rolling, you can *put* the dice however you please to make the very best move for your dinosaur, to help him win." Record her choice. Ask her why she chose this move and record her reason. Again, use probes as appropriate. Let her make that move for her dinosaur. Then say: "Now you can put the dice however you please to make the very worst move for my dinosaur, to try to make it lose." Record her selection. Ask for her reason and record her response. Make that move for your dinosaur.

Tell the child: "Now we will play the game in a different way. I will be in charge of this die (3+/3-) and you will be in charge of this one (number die). It's your dinosaur's turn and I will put this die on this sign (plus). Now you choose what you want your die to say for your dinosaur to help it win. (Record the child's choice.) You can make that move for your dinosaur. Now it's my dinosaur's turn to move. I'll put this die on this sign (minus). Put your die on what you want it to say for my dinosaur to try to make it lose." Record the child's choice and make the move for your dinosaur. Next put your die on a minus for the child's dinosaur and then on a plus for your dinosaur, following the same procedure as above.

Finally, have the child take one last turn by placing the dice on the signs she prefers. Look to see who is winning. (The child wins almost every time.)

You may find the use of cue cards helpful for recalling the script. Consistency in the script is important for ensuring that variations in the children's performance are not a function of variations in what you say.

—Scoring

Use Table 22 to score children after they have completed the activity. To calculate points for the different responses, see the instructions on the bottom of the table. Write the results for each child in each of the scoring categories, recording the number of points awarded in the small boxes at the top of each section. Under the "direction of move" and "counting" headings, put a check in the "all correct" column for a child who makes no errors, or write the number of errors made in the "number incorrect" column. (Note: Turns 12–14 are not scored. They are included to sustain the flow of the game.) Write the number of points awarded in the small box.

Under the "choice of dice" heading, fill in which die (5+/1- or 1+/5-) the child chooses. If she chose the 5+/1- die, check "yes" or "no" to indicate whether or not she could accurately explain why that was the best choice. An explanation such as "it (the die) has more forwards on it" indicates understanding. Examples of noncredited responses include "because it is lighter" and "because I like it." In the "choice of moves" columns, record the child's choice of sign and number (e.g., +3). (Note: The reasons that the child gives for her choices of best and worst moves are not scored so as not to place undue emphasis on verbal ability.) For the "choice on number die" section, record the child's choices of number. Record the child's total points in the last column. The maximum total is 22 points.

In reviewing children's scores, it is important to attend not only to the total score but also to the points earned in each of the categories. Children who have the same total score may have different abilities. The dimensions scored reflect understanding of rules, counting, strategy, and the ability to articulate reasons.

If a child earns no points, it may be because she does not understand the structure of a game. When this is the case, the game can become a learning experience for the child. Peers, as well as adults, can participate in teaching a child about the game.

—Preliminary Results: 1986–1987

One of the most striking features of playing the Dinosaur Game is the energy and enthusiasm that children bring to the task. The dinosaur theme is highly motivating to both boys and girls. Children seem to enjoy playing the game regardless of their level of skill. The element of competition provides further motivation for some children, while for others dramatic play is the more prominent factor.

The 1986–1987 class ranged from children who floated the dinosaur over the board, or moved a single step with each throw (no matter what number turned up on the die) to children who understood both rules and strategy. Children were more likely to earn points for either understanding rules or for counting than they were for both of these categories. Counting accurately seemed to be a more difficult task for children than moving their dinosaur piece in the correct direction. However, children who had difficulty counting accurately were still able to choose the appropriate strategic moves in the second part of the activity. This suggests that assessments that are limited to counting skills may underestimate a child's understanding of number.

For the choice of dice section, half of the 20 children were able to make the correct choice; but only half of that group were able to explain the reasoning behind their choice. As noted above, a response such as "because it has all the x's" was credited as correct. Examples of noncredited responses included "because I want to" and the explanation of one boy who chose the 5- die because "Those [minuses] keep going straight, and with the [plus], you'll keep going in different ways." He interpreted the signs quite literally, indicating a dependence and emphasis on visual cues that he exhibited during activities from other domains as well.

For the strategy question involving choice of move, most children found it easier to make correct choices for themselves and the adult when the directional die was placed on plus rather than minus. Many chose -1 for the adult's dinosaur and -3 for their own, perhaps because they thought that a smaller number was always less desirable than a bigger one and they did not try to combine that information with the directionality information.

TABLE 21: DINOSAUR GAME OBSERVATION SHEET

Child _____ Age _____ Date _____ Observer _____

Direction of move			Counting		Comments and Observations
Turn	Correct	Incorrect	Correct	Incorrect	
1					
2					
3					
4					
5					
6					
7					
8					
9					
10					
11					

Choice of dice: Which?_____ Why? _____

Direction of move			Counting		Comments and Observations
Turn	Correct	Incorrect	Correct	Incorrect	
12					
13					
14					

Choice of moves

Best move? _____ Why? _____

Worst move? _____ Why? _____

Comments and Observations

Choice on number die	3+/3-die	Child's choice on number die	Comments and Observations
For child's dinosaur	+		
For adult's dinosaur	–		
For child's dinosaur	–		
For adult's dinosaur	+		

TABLE 22: DINOSAUR GAME SUMMARY SHEET

Child (age)	Direction of move		Counting		Choice of dice		Choice of moves		Choice on number die				TOTAL
	all correct	number incorrect	all correct	number incorrect	Knows why 5+/1-? Y	N	Best move	Worst move	+ child's dino	– adult's dino	– child's dino	+ adult's dino	
Scoring	For turns 1–11 0–2 incorrect = 3 pts. 3 or more incorrect = 0 pts.		For turns 1–11 0–2 incorrect = 3 pts. 3 or more incorrect = 0 pts.		Chooses 5+/1- and knows why = 4 pts. Chooses 5+/1- and doesn't know why = 2 pts. Anything else = 0 pts.		Best move / Worst move: +3 / -3 = 4 pts. +3 / other = 2 pts. other / -3 = 2 pts. +2, +1 / -2, -1 = 1 pt. other / other = 0 pts.		3 = 1 pt.	3 = 3 pts.	1 = 3 pts.	1 = 1 pt.	22 possible points

77

❏ BUS GAME

—Purpose and Activity Description

The purpose of the Bus Game is to assess children's abilities to perform mental calculations and to record and organize number information for one or more variables. The first part of the game involves four trips in which passengers get on and off a bus. This session assesses a child's ability to increment and reduce without the use of chips. We look at whether a child can perform mental calculations in discrete steps, as well as whether the child can maintain a running tally in her head. The second part of the activity assesses notation skills. Children use chips to keep track of the number of passengers riding the bus. We chose the number of passengers by consulting prior studies indicating young children's competencies with small numbers (Gelman & Gallistel, 1986; Hughes, 1981).

The chips give the children something to manipulate and provide them with a ready-made notation system. Most children have had no experience making the kinds of quantitative judgments called for in this activity. Thus, part of the assessment involves a determination of whether they can figure out on their own how to use the chips to arrive at accurate answers.

Some children are more aware than others of the relevance of the chips for keeping track of number information, and the significance of the chips for generating the final tally. They may exhibit clever and creative problem-solving processes, but the strategies that they invent are not always fully under their control. Because this is a period of rapid growth in children's early number development, some of the more dramatic differences in children's performances most likely reflect different levels of development.

There are nonetheless significant variations in individual performances at the same level. Demonstrating an understanding of number principles is more important than the accuracy of the answer in this assessment. Random versus scorable error patterns also yield important information about a child's level of understanding.

The game can be left in the classroom once the assessment is finished, with one child playing the role of "boss," and one in the role of "conductor." The game can be played with or without the use of chips.

—Materials and Set-Up

The materials for the Bus Game include a bus, a game board, two sets of 10 chips, one green and the other blue, with containers, and cardboard passengers. The terrain on which the bus travels is a 20" by 33" foamcore board. (See illustration, p. 79.) We used colored construction paper to create a road along three sides of the board, as well as lakes, trees, and other scenery. Covering the landscape with clear contact paper makes the board more durable. A collapsible board makes both transporting and storing the board much easier.

There are four bus stops, 3" to 4" in height, each one mounted on a plasticine stand by the roadside and glued onto the board. The first bus stop, a large wooden ring called Circle Stop, is situated halfway down one of the 33" sides. The second stop, Pinecone Stop, is located at the end of that side. Feather Stop, a large peacock feather, is placed at the end of the second side (20") and Shell Stop, a large scallop shell, is located halfway down the third side. At the end of the third side is the station, made out of a cardboard box painted blue with a cut-out door, window, and a removable roof.

We constructed the bus out of a cardboard box (7" by 9" by 4"), covered with white foamcore. We also painted opaque gray windows onto its sides so that the passengers inside would not be visible. For decoration, we glued food advertisements on both sides of the bus, and drew a driver and meter on the front. Two cut-out doors on either side allow people to get on the bus, and a red exit door at the back flaps open, allowing passengers to get off. At the start of each trip, the bus should be placed at the beginning of the road, facing Circle Stop.

The people figures—10 adults and 6 children, ranging in size from 2" to 4"—are made out of sturdy cardboard and mounted on small wooden stands. Each figure has its own identity: Adults include a long-haired male hippie, a woman loaded down with shopping bags, and a construction worker, and children include a baby holding a doll, a schoolboy with books, and a boy in sneakers holding a basketball. Individuality of the figures greatly contributes to the appeal of the activity; of course, you can make up different characters to reflect your community.

—Procedure and Script

The assessment is conducted in one or two sessions, with one child at a time. The game can be played on the floor, with the child facing away from the rest of the classroom. If available, an observer can sit behind the child, but in full view of the chips to record the child's actions. If not, the adult playing the game with the child will need to record the responses to facilitate scoring later on.

Introduce the game to the children at group time as follows: "Today we have a new game in our classroom. It's called the Bus Game. You're going to play it two different times. One child at a time may play it with _____ [adult's name]. You will be the conductor who keeps count of how many people are on the bus as it travels around to all the bus stops." (Have the Bus Game available at group time for children to explore.)

Session I—This session, consisting of four trips, is conducted with the adult figures only and without the use of chips. It assesses the child's ability to perform calculations in her head. Have the child sit next to you, facing the board. Tell the child:

"This is the Bus Game, and this is the bus that drives around to all of these bus stops to pick up people. [*Move bus around route.*] First, it goes to Circle Stop, then it goes to Pinecone Stop, then it goes to Feather Stop, and what stop do you think it goes to next? [*Shell*] Your job is to be the conductor. The conductor keeps count of how many people are on the bus because when the bus gets to the station [*point to station*], the boss is going to want to know how many people are on your bus.

"You can keep count in your head of how many people are on the bus. The boss is going to call you at each stop and ask how many people are on your bus. So you need to remember inside your head how many people get on the bus. [*Move the bus along the road to Circle Stop, and place two people at the stop. Refer to Table 23, p. 84, for the correct number of people to place at each stop.*] Here we are at Circle Stop, and this many people are getting on the bus." Wait to put the people onto the bus until the child has taken note of them, making sure that the child cannot see them once they

are inside. (You may want to train yourself to say "*this many* people . . ." at each stop rather than the actual number of people.) Record the child's response in the space for "Stop 1" on the observation sheet (see Table 24).

For the next stop, place one person at Pinecone Stop, and move the bus there. Put the person on the bus. Speak into a pretend phone and ask, "Conductor _____ [*child's name*], how many people are on your bus now?" If the child responds, "Two," prompt, "How many altogether?" If the child still does not know how many, repeat the trip. If the child is still unsure, say, "Let's see," and open up the bus and count with her. Record this sequence under scaffolding and continue to write down all the child's responses on the observation sheet, along with your comments on her performance (e.g., if the child uses her fingers or counts in her head).

Then say, "So three people are on the bus now. Now the bus goes to Feather Stop, and at Feather Stop, this many people get on [*one*] and the boss says, 'Conductor _____ [*child's name*], now how many people are on your bus?'" Provide no further scaffolding and do not refer to any numbers.

For the second bus trip, say, "Now the bus is going to make another trip. This time people will get on the bus *and* they'll get *off* the bus too. You need to remember inside your head so you can tell the boss at each stop how many people are on the bus." Move the bus through the different stops as before, but without any scaffolding after the second stop.

For the third trip, say, "Now this time, people will only get *on* the bus, not off. But the boss does not have time to call you at each stop. So she's not going to be able to call you until the very end of the trip and you're going to need to keep remembering in your head the whole time, until you get to the station, how many people are on your bus." Proceed along the road, waiting until the station to ask for a calculation. Record any scaffolding needed for either this or the eighth trip.

For the fourth trip, say, "This time, people will get on *and* they'll also get *off* the bus. So you need to keep remembering the whole time because at the end the boss will ask how many people are on your bus." For these last two trips, record any visible strategies the child uses, such as finger counting, mumbling, or saying the number aloud at each stop. You can give occasional prompts such as "remember to count in

your head" if the child does not seem to be keeping a running total.

For the last part of this session, say, "I have a few more questions I want to ask you." Put four people on the bus, and ask the child, "How many people are on the bus now?" Then ask how many heads are on the bus, then noses, and finally, chins. Then ask how many *hands* are on the bus. Encourage the child to think about her answer if the immediate response is "four." Then ask how many feet are on the bus. Depending on the child's success with these questions, put one more person on the bus and ask, "Now, how many feet are on the bus?" Then ask for the number of hands and finally, heads. Record the child's responses and any strategies she uses that you can detect.

Session II—Once all of the children have had a first turn, reintroduce the game at group time: "Children can have a second turn at the Bus Game, but this time the game will be a little different."

Session II includes four trips using the chips. It assesses the child's ability to record and organize number information and to keep track of several variables. For the fifth bus trip, explain to the child, "You can be the conductor again, but we're going to do something a little different. To help you keep count of how many people are on the bus, you can use these green chips." Give the child a container of 10 green chips. "I will be in charge of the bus and the people."

The bus then begins its fifth trip around the board (see Table 23). Only adult figures are used on this trip. Move the bus along the road to Circle Stop, and place two people at the stop.

"Here we are at Circle Stop, and this many people are getting on the bus." Wait to put the people onto the bus until the child has counted out her chips. Remember to say, "This many people get on. . . ." rather than "Two people get on . . ." to allow the child to make the connection herself between the figures and her chips. Also, make sure children cannot see the figures inside the bus so that they will rely on their chips for their tallies. Record what the child does with her chips in the space for "Stop 1" on the observation sheet (see Table 25). Observe the child's use of chips at each stop, recording the number of chips she puts out. Also include relevant descriptive comments, such as noting if the child separates the chips by location.

If the child does not put out two chips at the first

stop, scaffold as follows: "Can you use your chips to help you remember that this many people get on the bus?" If the child still does not know what to do, first repeat, "What could you do to show that this many people get on the bus?", and then, if necessary, say, "Could you put out some chips?" Repeat the same scaffolding sequence at Pinecone Stop if needed, but if the child still is unable to use the chips, she is probably not ready for the activity, and you might want to discontinue it. Indicate on the observation sheet whenever scaffolding (S) is used.

Now place one person at Pinecone Stop and move the bus there. "And now we get to Pinecone Stop, and this many people get in." If the child forgets to use her chips, ask, "So, what are you going to do?" (This prompt does not need to be recorded as a scaffold.) Put the person on the bus. At Feather Stop, two people get in, and at Shell Stop one more person gets on the bus. For each stop, move the bus to the stop, place the people at the stop, let the child count out her chips, then put the people on the bus.

Finally, move the bus to the station and say, "Now the boss comes out of the station and says, 'Conductor _____ [child's name], please tell me how many people are on your bus now.'" If the child says thay she doesn't know or makes a guess, ask, "What do you think?" and then, "How about using your chips to help you get the answer?"

Record whether the child automatically refers to her chips for the total, or whether she needs scaffolding. If the child's total number of chips is different from her guess, ask which answer she wants to stick with. Record the child's final tally, then let the child take the people out of the bus, line them up, and count them. If the child's tally is incorrect, do not emphasize the inaccuracy of the answer. You might say something such as, "It looks like there are a lot of people on that bus" or "Look how many people can fit on the bus" or "There are more people than you thought there were!" Ask the child to return her chips to the container, and put the bus figures back in your pile.

For the sixth trip, say: "Now the bus is going to take another trip. This time people are getting on the bus *and* people are getting *off* the bus too. So here goes the bus to Circle Stop, and here's how many people are getting on at Circle Stop." Follow the procedure used in Trip 5, using only adult figures, and the numbers in Table 23. At the second and fourth stops, people are removed from the bus. At Pinecone Stop, say, "Something different is going to happen at Pinecone Stop. At Pinecone Stop, people are going to get *off* the bus."

If the child does not know to remove a chip, scaffold once, but no more: "How do you think you could use your chips to show that someone is getting *off* the bus?" Record the child's action and any scaffolding provided. When the bus gets to the station, say, "Now the bus arrives at the station, and the boss says, 'Conductor _____ [child's name], how many people are on your bus?'" Repeat the script and recording procedure used in Trip 5. If time is short, and the child does not seem interested, you do not need to empty out and count the people for each trip.

For Trip 7, say: "Now the bus is going to make another trip, only this time grownups are getting on the bus *and children* are getting on too. When the bus gets to the station, the boss is going to want to know how many *grownups* are on your bus and how many *children* are on your bus. So you can use these two sets of different-colored chips to help you remember how many grownups and how many children are on your bus."

Give the child the container of blue chips. Refer to Table 23 for the relevant numbers. For convenience, keep the adult and child figures in separate piles in front of you. When the bus moves to Circle Stop, place both grownups and children at the stop together, and say, "This many *grownups* and this many *children* are getting on." Wait until the child has put out all of her chips before placing the people on the bus. Record the colors used on the observation sheet. If the child does not understand how to use the two colors of chips and randomly chooses from the containers, scaffold once as follows: "Now remember, you'll need to remember how many *grownups* and how many *children* are on the bus." After this, provide no more scaffolding.

Follow the same script and recording procedure for the next three stops. At Shell Stop, say, "This many grownups get on and no children get on." When the bus gets to the station, have the boss ask for the number of grownups and the number of children, as well as how many *people* are on the bus altogether. Indicate on the sheet whether the child refers to the correct sets of chips for her tallies.

On the eighth trip, say: "Now the bus is going to make its last trip, and for this trip, both grownups and children are getting on. Sometimes they'll get off too. You can use both color chips again because the boss will ask how many *grownups* and how many *children* are on your bus." Use the same procedure and recording system as on the last trip, emphasizing that something different is happening at Pinecone Stop when people get off. If the child adds chips, scaffold once as on Trip 6, and record it. At the station, ask for the number of grownups, children, and people altogether.

In general, prompting can be provided as needed, but it should be differentiated from more formal scaffolding. Try to avoid the word *guess* when asking for an answer. A good general probe for children's responses is "How did you know that?" If a child is especially eager to move the bus or handle the people herself, explain that that part is your job, and that she can have a chance to play with the bus after you're through. You also can let the child move the bus to the first stop, and from the last stop to the station. Limiting the child's role keeps her from becoming too distracted by manipulating the people and bus as well as the chips.

—Scoring

Session I—Use the observation sheet for Session I (Table 24) to record the child's responses at each stop on Trips 1 and 2. Record the child's final tallies and any scaffolding provided. For Trips 3 and 4, record any strategies the child uses, such as counting aloud. For the additional questions, record the child's answers as well as any problem-solving strategies she uses to arrive at the answers. (The correct answers are written in parentheses for ease of scoring.)

Refer to the Bus Game Scoring Information, to fill out the "Bus Game Summary Sheet" (Table 27). Table 26 gives the point allotments for various responses. For both sessions, subtract a 1/2 point every time the child needs scaffolding.

Session II—Use the observation sheet for Session II (Table 25) to record the child's actions and your comments at each stop. Also record the child's final tallies. Indicate how the child uses her chips to begin with, whether she refers to the chips for the total, and what scaffolding is used. Record any other relevant information, such as whether the child can count accurately to 6. Use a similar procedure for each trip. For the third and fourth trips, record which color chips are used for adults and which for children.

As with Session I, refer to Table 26 to fill out the scoring sheet for Session II (Table 28). Although you can read across columns in each child's matrix to gain a sense for how individual children scored on each trip, you can gain a more analytic perspective by reading down the columns. The first column of scores ("final tally") reflects the child's ability to make sense of the information she has gleaned from the trips. The second column ("chip strategy") reflects effective use of problem-solving strategies. The third column ("refers to chips") refers to whether a child knows what kind of information is contained in her notation system, whereas the fourth column ("counting accuracy") reflects the child's counting skills. The total score for each child is recorded in the box on the lower right-hand corner of each scoring matrix.

—Preliminary Results: 1986–1987

The Bus Game revealed a range of abilities in the 1986–87 class. Because Session I was not conducted in full with these children, the results will focus primarily on Session II.

In the first trip in Session II, where children are asked to use chips to represent one variable—people getting on—the majority of children were able to use the chips accurately to determine a correct final tally. Errors occurred when people started getting off the bus, and when children were added to the passenger pool. Children who knew what to do in one of these situations did not always know what to do in the other. One common error made by approximately half of the children was to add chips for people getting off. Other strategies adopted when people got on *and* off the bus included turning over a chip for each person who got off and using a spatial arrangement: creating separate rows of chips to represent "on" and "off." But such strategies were fragile and difficult to sustain. Few children recovered once they started down a misguided path. One child learned from her sixth trip and removed chips for the final trip.

On the "two-variable" trips, about half of the children used the two sets of chips consistently to represent grownups and children, while others just randomly chose colors or implemented unsuccessful strategies. There was also a division between children who were aware of and used the number information the chips contained for final tallies, and those who needed scaffolding. One strategy children often fell back on was to "get to" the desired number any way they could. For example, if four adults got on the bus, and two chips were already laid out, the child simply added two more chips to "get to" 4.

Some children derived great satisfaction when their computations proved correct. They were highly attuned to number relationships, and invented short-cuts for counting their chips, dividing them into piles and pairing them up. For her final tally, one girl was keenly aware that the number of people on the bus should correspond to the number of chips, and spent a long time trying to figure out exactly where she had gone wrong. Whereas such children attended solely to the number information, others became much more involved with the characters getting on and off the bus, and were more interested in using the game for dramatic play.

—Further Suggestions for the Domain

To supplement the Dinosaur and Bus Games, teachers can provide a geometric reasoning activity, such as an activity using pattern blocks. Older or more advanced children can be challenged further on the Bus Game through a wide range of variations: having people get on and off at the *same* stop, using written notation, using larger numbers, adding more categories of people, adding fares, or graphing the popularity of different stops. On the Dinosaur Game, additional number dice can be added, the numbers can be made higher, or the symbols changed. Finally, as previously noted, we recommend maintaining a number notebook in the classroom to jot down short anecdotes describing children's spontaneous number reasoning.

TABLE 23: BUS GAME REFERENCE SHEET

SESSION I

TRIP 1
No chips/Adults on

1. Circle Stop   2 on
2. Pinecone Stop 1 on   (=3)
3. Feather Stop   1 on   (=4)
4. Shell Stop   2 on   (=6)
                  6

TRIP 2
No chips/Adults on and off

1. 3 on
2. 1 off   (=2)
3. 2 on   (=4)
4. 1 off   (=3)
    3

TRIP 3
No chips/Adults on
(final calculation only)

1. 3 on
2. 1 on
3. 2 on
4. 1 on
    7

TRIP 4
No chips/Adults on and off
(final calculation only)

1. 2 on
2. 1 off
3. 2 on
4. 2 off
    1

ADDITIONAL QUESTIONS
4 people on the bus:

1. Heads? (4)
2. Noses? (4)
3. Chins? (4)
4. Hands? (8)
5. Feet?   (8)

1 more on   (5)

6. Feet?   (10)
7. Hands? (10)
8. Heads? (5)

SESSION II

TRIP 5
Chips/Adults on

1. 2 on
2. 1 on
3. 2 on
4. 1 on
    6

(15 total)

TRIP 6
Chips/Adults on and off

1. 4 on
2. 1 off
3. 2 on
4. 2 off
    3

TRIP 7
2 chips/Adults and children on

1. 2 A on   1 C on
2. 1 A on   2 C on
3. 4 A on   3 C on
4. 2 A on   0 C on
    9 A   6 C

TRIP 8
2 chips/Adults and children on and off

1. 2 A on   3 C on
2. 1 A off   2 C off
3. 3 A on   2 C on
4. 2 A on   1 C off
    6 A   2 C

(8 total)

TABLE 24: BUS GAME OBSERVATION SHEET: SESSION I (NO CHIPS)

Child _____   Adult: _____

Age _____ Date _____   Observer: _____

Trip 1—Adults On	Trip 2—Adults On and Off	Trip 3—Adults On (Final Total Only)	Trip 4—Adults On and Off (Final Total Only)
Responses and comments:	Responses and comments:	Responses and comments:	Responses and comments:
Stop 1	Stop 1		
Stop 2	Stop 2		
Stop 3	Stop 3		
Stop 4	Stop 4		
Final tally:	Final tally:	Final tally:	Final tally:
Scaffolding? Y/N	Scaffolding? Y/N	Scaffolding? Y/N	Scaffolding? Y/N
		Strategy?	Strategy?

Additional Questions

heads(4) ___   hands (8) ___   feet (10) ___   Comments:
noses(4) ___   feet (8) ___   hands (10) ___
chins(4) ___   heads (5) ___

85

TABLE 25: BUS GAME OBSERVATION SHEET: SESSION II (WITH CHIPS)

Child _____

Age _____   Date _____

Adult: _____

Observer: _____

Trip 5—Adults On	Trip 6—Adults On and Off
Actions and comments:	Actions and comments:
Stop 1 (S *: 1 2 3)	Stop 1
Stop 2	Stop 2 (S: 1)
Stop 3	Stop 3
Stop 4	Stop 4
Final tally: ____ (S: 1 2)	Final tally: ____ (S: 1 2)
chip strategy:	chip strategy:
refers to chips for total:	refers to chips for total:
counting:	counting:

* S = number of times scaffolding is used

86

might work for a long time to depict a spider as accurately as possible. Such children may use information they have learned in other contexts to formulate conclusions about classroom events. Observations of a cricket hitting the top of its container might generate a conclusion that "the cricket can jump higher than the bottle it is in."

Characteristics of unusual ability in the science domain include the ability to relate and compare information, to assign meaning to observations, and to formulate and test hypotheses. The emerging scientist is eager to explore the world and poses many questions in her search for a larger store of knowledge. When presented with an impossible task such as making a circle out of squares, such as a child is sensitive to the "it won't" as opposed to the "I can't" aspect of the exercise. The Spectrum activities attempt to capture the child who enjoys identifying the structure and pattern of things and who is interested in finding and solving problems.

We address three end states in the science domain. First, the naturalist demonstrates an interest in and understanding of natural phenomena, and also possesses sensitive observation skills. The proposed Discovery Area encourages observation, description, and classification by introducing children to a variety of living things and inanimate objects. We decided against including a more structured activity for this component of the domain since sensitive observation of one's surroundings is often exhibited over time.

The Treasure Hunt Game, reflecting the second end state, the experimental scientist, addresses the ability to go beyond observation and to use the data presented to infer governing rules, a key element in scientific thinking. The Sink and Float Activity taps abilities similar to those addressed by the Discovery Area and the Treasure Hunt Game: careful observation, simple hypothesis formation, and experimentation.

Finally, the Assembly Activity elicits skills characteristic of the third end state, the mechanic, such as recognition of causal and functional relationships. Children who excel in this activity are likely to be interested in how things work and enjoy trying to fix things that are broken.

☐ DISCOVERY AREA

—Purpose and Activities Description

The purpose of the Discovery Area is to provide a year-round calendar of activities and projects that encourage children to observe, explore, and experiment with natural phenomena. The activities and the assessment for the Discovery Area are less structured than are the other activities in the science domain. Children are exposed to a variety of natural science activities throughout the school year instead of to a single formal activity. Teachers assess children's competence by making formal and informal observations of the main cognitive components involved in scientific exploration and observation.

The cognitive components addressed in the Discovery Area include *close observation, identification of similarities and differences, hypothesis formation, experimentation,* and *interest in or knowledge of the natural world.* Indoor and outdoor activities in the area provide teachers with a variety of opportunities to observe these components. Since not all children exhibit interest in the same phenomena or domain of experience, it is important to present a range of natural science experiences for children to pursue. Teachers should take note of those children who demonstrate a strong interest in or aptitude for particular subject matter or activities, such as rocks, animals, or conducting experiments.

A monthly schedule of Discovery Area activities is outlined on pages 97–99. We have also included a section with activities that can supplement or replace those listed in the calendar, depending on children's interests, available equipment, climate, and the terrain around your school.

—Materials and Set-Up

The materials and set-up for the Discovery Area will depend on the activities you select. Although a selection of basic materials and equipment is outlined in the following list, no one set of supplies is essential. The more limited the surrounding natural setting, the more the teacher will have to introduce into the classroom. Many materials in the Discovery Area can be found in the school yard (e.g., leaves, earth, stones, wood), collected by children (e.g., shells, rocks, metal objects), or donated by parents (e.g., fur, old magazines, yarn, containers).

The best kinds of materials are those that children can use in a variety of ways, such as clay, sand, wood, ice cubes, seeds, and pond water. Because these materials exist in many forms, weights, colors, and textures, they invite and enable children's observation and experimentation. Also, because these materials can be shaped and transformed by children's actions, they are usually provocative enough to capture children's attention without direct adult supervision (Pitcher, Feinburg, & Alexander, 1989).

If possible, the Discovery Area should consist of one or two small tables in a corner of the room, with shelf or windowsill space to display individual collections. At any given time, two or more items should be available for children to observe and explore. New items or activities should be added every few weeks to keep children interested in returning to the area. When new materials are introduced, be sure that all the children know how to handle them and where to store them.

BASIC MATERIALS AND EQUIPMENT FOR THE DISCOVERY AREA

GENERAL EQUIPMENT

- magnifying glasses
- clear sorting containers
- tweezers
- eyedroppers
- collection boxes
- microscopes
- mirrors
- magnets

WATER TABLE EQUIPMENT

- assorted sieves
- assorted funnels
- assorted plastic bottles
- assorted plastic containers
- eggbeater
- assorted floating and sinking materials
  (e.g., corks, rocks, sponge, washers; see box on p. 109)
- food coloring

MEASUREMENT EQUIPMENT

- thermometers
- meter sticks and rulers
- cooking measures
  (e.g., spoon sets, cup sets)
- scales

ANIMAL EQUIPMENT

- cages, boxes, tubs
- insect cages or jars
- bird houses
- aquarium

GARDEN AND PLANT EQUIPMENT

- box tops, tubs, or trays
- plant pots, boxes, egg cartons
- hand tools
  (e.g., trowel, hand-held cultivator, spades)

SPECIMENS

- fossils
- seeds
- rocks and pebbles
- shells
- feathers
- bones
- fur

RECORDING MATERIALS

- tape recorders
- markers
- pencils
- paper
- sequence cards

—Procedure and Script

Introduce the Discovery Area to the children at the beginning of the school year. Start by establishing a "check in" system to limit the number of children in the area. You might want to hang photographs or name tags in a special place. You also can generate rules for use of the area with the children's help. Rules should be clear and concise with emphasis on issues of safety, sharing, and storage of materials. Most of the activities in the Discovery Area are open-ended and children should feel free to use the materials as needed.

Before starting the activities (see suggestions that follow), demonstrate and describe different ways to use the equipment and materials in the Discovery Area. For example, have children listen to the insides of shells as well as examine them closely with magnifying glasses. After this introduction, encourage the children to use the equipment in conjunction with new and ongoing exercises. Materials can be used in both freeplay and structured exercises. For example, in addition to conducting the structured Sink and Float assessment described on pages 110–114, give children ample time just to play at the water table—filling, pouring, siphoning, and so on.

—Scoring

As noted above, the Discovery Area is a less structured assessment than many of the other Spectrum assessment activities. The assessment is similar to the Creative Movement Curriculum, the Peer Interaction Checklist, and the Art Portfolio in that they all entail looking at children's activities and work over time. The assessment of a child's natural science abilities derives primarily from the teacher's formal and informal observations. The Discovery Area Scoring Criteria listed in Table 29 are designed to guide teachers' observations.

Before observing children in a natural science activity, carefully study the scoring criteria in Table 29 (p. 101) to familiarize yourself with the definitions. Use the Discovery Area Observation Sheet (Table 30) while scoring, keeping as detailed notes as possible regarding the child's questions, statements, interests, observations, and problem-solving strategies. The Discovery Area Observation Sheet does not result in a quantitative score; rather, it provides teachers with an overall impression of the child's strengths and interests in the domain of natural science.

Child: _____

Trip 7—Adults and Children On

Actions and comments:

chip color: _____   Adults _____ | Children _____

Stop 1 (S: 1)

Stop 2

Stop 3

Stop 4

Final tally: A _____   C _____   Total _____

chip strategy:

refers to chips for total:

counting:

Trip 8—Adults and Children On and Off

Actions and comments:

chip color: _____   Adults _____ | Children _____

Stop 1

Stop 2 (S: 1)

Stop 3

Stop 4

Final tally: A _____   C _____   Total _____

chip strategy:

refers to chips for total:

counting:

TABLE 26: BUS GAME SCORING INFORMATION

SESSION I   (Maximum = 22 pts.— subtract 1/2 pt. each time child needs scaffolding)

TRIP 1

Number Correct:	3	=	gets last 3 stops correct
	2	=	gets 2 out of last 3 stops correct
	1	=	gets 1 out of last 3 stops correct
	0	=	gets first stop correct but others wrong

TRIP 2

Number Correct:	3	=	gets last 3 stops correct
	2	=	gets 2 out of last 3 stops correct
	1	=	gets 1 out of last 3 stops correct
	0	=	gets first stop correct but others wrong

TRIP 3

Final Tally Correct:	3	=	yes
	0	=	no (or a guess)

TRIP 4

Final Tally Correct:	3	=	yes
	0	=	no (or a guess)

ADDITIONAL QUESTIONS:

2 pts. each for last 5 questions (first 3 are not scored)
(4 people: hands/feet; 5 people: feet/hands/heads)

SESSION II   (Maximum = 34 pts. — subtract 1/2 pt. each time child needs scaffolding)

TRIP 5

Final Tally Correct:	2	=	yes
	0	=	no
Chip Strategy:	3	=	effective
	1	=	other (e.g., tries to "get to" the correct answer)
	0	=	random
Refers to Chips:	1	=	yes
(for Totals)	0	=	no
Counting Accuracy:	1	=	yes
	0	=	no one-to-one correspondence

TRIP 6

Final Tally Correct:	2	=	yes
	0	=	no
Chip Strategy:	3	=	effective
(refers only	1	=	other (e.g., turns over chips to make separate piles)
to subtraction)	0	=	random

Refers to Chips:	1	=	yes
(for Totals)	0	=	no
Counting Accuracy:	1	=	yes
	0	=	no one-to-one correspondence

TRIP 7

Final Tally Correct:	2	=	all of answer correct
	1	=	gets adult or child tally correct or total wrong or both
	0	=	gets all parts incorrect
Chip Strategy (A):	2	=	separates by color
(refers only to color)	1	=	can't sustain strategy
	0	=	random; no apparent strategy
Chip Strategy (B):	3	=	effective
(refers only to addition)	1	=	other
	0	=	random
Refers to *Different*			
Color Chips for Totals:	1	=	yes
	0	=	no
Counting Accuracy:	2	=	yes
	1	=	misses a number when counting; makes a minor counting mistake
	0	=	no one-to-one correspondence

TRIP 8

Final Tally Correct:	2	=	all of answer correct
	1	=	gets adult or child tally correct and/or total wrong
	0	=	gets all parts incorrect
Chip Strategy (A):	2	=	separates by color
(refers only to color)	1	=	can't sustain strategy
	0	=	random; no apparent strategy
Chip Strategy (B):	3	=	effectively uses subtraction
(refers only to subtraction)	1	=	separates chips into piles or turns over chips: some attempt to distinguish between addition and subtraction but unable to use system effectively
	0	=	random
Refers to *Different*			
Color Chips for Totals:	1	=	yes
	0	=	no
Counting Accuracy:	2	=	yes
	1	=	misses a number when counting; makes a minor counting mistake
	0	=	no one-to-one correspondence

Child (age)	Trip 1	scaffolding	Trip 2	scaffolding	Trip 3	scaffolding	Trip 4	scaffolding	Additional Questions					Total: Session I	Total: Session II	Total: Sessions I & II	Comments
									hands	feet	feet	hands	heads				

TABLE 27: BUS GAME SUMMARY SHEET SESSION I

TABLE 28: BUS GAME SUMMARY SHEET SESSION II

Child (age)	Trip	final tally	chip strategy A	chip strategy B	refers to chips	counting accuracy	scaffolding	Subtotal
	5							
	6							
	7							
	8							
	Total							
	5							
	6							
	7							
	8							
	Total							
	5							
	6							
	7							
	8							
	Total							
	5							
	6							
	7							
	8							
	Total							
	5							
	6							
	7							
	8							
	Total							

Child (age)	Trip	final tally	chip strategy A	chip strategy B	refers to chips	counting accuracy	scaffolding	Subtotal	Comments:
	5								
	6								
	7								
	8								
	Total								
	5								
	6								
	7								
	8								
	Total								
	5								
	6								
	7								
	8								
	Total								
	5								
	6								
	7								
	8								
	Total								
	5								
	6								
	7								
	8								
	Total								

CHAPTER 4
SCIENCE DOMAIN

—INTRODUCTION

Most children do not require a formal introduction to the science domain. They are spontaneously interested in many aspects of their environment: people, plants, animals, and features of their own immediate physical surroundings. Children discover simple causal relationships all around them, from turning on a light to pushing a swing to blowing a whistle. Infants exhibit a beginning sense of cause and effect when, for example, they shake their crib and the mobile hanging above their head begins to move. But determining which part of an interaction is cause and which is effect may remain puzzling for years to come.

From the work of Piaget, we know that a child's understanding of the world develops with age as a result of her active exploration of the environment (Ginsburg & Opper, 1979). The infant's emerging understanding of categories turns into the young schoolchild's growing recognition of classes and sets. From observing and manipulating objects, the preschool child starts to identify predictable patterns of interaction and behavior. Ability in science is based more heavily on real world experience than ability in such domains as mathematics and music, and takes a longer time to emerge. Children usually are not assessed until elementary, or even junior high, school when the curriculum shifts from an emphasis on process to product, and becomes more content oriented.

The physical sciences, including chemistry and physics, explore the world of material objects and the evolution of physical systems. Natural sciences such as biology investigate the forms and phenomena of living things including their origin, growth, and structure. Because the role of science and technology is becoming increasingly important in our lives, schools in the future are likely to increase their focus on the physical, as well as the natural sciences. Areas of the typical preschool classroom that accommodate different facets of science include the block area, water table, sand table, and sometimes a natural science, woodworking, or cooking area.

—CONCEPTUALIZING THE SCIENCE ACTIVITIES

Ability in science manifests itself in different ways. Some children want to find out how things work, others are more concerned with how things grow, and still others mainly are interested in classifying things into categories. For example, some children may focus their energy on classifying objects according to whether they sink or float, whereas others are more interested in making things that sink out of objects that ordinarily float. Children also may bring a scientific approach to other domains. For instance, a child who does not show much interest or skill in drawing might work for a long time to depict a spider as accurately as possible. Such children may use information they have learned in other contexts to formulate conclusions about classroom events. Observations of a cricket hitting the top of its container might generate a conclusion that "the cricket can jump higher than the bottle it is in."

Characteristics of unusual ability in the science domain include the ability to relate and compare information, to assign meaning to observations, and to formulate and test hypotheses. The emerging scientist is eager to explore the world and poses many questions in her search for a larger store of knowledge. When presented with an impossible task such as making a circle out of squares, such as a child is sensitive to the "it won't" as opposed to the "I can't" aspect of the exercise. The Spectrum activities attempt to capture the child who enjoys identifying the structure and pattern of things and who is interested in finding and solving problems.

We address three end states in the science domain. First, the naturalist demonstrates an interest in and understanding of natural phenomena, and also possesses sensitive observation skills. The proposed Discovery Area encourages observation, description, and classification by introducing children to a variety of living things and inanimate objects. We decided against including a more structured activity for this component of the domain since sensitive observation of one's surroundings is often exhibited over time.

The Treasure Hunt Game, reflecting the second end state, the experimental scientist, addresses the ability to go beyond observation and to use the data presented to infer governing rules, a key element in scientific thinking. The Sink and Float Activity taps abilities similar to those addressed by the Discovery Area and the Treasure Hunt Game: careful observation, simple hypothesis formation, and experimentation.

Finally, the Assembly Activity elicits skills characteristic of the third end state, the mechanic, such as recognition of causal and functional relationships. Children who excel in this activity are likely to be interested in how things work and enjoy trying to fix things that are broken.

☐ DISCOVERY AREA

—Purpose and Activities Description

The purpose of the Discovery Area is to provide a year-round calendar of activities and projects that encourage children to observe, explore, and experiment with natural phenomena. The activities and the assessment for the Discovery Area are less structured than are the other activities in the science domain. Children are exposed to a variety of natural science activities throughout the school year instead of to a single formal activity. Teachers assess children's competence by making formal and informal observations of the main cognitive components involved in scientific exploration and observation.

The cognitive components addressed in the Discovery Area include *close observation, identification of similarities and differences, hypothesis formation, experimentation,* and *interest in or knowledge of the natural world.* Indoor and outdoor activities in the area provide teachers with a variety of opportunities to observe these components. Since not all children exhibit interest in the same phenomena or domain of experience, it is important to present a range of natural science experiences for children to pursue. Teachers should take note of those children who demonstrate a strong interest in or aptitude for particular subject matter or activities, such as rocks, animals, or conducting experiments.

A monthly schedule of Discovery Area activities is outlined on pages 97–99. We have also included a section with activities that can supplement or replace those listed in the calendar, depending on children's interests, available equipment, climate, and the terrain around your school.

—Materials and Set-Up

The materials and set-up for the Discovery Area will depend on the activities you select. Although a selection of basic materials and equipment is outlined in the following list, no one set of supplies is essential. The more limited the surrounding natural setting, the more the teacher will have to introduce into the classroom. Many materials in the Discovery Area can be found in the school yard (e.g., leaves, earth, stones, wood), collected by children (e.g., shells, rocks, metal objects), or donated by parents (e.g., fur, old magazines, yarn, containers).

The best kinds of materials are those that children can use in a variety of ways, such as clay, sand, wood, ice cubes, seeds, and pond water. Because these materials exist in many forms, weights, colors, and textures, they invite and enable children's observation and experimentation. Also, because these materials can be shaped and transformed by children's actions, they are usually provocative enough to capture children's attention without direct adult supervision (Pitcher, Feinburg, & Alexander, 1989).

If possible, the Discovery Area should consist of one or two small tables in a corner of the room, with shelf or windowsill space to display individual collections. At any given time, two or more items should be available for children to observe and explore. New items or activities should be added every few weeks to keep children interested in returning to the area. When new materials are introduced, be sure that all the children know how to handle them and where to store them.

BASIC MATERIALS AND EQUIPMENT FOR THE DISCOVERY AREA

GENERAL EQUIPMENT

magnifying glasses
clear sorting containers
tweezers
eyedroppers
collection boxes
microscopes
mirrors
magnets

WATER TABLE EQUIPMENT

assorted sieves
assorted funnels
assorted plastic bottles
assorted plastic containers
eggbeater
assorted floating and sinking materials
    (e.g., corks, rocks, sponge, washers; see
    box on p. 109)
food coloring

MEASUREMENT EQUIPMENT

thermometers
meter sticks and rulers
cooking measures
    (e.g., spoon sets, cup sets)
scales

ANIMAL EQUIPMENT

cages, boxes, tubs
insect cages or jars
bird houses
aquarium

GARDEN AND PLANT EQUIPMENT

box tops, tubs, or trays
plant pots, boxes, egg cartons
hand tools
    (e.g., trowel, hand-held
    cultivator, spades)

SPECIMENS

fossils
seeds
rocks and pebbles
shells
feathers
bones
fur

RECORDING MATERIALS

tape recorders
markers
pencils
paper
sequence cards

—Procedure and Script

Introduce the Discovery Area to the children at the beginning of the school year. Start by establishing a "check in" system to limit the number of children in the area. You might want to hang photographs or name tags in a special place. You also can generate rules for use of the area with the children's help. Rules should be clear and concise with emphasis on issues of safety, sharing, and storage of materials. Most of the activities in the Discovery Area are open-ended and children should feel free to use the materials as needed.

Before starting the activities (see suggestions that follow), demonstrate and describe different ways to use the equipment and materials in the Discovery Area. For example, have children listen to the insides of shells as well as examine them closely with magnifying glasses. After this introduction, encourage the children to use the equipment in conjunction with new and ongoing exercises. Materials can be used in both freeplay and structured exercises. For example, in addition to conducting the structured Sink and Float assessment described on pages 110–114, give children ample time just to play at the water table—filling, pouring, siphoning, and so on.

—Scoring

As noted above, the Discovery Area is a less structured assessment than many of the other Spectrum assessment activities. The assessment is similar to the Creative Movement Curriculum, the Peer Interaction Checklist, and the Art Portfolio in that they all entail looking at children's activities and work over time. The assessment of a child's natural science abilities derives primarily from the teacher's formal and informal observations. The Discovery Area Scoring Criteria listed in Table 29 are designed to guide teachers' observations.

Before observing children in a natural science activity, carefully study the scoring criteria in Table 29 (p. 101) to familiarize yourself with the definitions. Use the Discovery Area Observation Sheet (Table 30) while scoring, keeping as detailed notes as possible regarding the child's questions, statements, interests, observations, and problem-solving strategies. The Discovery Area Observation Sheet does not result in a quantitative score; rather, it provides teachers with an overall impression of the child's strengths and interests in the domain of natural science.

ACTIVITIES CALENDAR

The following is a suggested natural science activities calendar. The selection and sequence of activities are based on seasonal changes, children's interests, and manageability of the activity either inside or outside the classroom. We do not describe the activities in full, since many teachers already offer similar curricula in their classrooms.

SEPTEMBER

1. Set up space for Discovery Area

2. Introduce materials that will be in area

3. Introduce idea of collection boxes

   Collection boxes are used to collect things of interest outside for further examination. Leaves, rocks, moss, and other natural curiosities can be collected and further explored under the magnifying glass or microscope, with peers, teachers, or both.

4. Make collection boxes as an art activity

   Use shoe boxes and various materials for decorating and labeling.

OCTOBER

1. Fall nature walk

   Explore fall phenomena with children. Discuss the colors of leaves and what has happened to them. Where are all the birds and colors of summer? How have things changed since summer? Bring along collection boxes.

2. Discussion about nature walk and collection box items

   Children can sit in a large circle, with sheets of newspaper on the floor in front of them on which to empty out two "favorites" from their collection boxes.

3. Leaf collage

   Sprinkle crayon shavings onto a piece of waxed paper. Place several leaves on the paper with another piece of waxed paper over it. Iron the waxed paper and tape the collage to the window.

4. Halloween pumpkin field trip

   Select a small pumpkin for each child to decorate and take home. Carve a large class pumpkin, dry the seeds, and roast them. The class pumpkin can remain in the Discovery Area. Children can observe and discuss its decay as an ongoing activity.

NOVEMBER

1. Feeding birds and squirrels

   Buy birdseed and nuts. Ask children to bring in bread scraps.

2. Make a class bird feeder

   To make simple bird feeders, combine one part peanut butter to one part shortening; spread the mix onto pinecones; and roll the pinecones in birdseed. Attach bright yarn and hang the pinecones from trees, or store them in plastic wrap for children to take home.

DECEMBER

1. Create a class minimuseum

Cut tops off milk cartons and place them in a large shallow box. Have children collect or donate different outdoor objects such as rocks, leaves, or shells. Fill the milk cartons with the specimens. Give the children magnifying glasses to observe the different objects more closely.

2. Snow experiment

Bring a container of snow into the classroom. Place snow under the microscope to see what it looks like as it melts.

JANUARY

1. Winter nature walk

Where are the leaves? What's under the snow? Why is the ground so hard? Can children imitate the sound of walking on the snow?

2. Make snowpeople

Divide the classroom into several small groups. Have each group make its own snowperson. Encourage children to work together for the group project. Observe the change in shape of the snowpeople over time.

FEBRUARY

1. Make snow castles

Encourage children to generate their own ideas for building snow castles. How long will the castles take to melt?

2. Ice experiment

Get two ice cube trays. Pour tap water into one tray and salt water into the other. Place both trays outside over night and see which one freezes and which one doesn't. Take the ice cubes back to the classroom and use different materials (cotton, paper, cloth, rubber, etc.) to wrap the ice. Compare different materials to see which one melts the ice cubes the fastest.

3. Snow arts

Paint on the snow and observe how the color changes while the snow melts.

MARCH

1. Tadpoles

Tadpoles can be found in lakes and ponds or they can be purchased from a biological supply company. Watching them develop into frogs is an excellent long-term naturalist activity. Children can see how an organism changes at different stages of life, and also learn how to take care of animals by feeding them and changing the water.

2. Spring nature walk

Discuss the idea of seasonal change with children: Where is the snow? How many green things can you find? List several observable changes from winter to spring, in such areas as children's dress, the natural environment, and animal life.

3. Grow an amaryllis bulb

Put an amaryllis bulb and a ruler with a piece of paper attached to it in a flower pot. Introduce children to the concept of measuring by having them record the change in height of the amaryllis.

APRIL

1. Seeds and plants

Test whether there is a relationship between the size of seeds and speed of germination. Design a series of experiments to find out how air and light affect the germination of seeds and the growth of plants.

2. Earth Day nature walk

Give children gloves, and have them take a walk to pick up trash. Create a group project "junk sculpture." Talk with children about how to protect the environment.

MAY

1. Transfer plants to outdoor garden

2. Sky investigation on a cloudy day

Read cloud and weather books. Have children sit or lie on the ground, looking up at the sky. What do the shapes of the clouds look like?

JUNE

1. Spring/summer nature walk

Focus on bug collecting. Bring nets, if available, for conducting "sweeps" of areas of grass, bushes, and meadows. A sweep entails sweeping the net through an area and gathering up the top of the net to investigate the insect life in that particular area. After carefully observing, let the insects go.

2. Baby visit

Invite babies and toddlers to visit the preschool classroom. What's different about the way a newborn or a toddler moves? How are they different from you? Can you think of any other differences between you and babies? Any similarities? What did you look like when you were a baby?

ADDITIONAL ACTIVITIES

Most of the activities suggested below can be conducted more than once. These activities allow teachers to observe children's developmental progress in understanding scientific phenomena and mastering experimental methods.

Each time you present an activity, you can vary either the material being used or the concept being introduced. Since most of these activities are child directed, after a short introductory period you can allow children to explore the materials on their own.

1. Bubbles

   Use dishwashing detergent (Joy or Dawn work best) to make a bubble solution. Shape pipe cleaners into circles, squares, and triangles and use them as wands. Ask children to predict what shape the bubbles will be. Make more wands from funnels, spools, or strawberry baskets.

   You also can cut different shapes into the center of plastic plates or the bottoms of cups. A long string, woven through two straws and knotted with a small knot (make sure the knot is wedged inside one of the straws) will create different-sized bubbles. You can either blow through the straws, or gently sway them up and down, and then bring them together to form a bubble.

2. Magnets

   Give children magnets and a variety of materials such as nails, pins, pencils, and aluminum. Ask them to conduct experiments to find out what kind of objects magnets attract. Then give children a variety of materials such as straws, rulers, string, tape, wire, and magnets. Ask them to find ways to move a metal toy car across the table without touching it.

3. Human senses

   Pour different liquids (e.g., vinegar, apple juice, honey water, sugar water, salt water, water, coffee, cola, and soy sauce) into different bottles.

   Ask children to describe the colors of the liquids. What sense are they using to detect differences among the bottles? What other senses could they use? Give the children labels (with words or pictures) and ask them to match the labels with the right bottles. Encourage them to use their senses of smell, sight, and, if you wish, taste.

4. Learn about the fat content of food

   Present different kinds of food such as bacon, peanuts, mayonnaise, butter, leafy vegetables, and bread to the children. Ask them to rub each food firmly on a sheet of paper. Then, hold the paper up to the light and observe the spot where the food was rubbed. Record children's observations.

TABLE 29: DISCOVERY AREA SCORING CRITERIA

CLOSE OBSERVATION

1. engages in close observation of materials by using one or more of the senses to learn about the physical characteristics of things in the environment

2. notices changes in an object over time

    (e.g., new leaves on plants, buds on tree, tadpole has legs now, etc.)

3. shows interest in recording observations through drawings, charts, sequence cards, and so on.

IDENTIFICATION OF RELATIONSHIPS

1. notices similarities and dissimilarities between objects and likes to compare and contrast materials, events, or both

    (e.g., compares and contrasts crabs and spiders)

2. classifies objects according to various criteria

    (e.g., by color, shape, size, texture)

HYPOTHESIS FORMATION

1. makes predictions based on observations

2. asks "what if"—type questions about natural objects or events

3. offers explanations for why things are the way they are

EXPERIMENTATION

1. follows up on hypotheses (of one's own or others) by generating ideas for experiments or setting up simple experimental situations

    (e.g., puts a large and a small rock in water to see if one sinks faster than the other)

2. explores objects or relationships by manipulating pertinent variables or combining materials in ways that are novel

    (e.g., watering a plant with paint instead of water)

INTEREST IN NATURALIST ACTIVITIES

1. shows interest in natural phenomena or related material over extended period of time, with strong intrinsic motivation to direct own learning process

2. asks questions regularly about things one has observed

3. likes to report on one's own or others' experiences with the natural environment

KNOWLEDGE OF THE NATURAL WORLD

1. demonstrates an unusual amount of knowledge about a particular natural object or phenomenon

    (e.g., bugs, dinosaurs)

2. spontaneously offers relevant information about various natural phenomena and often answers questions raised by teachers or others about the natural environment

TABLE 30: DISCOVERY AREA OBSERVATION SHEET

Child _____   Age _____   Observer _____   Date _____

Components	Observations
Close Observation: 1. Uses different senses 2. Notices changes in object over time 3. Records observations in various ways 4. Other	
Identification of Relationships: 1. Compares/contrasts materials, events, or both 2. Classifies objects based on various criteria 3. Other	
Hypothesis Formation: 1. Predicts based on observations 2. Asks "what if" – type questions 3. Offers explanations for why 4. Other	
Experimentation: 1. Sets up experimental situations 2. Manipulates materials in novel ways 3. Other	
Interest in Naturalist Activities: 1. Shows strong intrinsic interest in natural phenomena 2. Asks questions about things being observed 3. Reports experiences with the natural environment 4. Other	
Knowledge of the Natural World: 1. Demonstrates an unusual amount of knowledge 2. Offers information and answers questions 3. Other	

❑ TREASURE HUNT GAME

—Purpose and Activity Description

The purpose of the Treasure Hunt Game is to give children the opportunity to draw logical inferences and to generate a rule connecting two sets of data. In this game, children hunt for "treasures" hidden under flags on a game board island. The children are encouraged to try to figure out the rule governing where the treasures have been hidden: bones are under orange flags, jewels under red flags, rocks under green flags, whereas the blue flags contain no objects at all. Once they have detected this pattern, the children can use the information to predict where the remaining objects are hidden.

During the game, children store the treasures in a color-coded box. Thus, the teacher can observe which children are able to classify the objects according to color. Although many children are able to sort the treasures into the correct sections, they may have difficulty using the information to predict where they will find the next treasure. Some may make predictions based on the actual color of the object itself (e.g., speculating that a brown flag will hide a brown rock), or they may base a prediction on whether or not they like a certain color. The blue section (corresponding to the blue flags that do not contain any treasures) is the most challenging for children to interpret because it contains no items.

Although verbalization is purposely not emphasized in this game, children are asked if they can articulate the rule after the first three turns, and again at the end of the game. On the sixth turn, teachers can note whether a child is able to infer where the rock can be found based on her knowledge of where the other treasures were found. For children who identify the rule immediately, further challenge can be provided by playing the game a second time and switching the objects associated with different flags or substituting new objects.

In longer versions of the game, some children might be able to use the knowledge that there are four treasures of each type to recognize when they have finished collecting all of the objects in one category, or to figure out which treasures are left. Children also will vary on how clearly they are able to articulate the underlying rule.

—Materials and Set-Up

The materials for the Treasure Hunt Game include a game board made from a 3' by 2' by 3" shallow cardboard box with an oversized rectangular top (1" overhang); blue cellophane and green contact paper; three or four small trees; 16 yogurt cups with the lids colored green; 16 flags made out of triangular felt pieces attached to thin wooden dowels (4 1/2" each) set in lumps of plasticine; three kinds of treasure (e.g., four rocks, four jewels, four bones); and an empty tissue box in which children can keep their treasures. You also will need a set of 12 cards depicting either a colored flag or a type of treasure. (See illustration p. 104.)

Cover the oversized cardboard top with the blue cellophane to give the illusion of water. Then place an irregularly shaped "island" made out of green contact paper onto the "ocean." Scatter three or four small trees throughout the island. Cut 16 holes (3" in diameter each) out of the island into which you can place the empty yogurt cups.

Make sure that the green-colored tops rest just above the island surface. Place a flag beside each hole. There should be four flags each of red, blue, orange, and green felt. Put jewels in the holes by the red flags, small rocks in the holes by the green flags, and bones in the holes by the orange flags. You can use costume jewelry (diamonds, rubies, brooches) for the jewels, and rabbit bones (available from most science supply companies) for the bones. At the start of the game, give children the set of 12 cards in the following sequence :

1. red flag	7. green flag
2. orange flag	8. blue flag
3. blue flag	9. bone
4. orange flag	10. rock
5. red flag	11. blank (empty)
6. rock	12. jewel

You also should provide children with a small box (the empty tissue box) in which they can keep their treasures. Divide the box into four sections with different-colored construction paper corresponding to the four colors of the flags.

Each child can be assessed in one session, usually lasting about 10 minutes. Record the child's responses on the observation sheet (see Table 31, p. 107). If time allows, children can play different versions of the game tailored to their individual levels of interest and understanding.

TREASURE HUNT GAME

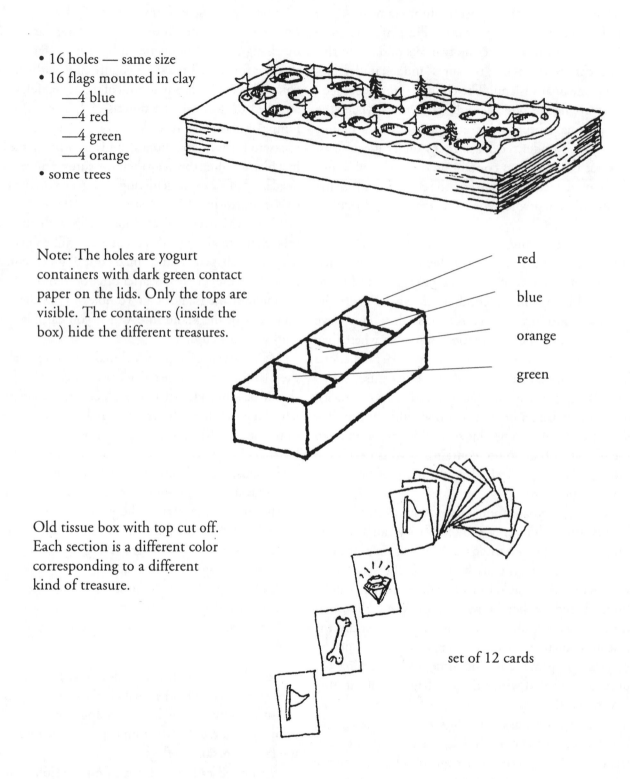

- 16 holes — same size
- 16 flags mounted in clay
  - —4 blue
  - —4 red
  - —4 green
  - —4 orange
- some trees

Note: The holes are yogurt containers with dark green contact paper on the lids. Only the tops are visible. The containers (inside the box) hide the different treasures.

red

blue

orange

green

Old tissue box with top cut off. Each section is a different color corresponding to a different kind of treasure.

set of 12 cards

Some cards have flags on them. Others have a picture of the treasure type.

—Procedure and Script

Because of the challenge it presents for some children, the Treasure Hunt Game is best introduced in the latter half of the school year. At group time, introduce the game as follows: "This week we have a new game in the class called the Treasure Hunt Game. This game is a little like a puzzle because children try to figure out where treasures are hidden. Everyone will have a turn to play the game with _____ [*adult's name*]." If you want to display the game for children before conducting the assessment, make sure they do not pull off the lids and discover where the treasures are hidden.

Refer to Table 31 as you read through the following script. Have the child sit next to you in front of the board. Tell her: "This is a treasure hunt game. You're going to have a lot of turns to find different treasures under these flags. There are jewels, rocks, and bones. There also are some holes that are empty. You need to figure how to find *all* of the treasures by remembering where you find *each kind* of treasure."

Next, give the child the cardboard box and say: "This box can help you. It has a red, orange, green, and blue part just like there are red, orange, green, and blue flags (point to flags). It can help you keep track of your treasures and where you find them. These cards will tell you what to do."

Place the cards face down in a pile in front of the child and have her turn over the top card (a red flag). Tell her this means that she should look under a red flag. When she finds a jewel, say (once), "Oh, you found a jewel under the red flag." If the child does not put the jewel into the red part of the box, ask her (once), "Where are you going to put that?" If she still does not use the red section, say, "Remember you found that under the red flag."

Have the child turn over the next card (orange flag) and tell her that it means that she should look under an orange flag. When she finds the bone, say, "Oh, you found a bone under the orange flag." As in the first turn, if the child does not put the bone in the orange section of the box, ask her, "Where are you going to put that?" If she still does not use the orange part, say, "Remember, you found the bone under the orange flag." When the child turns over the next card (blue), and looks under the blue flag and discovers it is empty, say, "Oh, there was nothing under the blue flag." Do *not* make any more reinforcing statements after this turn.

For the next part, say, "Now we're going to do this a little differently. *Before* you look, I want you to tell me what you think you'll find." When the child picks up the next card, it is very important to ask her *before* she looks under the flag *what* she thinks she'll find and *why*. If her prediction is correct, ask her, "How did you know that?" Do not scaffold for the box. Follow this procedure for each card, making sure you stop the child at each turn before she looks in a hole.

On Turn 6, say, "This card asks you to look for a rock. *Where* do you think you'll find a rock?" "Why?" Again, if the child's prediction is accurate, you can ask, "How did you know that?" Continue following this procedure, asking the "what" or "where" questions and as many "why's" as you think appropriate for the remainder of the game. If, after Turn 8, the child still does not know how to use the box, scaffold once saying, "See if there is a way your box can help you [to figure out where you can find a bone]." You also can offer comments of basic support such as, "Try to remember . . ." if the child seems carried away by her eagerness to find the treasures.

After the last turn, ask the child if she can tell you what the rule for the game is, or what the secret is for knowing where to find the treasures. As a form of closure (and if the child shows interest), have her look under the remaining flags for the last three treasures. If time allows, you also can have her help you replace the covers on the yogurt cups. If she has identified the rule, ask her not to tell other children the secret of the game until they have had their turn too. If keeping the rule a secret proves too difficult, you can switch the treasures around for different children.

—Scoring

Again, refer to Table 31 for this section. For the first three turns, record any scaffolding you provide about how to use the box. Also, for the first six turns, indicate under "box placement" whether the child places her treasures in the correct sections. For each card, starting with card 4, record in the appropriate boxes the child's predictions or the color flag under which she looks, and her reasons. Also beginning with Card 4, indicate with a check in the appropriate column whether the response is correct or incorrect, and record under "checks Box" whether the child refers to the box when figuring out what she will find or where she will look. After Turn 8, record whether further scaffolding for the box was provided. In the space at the bottom of the page, record the child's answer to the final question about how she knew where the different treasures were. Include any other comments you may have regarding the child's performance.

Note at what point the child breaks the code, in other words, when she discovers that the different kinds of treasures are hidden according to the colors of the flags. This breakthrough should be evident either when she begins to make correct responses consistently (allowing for errors due to haste or impulsiveness), or when she is able to verbalize how she knows where to look or what she will find. Use Table 32 to compile the children's scores. If a child breaks the code at cards 4, 5, or 6, allot 15 points; at Cards 7, 8, or 9, allot 10 points; at Cards 10, 11, or 12, or immediately after the game has ended, allot 5 points. If at any point the child shows that she understands that blues are empty, either through verbal explanation or correct choices with the "blue/empty" questions, allot 3 points. If she is able to articulate the underlying rule either during the game or in response to the final question, place an asterisk in the appropriate box. Finally, comment on whether or not the child referred to the box when making her predictions.

—Preliminary Results: 1986–1987

Of the 19 children in the 1986–1987 class, 10 learned the rule to the game by the end of the activity, and 5 were able to articulate it. The most general statement of the rule was provided by one girl who said, " 'Cause all the colors in the first place are in the second place." Whereas most children who understood the rule linked a specific object to a specific color, this girl was able to identify and articulate the more general concept—that color was the relevant variable.

Some of the children who were the most successful seemed to suspect or expect a link between the color of the flag and the type of treasure early on. When asked what they expected to find under a particular flag or where to find an object, they often checked the box to guide their guesses. When they were asked why they made a particular choice, they offered such responses as "because the rock's always in the green" or "because I had a jewel in the red one." At times, they answered, "I don't know" to the "why" questions, even though they made the right choice and seemed to know the rule. One child who seemed to be on the verge of breaking

the code suddenly lost it for no apparent reason.

Several of the children who did quite well also found it difficult to figure out that the holes of the blue flags were empty. They would become confused when they looked in the box and saw no objects in the blue section. Similarly, they often had trouble figuring out which color flag stood next to an empty hole.

While most children referred to the box, some also relied on their memory. One child never referred to the box, and repeatedly would ask herself, "Now, where did I find that before?" Another child was successful as long as she reflected on her choices and checked the box; however, when she acted quickly or without checking the box, she was often wrong. One girl reorganized the box midway through the game, categorizing the treasures into the appropriate sections, but then remained unable to capitalize on the information later on.

The children who never discovered the rule made random choices. They sorted the treasures into the box accurately, but did not refer back to the box. They were quite content with the treasures they found even if the objects did not match their predictions. Some children responded to irrelevant color cues on the cards, for example, predicting "green" when they saw green grass under the rock, or "white" when they saw a blank card. One child was so fascinated by the jewels that he was distracted from attending to the other aspects of the game. This boy was unusually sensitive to visual cues in other domains as well.

For further challenge, four children tried a version of the game in which jewels were switched with empty holes and the box was removed. They performed almost as well as in the first game. One child recognized the switch of jewels for "empties," even though she had played the two versions of the game three days apart. A more advanced version of the game was tried with numbers attached to the flags, and treasures hidden according to number instead of color. This version was very difficult for children because they were unable to switch their focus from color to number. Only one child was able to break the code. This variation could be used for children who perform exceptionally well. An option for children who never discover the rule is for the adult to explain the rule ("all the jewels were under the red flags, all the bones were under the orange flags"). Then tell the children that this time you will hide jewels, bones, and rocks under different-colored flags, and let them play the game again.

TABLE 31: TREASURE HUNT GAME OBSERVATION SHEET

Child: _____

Observer: _____

Date: _____

Age: _____

BOX SECTIONS

COLOR	red	blue	orange	green
OBJECT	jewel	empty	bone	rock

SEQUENCE OF CARDS	CHILD'S PREDICTION	C	I	SCAFF	BOX PLACEMENT	CHECKS BOX	"WHY" RESPONSES OR IF RULE ARTICULATED
1. red							
2. orange							
3. blue							
4. orange							
5. red							
6. rock							
7. green							
8. blue							
9. bone							
10. rock							
11. empty							
12. jewel							

Reasons/Rule Articulated:

107

TABLE 32: TREASURE HUNT GAME SUMMARY SHEET

Child (age)	Breaks Code	Learns Blues	Verbalizes Rule	Use of Box	TOTAL	Comments

DISTRIBUTION OF POINTS:

Breaks code at turns 4, 5, or 6 = 15 points
              at turns 7, 8, or 9 = 10 points
              at turns 10, 11, or 12 = 5 points

Learns blues are empty = 3 points

Verbalizes rule = *

Use of box: write comments

Maximum score = 18 points

❑ SINK AND FLOAT ACTIVITY

—Purpose and Activity Description

The purpose of the Sink and Float Activity is to assess children's abilities to think like a scientist in terms of making careful observations, identifying relationships between variables (such as weight and likelihood of floating), and generating and testing hypotheses by conducting simple experiments.

The activity was adapted from the Elementary Science Study Unit (1986) produced by Delta Education. In the assessment, children are presented with a tub of water and a variety of materials. To start off, children are asked to predict which of these materials will sink and which will float; test their predictions; and then generate a hypothesis about why the materials behaved as they did. In another task, children are asked to figure out a way to make sinking objects float and floating objects sink. The assessment also includes a period of free play and experimentation to see if, left to her own devices, the child will initiate scientific investigations (e.g., how many items can a sponge hold before it sinks?) or engage in other types of play (e.g., tell a story with the Fisher Price people).

The cognitive processes involved in this activity include observing, comparing, classifying, and generating and verifying predictions based on close observations. Children also may learn about the buoyancy of various objects and the concepts of density and displacement. In the course of the activity, some children conduct very simple experiments. They may try to distinguish relevant from irrelevant variables in each step of the task. For example, they may try to group objects into "sinkers" and "floaters" according to variables like weight and shape. Or, they may try to see what happens when they drop items from different heights, or combine materials that sink with those that float.

The kinds of explanations that children offer for their observations often indicate whether they are able to use the available information effectively. Are their hypotheses and predictions based on their observations, or are they randomly generated without reference to their information base? Because children at this age can express their hypotheses verbally or nonverbally, the activity is scored both on verbalized questions and ideas as well as nonverbal play. Many of the processes tapped by this activity also are addressed in the Discovery Area.

—Materials and Set-Up

The materials and the set-up for this activity are derived in large part from the Elementary Science Study Unit (1986). The activity is conducted with one child at a time, and lasts about 15 minutes. If children want more time playing with the materials, they can either be encouraged to return after all of the children have had a turn, or they can continue exploring similar materials at the water table.

The Sink and Float Activity is conducted using a two- to three-gallon plastic tub, half filled with water, and placed on a towel. The surface of the table or floor should be an area you would not mind getting wet. Keeping a second towel nearby helps both materials and people stay relatively dry. You might ask children to wear aprons as well.

The following is a list of materials used in the activity:

- 1 plastic marble and 1 plastic egg (for use in demonstration)
- 2 small wooden blocks
- 2 small bolts with nuts
- 2 clear plastic film canisters with tops
- 2 small corks or pieces of foam rubber
- 2 small rocks
- 2 Fisher Price people
- 2 opaque plastic film canisters with tops
- 2 washers or coins
- 1 kitchen-size sponge or piece of styrofoam

To prevent children from getting distracted, place the preceding materials in a small bag or box and out of the children's sight before beginning the activity. Record children's responses (verbal and nonverbal) on the observation sheet provided in Table 33 (pp. 114–115).

A few weeks prior to the assessment, equip the water table with sinking and floating materials. Although the exact assessment items listed above probably should not be used, provide materials that are familiar to children, but not typically used at the water table. The objects should vary in weight, size, shape, composition (plastic, metal, wood) and density. Possible materials include oil-based clay, aluminum foil (when rolled up, it sinks; when flat, it floats), paper clips, marbles, plastic straws, and plastic caps. You also might want to provide rulers or a scale so children can examine the different dimensions and properties of the items. The liquid in which they are floated can be changed by adding salt, cooking oil, and so on.

Introduce the Sink and Float Activity as follows: "Today we have a new game in the class for children to play with. It has different objects that sink and float. One child at a time will have a turn to play the game with _____ [*adult's name*]."

Part I: Warm-up: Predictions and Sorting

A. Prediction—Begin the activity by explaining to the child: "There are a lot of different things in this bag that we can put in the water. I'm going to take them out of the bag one at a time, and I want you to tell me whether you think each one will *sink* or *float* when you put it in the water. Let me show you what I mean." Demonstrate with the marble and plastic egg. (This will help children who may not be familiar with the terminology of "sink/float.")

To conduct the assessment, take the items (one of each pair) out of the bag in the order in which they are listed in Table 33. Give each object to the child to place in the water, making sure she makes a prediction *before* putting the object in the water. Starting with Turn 4, ask her why she made her particular prediction, and record her answer in the space provided on the observation sheet.

Remove each item from the water before the next one is placed in it so the child can focus on each object individually. As the child goes through the list of eight items on the observation sheet, check off the predictions that were correct, and record the explanations. Although the predictions will not be scored, they provide useful information about a child's familiarity with the concepts of floating and sinking.

B. Sorting—Remove the last item from the water. Ask the child to sort the items into two groups of things that float and things that sink. Ask her why she placed the objects into the two piles. You can probe with "What is the same about all of the sinking/floating things?" or "Why do these things sink, but these float?" Record which objects the child placed in each group and her reasoning. Have the child test the items in each group and ask her for a possible explanation of why misplaced items did not behave as expected. Record the child's responses.

Part II: Free Experimentation

Take all of the materials out of the water and the bag and place them on the table. Ask the child, "What ideas would you like to try out with these materials?" or "Is there something you would like to make these things do in the water?" This section is intended to elicit the child's own ideas without significant input from the adult, to see how the child approaches the materials: Does she engage in experimentation, classification and sorting, or dramatic play? Allow about 5 to 7 minutes for free play with the materials. If the child appears at a loss, encourage her to follow up on her own comments and questions by experimenting with the materials, but do not scaffold further.

Record the child's activity in as much detail as possible on the observation sheet, including her questions and remarks as well as her actions. If the child is reluctant to stop playing after the allotted time, tell her that she should finish up with one last thing, and that you have just a few more things you'd like to try. Then she will be able to play on her own again. If the child has no ideas, proceed to Part III.

Part III: Structured Experimentation

A. Transforming Floaters into Sinkers and Sinkers into Floaters—Remove all of the items from the water. Begin this section by saying, "Now that you know what some of these things do when they're put in the water, I want to see if you can think of a way to make one of the floating things sink to the bottom, and one of the sinking things float on top of the water." Take one of the clear film canisters and ask, "How do you think you can make this container sink to the bottom and stay there *without holding it under with your hand*?" Check off which strategy the child uses on the observation sheet, describing it in as much detail as possible. If the child simply verbalizes an idea, encourage her to follow up on it by trying it out. Then, ask her why she thinks her strategy either did or did not work. Also encourage her to think of additional ways to sink the canister.

Once again, remove all items from the water, but this time, encourage the child to think of how she could make a sinking item float. Use the washer, coin, or small rock for the sinking object. Again, ask the child why she thinks her strategy either did or did not work. Record the child's strategies in the space provided in Table 33.

B. Guess the Hidden Object—For this half of Part III, place all of the materials except the opaque canister in the bag so that they are out of the child's sight. (This insures that the child will not be able to see which item is missing.) Tell the child, "I have an idea for a game we can play with the different things we've put in the water. I'm going to hide something in this container, and I want to see if you can guess what is inside."

Place one of the sinking objects (e.g., bolt) inside the canister without the child seeing what it is, and place the canister in the water. Ask the child to guess what is inside the canister without taking it out of the water. Also ask what the reasons are for each guess she makes. Record both the child's guess and rationale on the observation sheet. Note if the child finds a way to figure out exactly which item is inside.

If the child is unable to make a guess about the contents of the canister, ask her whether seeing that the container is at the bottom of the tub gives her any clues. If no ideas are forthcoming, let her take the canister out of the water to feel how heavy it is, or shake it to find out what it sounds like. Again, record her guesses and rationales. Finally, let her open the canister to discover its contents.

Next, repeat the same activity, only this time using a floating object (e.g., Fisher Price person). To bring the activity to a close, ask if there is one last thing the child would like to try with the materials, or if she has any questions she would like to ask.

—Scoring

Refer to Tables 33 and 34 for this section. Record the child's responses and actions on Table 33. After completing the activity, use Table 34 to figure out and record each child's score. For Part I A, do not score the child's predictions. To score the rationales for Turns 4 – 8, award 2 points if the child is able to give plausible explanations for three or more of her predictions.

For Part I B, allot 3 points for sorting five to eight items correctly; add 2 more points if the child's rationale identifies a relevant variable like weight. Note in particular if the child is able to offer an explanation for any discrepancies, like why the rock sinks even though it may be lighter than the Fisher Price people.

Technically, factors such as density, volume, and surface area are the relevant variables for determining the buoyancy of an object; but *weight* can be scored as relevant for children at this level. (The formal definition of buoyancy is "the upward pressure exerted upon a body by the fluid in which it is immersed, which is equivalent to the weight of the fluid which the body displaces.") Rationales of "these sink, but these float" or identifying color, size, or shape as a variable should be noted, but not awarded any points.

In Part II, try to record all play and remarks the child makes. Since not all responses reflect genuine investigative efforts, award 3 points for a "scorable" question or comment, or for an example of experimental play. The examples on the next page which distinguish scorable from nonscorable responses will help you in attributing points. (The examples are not intended to be exhaustive, but rather indicate the range of how a child might respond.) In general, whenever a child identifies a relevant variable either through questions, comments, or play, 3 points are allotted. Whether the variable is identified in the form of a question, comment, or action is not important; they are weighted equally. In the interests of time and setting a reasonable limit for the total possible score in this part of the activity, a maximum of 15 points is allowed for this section.

In Part III A, mark which strategy the child uses in the space provided, and any rationales given. Award three points for each idea or action that succeeds in making the sinking item float or floating item sink. Award 1 point for plausible rationales offered for why a particular strategy either did or did not succeed.

For Part III B, record all guesses the child makes for what is hidden inside the opaque canister and the reasons for her guesses. Award 2 points if she correctly identifies either a sinking or floating item for the two steps of this part of the activity. Award an additional

EXAMPLES OF RESPONSES

Questions that can be scored (3 points):

What will happen if I take the top off the container?

What will happen if I put the rock inside the container?

Why do all the wooden things float?

Why do some things sink deeper down than others?

Why does the sponge get heavy when it gets wet?

Why do things stick together when they're in the water?

I bet the sponge will sink with a lot of sinking things on it.

Nonscorable questions:

Where did you find these rocks?

How many blocks are there in the water?

Can I pretend the sponge is a raft in a swimming pool?

Experimental play (3 points):

Child tries to sink a canister by filling it with water.

Child places washers on top of a wooden block in order to hold it under water.

Child tries to find out how many heavy items a sponge can hold without sinking.

Child tries to sink a floating item by releasing it from high in the air.

Child is interested in the size of a splash that an object makes when dropped in the water from different heights.

Nonscorable play:

Child pretends to wash all the materials.

Child pretends the tub of water is a swimming pool for the Fisher Price people.

Child uses materials as storytelling props.

Child makes a diving board for Fisher Price person.

(Note: Of course, nonscorable play and questions may provide valuable information about a child's other areas of interest or strength.)

point if she is able to identify precisely the item inside the canister. Record any rationales given, but do not score them.

—Preliminary Results: 1987–1988

Of the 17 children who participated in the Sink and Float Activity, 4 children received a score of "high"; 10 ranged from "medium-high" to "medium-low"; and three were in the "low" group. The children in the highest group were able to use their observations of the materials in Part I to help them predict which items would sink and which would float. One boy carefully examined the objects, feeling them, squeezing them, and asking himself which ones looked alike. Another compared which items floated deeper than others. A third explained, "Heavy things sink, you know—it's gravity." He defined gravity as "when something falls off a cliff . . . when something goes down." The children in the lowest group, on the other hand, made random guesses, were unable to generalize the information they did have, and could not offer any rationales for their observations.

In Part II (Free Experimentation), children ranged from having no ideas at all to both positing and testing numerous different ideas. Some children engaged in exploratory play, but did not seem interested in trying out their own experiments. They simply wanted to wash the materials or to place things in the water and then remove them one by one. A couple of children voiced ideas of their own, but were reluctant to try them out, even after encouragement by the adult. However, almost half of the children experimented with many different ideas, even after they had accomplished their intended goal. Their ideas included trying to balance different materials, seeing how many items an object like the sponge could hold, dropping items from different heights, and making floating things sink and sinking things float. One child noticed that the two wooden blocks stuck together when placed in the water. He systematically took other pairs of objects to see if they also would stick together. This child was so intrigued with the activity that he helped to set it up for the other children each day, and checked to see if any new materials were available. He then asked his classmates afterwards what they did with the materials.

In Part III A, 10 of the children were able to make the canister sink and the washer float. They tried putting heavy items either inside or on top of the canister to make it sink, and they floated the washer on a floating item such as the sponge or inside one of the canisters to make it float. Some of these children continued to generate additional ideas even after they completed the task successfully. Some of the less successful attempts at making the canister sink included throwing it into the water, and adding items that were not heavy enough to weight it down. Unsuccessful attempts to make the washer float included putting lighter items on top of it, and trying to get it to balance on top of an unstable floating item.

In Part III B, some children did not make any guesses, but most could say that the hidden item must be either heavy or light depending on whether the canister sunk or floated. As one child explained, "I knew it wasn't a heavy thing because heavy things drowned." A few children were able to figure out exactly what the item was: one boy tested potential "hidden objects" by putting them into the water and observing whether they sank or floated, and then shaking the canister to hear what kind of noise was generated.

As with some of the other Spectrum activities, some children brought their own strengths to the task. One boy created a rich narrative about the "Great and Famous Sponge Man," while another was very interested in the feel of the different materials, and how they could be fashioned into a sculpture both in and out of the water.

TABLE 33: SINK AND FLOAT ACTIVITY OBSERVATION SHEET

Child _____   Observer _____

Age _____   Date _____

I. WARM-UP: PREDICTIONS AND SORTING

A. Predictions:

Predictions (mark *S* or *F*)		**Rationale**
1. Wooden block	___	
2. Nut and bolt	___	
3. Clear canister	___	
4. Small cork	___	(why?) _____
5. Small rock	___	(why?) _____
6. Fisher Price person	___	(why?) _____
7. Opaque canister	___	(why?) _____
8. Coin/washer	___	(why?) _____

Closure: So, why do you think some of these sank/floated?

B. Sorting:

Floating Things: **Sinking Things:**

Rationale (e.g., weight, size, shape, color, sink/float, or other—describe):

Rationale (for why misplaced items did not do as expected):

II. Free Experimentation

Describe in as much detail as possible child's play, comments, and questions, and indicate by an *E* those that can be considered experimental or scorable (see Scoring section).

III. Structured Experimentation

A. 1. *"How can you make the container sink?"*

      a. places sinking item(s) inside canister ____

      b. piles materials on top of canister ____

      c. other (describe):

2. *"How can you make the coin/rock float?"*

      a. places sinking item on top of a floating item (i.e., cork, sponge) ____

      b. places sinking item inside container ____

      c. other (describe):

B. 1. *"Guess what's inside the container."*

               Child's Guess/Why?

Bolt:

Fisher Price:

Additional Comments:

TABLE 34: SINK AND FLOAT ACTIVITY SUMMARY SHEET

Child (age)	I A Rationale: 3 correct = 2 pts.	I B Sorting 5–8 items = 3 pts.	Correct Rationale = 2 pts.	II Each Scorable Response = 3 pts	III A Each Successful Idea = 3 pts.	Plausible Rationale = 1 pt.	III B Correct Guess = 2 pts.	Exact ID = 1 pt.	TOTAL

◻ ASSEMBLY ACTIVITY

—Purpose and Activity Description

In the Assembly Activity, the teacher presents the child with objects of increasing mechanical complexity and asks the child to take them apart and put them back together. Because real gadgets are so appealing to children of this age, authentic machines are used instead of play materials. The materials for the assessment include two food grinders of varying complexity and a small oil pump. Other gadgets can be used as long as they contain a small number of relatively large parts and can be taken apart and used safely.

Successful completion of the activity depends on a range of observation and problem-solving skills: Do the children notice which pieces come off? Do they learn how to reassemble them, inferring relationships based on sensitive observation? Do they exhibit an understanding of how the gadget works? Can they use a trial-and-error approach effectively, using relevant feedback from their actions to modify their next step? Do they recognize when a part is in the wrong place or when the machine does not work? The activity also allows the teacher to look at a child's fine motor skills and visual-spatial abilities. A child may identify where pieces should be placed either through spatial reasoning and use of positive and negative space, or by noticing equivalence between slots and parts in size, shape, and number.

Children are not required to use verbal skills to complete the activity successfully. While we include several open-ended questions—such as asking what the child thinks the gadget is or does—the child is never penalized for her answer. The Assembly Activity is particularly relevant for observation of such working styles as attention to detail, focus, and planfulness.

The objects are sequenced from easiest to hardest. If the child experiences difficulty and frustration with the first grinder, she may choose to end the activity. Few children make it as far as the pump, the most complex gadget. Variations on this activity include providing disks of different sizes so children can see how the each grinds food more or less coarsely. If children require further challenge, both grinders can be taken apart and the pieces laid out on the table. Children can be asked to group pieces together. Their problem-solving approaches may range from systematically matching pieces by function to random grouping.

—Materials and Set-Up

As noted above, the materials for the Assembly Activity are two meat grinders and a small oil pump. (See illustrations, pp. 119–121.) The grinders are relatively old models that are held together by nuts and bolts. They can be taken apart and reassembled without the use of tools. Mechanical objects manufactured more recently are likely to have the nuts and bolts replaced by rivets that cannot be taken apart.

The activity is designed to be completed in one session. The grinders are clamped to a table, at which the child either sits or stands, with the teacher seated to one side. A small tray is provided so that the smaller pieces of the grinder and pump do not roll off the table.

The first grinder is operated by turning a handle, which in turn rotates the spiral core, pushing the food through a series of small holes and into the spokes of the grinding disk. The spokes cut the food into small pieces. The grinding disks are available in different shapes for different kinds of food—nuts, carrots, meat, and so on. This grinder contains five removable pieces, fastened together by one main nut. Once this main nut has been unscrewed, the washer and grinding disk can be pulled off and the inner grinding mechanism removed. The handle, made of two parts, also can be taken off, but it is possible to take apart and put the grinder back together without ever detaching the handle.

The second and larger grinder contains several main fasteners, a handle attached by a thumbscrew bolt that has to be removed in order for one to take apart the inner grinding mechanism, and a bridge fastened to the front of the grinder by two wing nuts on either side. Two other pieces can be removed although they are not functionally related to the other parts: the top grinder bowl twisted onto the main body and a front guard covering the grinding plates.

The oil pump is a smaller and lighter object with much smaller parts. There are three main components that must be reassembled in a very specific and not at all obvious order, as well as several small parts that are not functionally related. Several of the pieces are hidden from view when the pump is assembled. The pump can be reassembled in a number of ways, some of which are more effective than others. In general, children should not be presented with the pump unless they have demonstrated great skill with the grinders.

The main criteria for selecting gadgets of varying complexity are listed below. Although you may not be able to find objects that meet all of the criteria, use the following as guidelines for selecting appropriate materials. Practice taking apart and assembling the objects yourself before conducting the assessment with children.

• Object 1 (Simple mechanism with limited number of parts)

  total of 4–6 removable parts

  1 main fastener

  1 component that can be put together independently and then attached to the object (such as the grinder handles)

• Object 2 (Complex mechanism with more parts than Object 1)

  total of 8 to 12 removable parts

  2 or 3 main fasteners

  washers or other pieces whose functions may not be obvious

  1 or 2 components that can be assembled independently (see Object 1)

• Object 3 (Complex mechanism that is put together differently than the first two gadgets, e.g., uses springs instead of gears)

  1 or more main fasteners

  some parts which are hidden from view

  washers or similar parts

  2 or more separate components that can be put together in more than one way, some of which work better than others

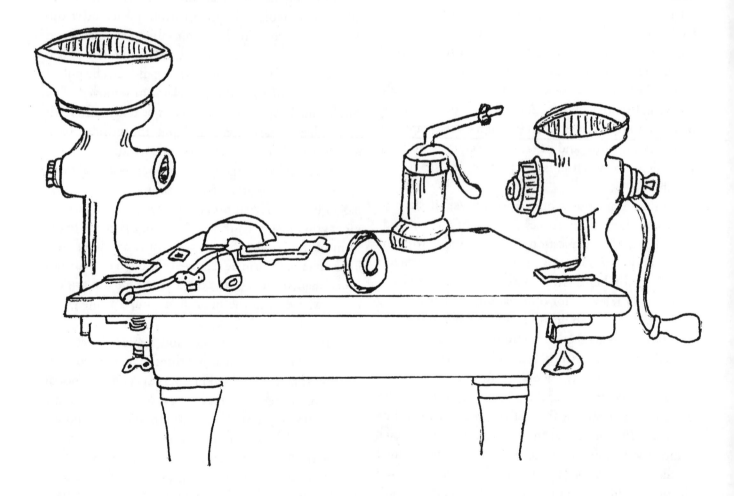

ASSEMBLY ACTIVITY: (left to right) Grinder 2, oil pump, Grinder 1

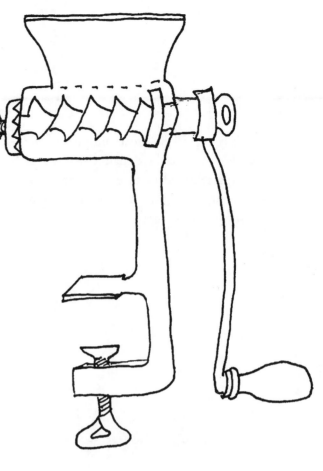

Grinder 1 is the first and simplest object. This grinder has five removable parts, including one main fastener.

GRINDER 1

Grinder 2 is larger and more complex than Grinder 1. This grinder has nine removable parts. (Grinder bridge is not shown in this illustration.)

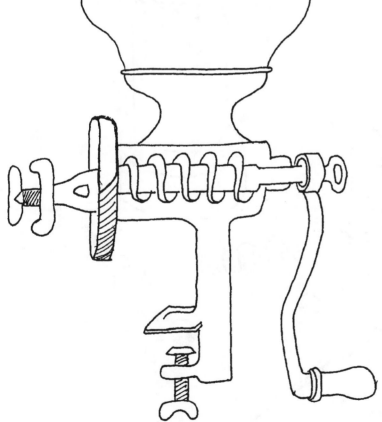

GRINDER 2

The oil pump is the most complex of the three objects. The three main components must be assembled in an order that is not self-evident, presenting children with a more sophisticated challenge.

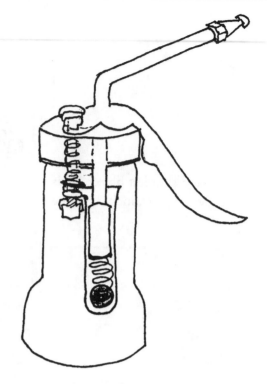

OIL PUMP ASSEMBLED

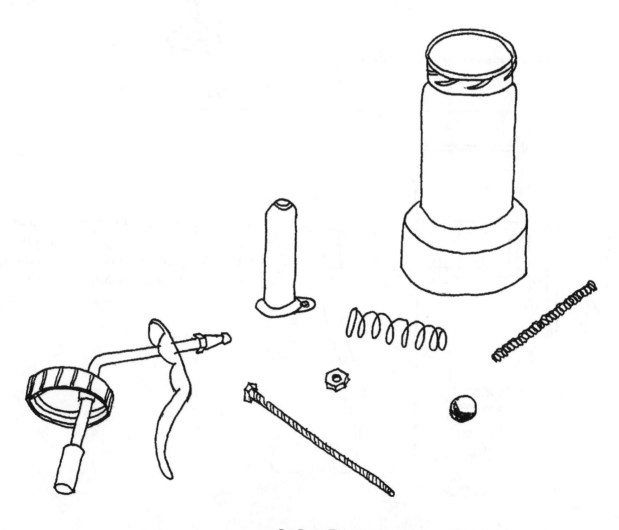

OIL PUMP DISASSEMBLED

—Procedure and Script

A few weeks before the Assembly Activity is introduced, present children with nuts and bolts, hinges, door knobs, a variety of screwdrivers and wrenches, and other simple hardware. You might also introduce books about tools or machines, and discuss children's experiences using machines or building things with tools. Try to make sure that every child has a chance at free play with the tools and parts, always with an adult observer nearby to insure safety.

When introducing the assessment activity, place the grinders within children's view. Explain, "This week, children are going to be able to play with different kinds of gadgets. These gadgets can be taken apart and put back together again." Conduct the activity with one child at a time at a small table in a relatively quiet corner of the room. Make sure that the outer screws of the food grinder are securely fastened for each child, but not so tightly that children will have difficulty unscrewing them.

Begin the activity by asking the child if she has ever seen this object or has any idea what it is. If not, explain to her that it is a meat grinder, and have her twirl the handle to see how it works. Then say, "Now, let's see if you can take the *whole thing* apart and put the *whole thing* back together again. First, look carefully all around it and see how the pieces fit together and come apart. After it's all taken apart, it needs to all be put back together again." For safety reasons, sit close to the grinder. You may need to place your hand under the handle to prevent it from falling off when the fastening screw is removed. Do not allow children to unscrew the clamp fastening the grinder to the table. Also, make sure that the child does not pinch her hand with the grinding plates when she tries to fit together the pieces.

If the child has trouble getting started, you can try to ease her into the activity and help her focus by talking with her about the object. You can ask her what kinds of tools her parents have at home and whether she has used them. For the rest of the activity, let the child proceed at her own pace while you remain in the background as much as possible. Show interest and provide support for the child's effort, but do not constantly direct her activity. For consistency in scoring, present every child with the second grinder unless it is clearly too difficult and would only result in frustration.

In general, scaffolding offered for any part of the activity proceeds from the general to the specific (see Table 35, p. 124). Thus, if a child does not know how to begin, suggest, "Well, let's take a look at all the pieces." Or you could say, "There are some pieces of this grinder that come apart. Can you find them?" Also, you might try, "Are there any (other) pieces you can see that come apart?" or "Let's look in the back and in the front." If more help is needed, ask, "What do you think would be a good part to take off first?" or, "Where do you think would be the best place to start?" On a more specific level, you might point to the main fastener and say, "Try taking this off," or, "Let's see what this might do." Record the scaffolding you provide on the observation sheet.

Children who do not require such extensive scaffolding to start may need help along the way. If they fail to remove all of the pieces, you can either suggest simply, "Look carefully," or say, "Look and see what else is attached. Look at *all* the pieces." If the child has finished removing the pieces and some parts still remain attached, ask, "Is there anything else that comes off?" If they have difficulty when trying to reassemble the object, ask them, "Where do you think that might go?" or, "What other ways can you hold/move that to make it fit?" or, "Can you think of another way that these might go together?" Comparing the grinder to a puzzle also helps: "It's like a kind of puzzle and you have to fit the pieces back in."

Let the child know that she can ask you for help in screwing on or off a small or difficult piece. If a child lacks the fine motor skills necessary for screwing on or off a nut or bolt, start it for her and let her finish turning it. Also, inform the child if she is trying to take something apart that does not come apart. If a composite piece lying on the table can be separated further, suggest that the child reexamine the pieces on the table. Reattaching the handle is especially difficult for some children because they do not know which way it should be held. One possible clue lies in the different-size holes for attaching the handle. Comments such as "Let's look at the holes and see which one is bigger" aid the child in figuring out how to secure the handle.

In general, use your own judgment about the degree of scaffolding needed. If a child attaches a piece incorrectly, it is not necessary to correct her. For those children completely at a loss, you may want to help them take the object apart and put it back together (but to not score them). At the end of the activity, suggest to the child that she give the handle a good turn to make sure that it works.

—Scoring

The observation sheet refers only to the two grinders, since very few, if any, children are presented with the oil pump during the assessment. If you use other mechanical objects, the scoring system may require minor modifications. Table 35 provides different levels of scaffolding that can be used throughout the activity. Before conducting the activity and filling out the score sheet, familiarize yourself with the scoring criteria in Table 36. Then, score the child either during or immediately following the activity with the observation sheet in Table 37. If possible, it may be helpful to videotape the child and score from the tape as needed. Then transfer the scores to the summary sheet provided in Table 38.

The scoring system includes the following categories: sense of relationship of parts to whole, problem solving, attention to detail, and fine motor skills. Children are scored low, average, or high in each category for each of the objects.

—Preliminary Results: 1986–1987

Eighteen of the 20 children in the 1986–1987 class volunteered to work on the grinders. There were no apparent gender differences in interest or skill. Nor was age a discriminating factor: some of the youngest children gave the strongest performances, and exhibited uncharacteristically high focus and investment in the task.

Children demonstrated a wide range of abilities: some did not know how or where to begin, whereas others recognized immediately how the grinders came apart. These children also remembered where the pieces should be reattached, or systematically fit them into place through trial and error. The children using a more random and haphazard approach tried to fit parts almost anywhere; one child complacently stuck a remaining washer onto the bottom tip of the handle, accurately surmising that it would not fall off. Some children seemed surprised when pieces slipped off after they removed the fastening nut or bolt. They left parts loosely attached, and could not figure out which way the screws should be turned. These same children also appeared equally satisfied regardless of whether parts were missing, fastened on backwards, or placed in the wrong position. One girl reassembled the grinding mechanism in the correct order, but fit it into the shaft backwards. Another common mistake was to try unscrewing parts that could more simply have been pulled off.

The more planful children learned how to twist a screw on or off by themselves. They used the first grinder as a reference for the second grinder, rather than treating the latter as an entirely new challenge. They solved problems quickly, seemed to have a sense for when the task was completed, and persisted with problem spots, seeking help only after several of their own attempts failed.

Many of the children enjoyed talking as they proceeded through their task. Some derived great pleasure from the problem-solving nature of the activity; for others, it was tiring. As one boy told us, "It's always hard to remember things when you're four." One child conducted his own experiment, letting the grinder handle fall and swing from different heights. Some children also offered suggestions for what the grinder was: "gas compressor," "you put wood in there and it would come out grinded up," "water fountain," and "it makes tuna fish."

—Further Suggestions for the Domain

You can set up your classroom to encourage scientific discovery. A block area for building towers, bridges, and other structures helps children acquire the basis for understanding such concepts as weight, distance, and gravity as well as geometric concepts of length, width, and area. A water table encourages experimentation with funnels, siphons, and objects that sink or float, whereas a natural science area can display a changing collection of shells, nests, seeds, and small animals.

You can also provide equipment such as magnifying glasses, magnets, and mirrors. (See the Discovery Area section of this chapter.) You can also apply simplified versions of the scientific method to activities in other domains. For example, ask children to predict what will happen when two colors of paint are mixed together, to generate hypothesis-testing in the art area.

A list of additional activities, designed to foster skills needed by different types of scientists follows. Of course, children should be free to use the activities and materials to pursue their own interests. For example, a child interested in the mechanical sciences could use water table materials to investigate causal mechanisms, forces, and conservation, whereas a child interested in the natural sciences may explore the qualities of materials provided in the Machine City or the Construction Center.

Experimental Scientist

Provide equipment in the block area that invites experimentation. Possible materials include ramps, balls, and pulleys.

Marble Machine: Have children create their own marble machines by pounding nails into a wooden board and attaching rubber bands to the nails. The marbles can be sent down the board through the rows of stretched rubber bands as in a pinball machine. Observe how children position the rubber bands when playing with the machine. Encourage children to create new paths for the marbles.

Naturalist

Discovery Area [see Discovery Area section]: This area contains rocks, fossils, human-made materials, and plant and animal life. The focus is on encouraging children's own discoveries. Plant and animal observation activities include observing, describing, and recording new developments in a daily log.

Engineer/Mechanic

Machine City: Provide gadgets for structured free play such as telephones, clocks, door knobs and hinges, radios, old typewriters, and tape dispensers. Children can take apart and put the gadgets back together.

Repair Center: Include working and broken models of simple machines such as a flashlight. Give children a slightly broken machine and let them figure out why it doesn't work. You also can notice which children are more drawn to the Repair Center or Machine City, and which to the Discovery Area.

Construction Center: Give children toothpicks, plasticine, and popsicle sticks with holes in one or both ends and ask them to create their own constructions. Or, make available commercial materials like Construx, Tinkertoys, or Legos to encourage openended construction activities.

Exploring the Classroom: Have children inspect cabinet closures, pipes under sinks, window locks, door locks, drawers. Invite children to figure out what makes the cabinet door stay closed, how a drawer rolls, and so on. Let them try locking and unlocking the door. Provide materials (e.g., plastic tubing, clamps, plastic pumps) in the water table that enable children to recreate the workings of the sink pipes. You also can conduct investigations in other areas of the school (e.g., playground, director's office).

TABLE 35: ASSEMBLY ACTIVITY SCAFFOLDING SUGGESTIONS

GENERAL:

"Let's see if you can take the whole thing apart and put it all back together again."

"This is like a kind of puzzle; you take the pieces off and then put them back together again."

"There are some pieces of this grinder that come apart. Can you find them?"

"Are there any (other) pieces you can see that come apart?"

"Look carefully. Do you see any other pieces that come off?"

"What are you trying to do here?"

"Look and see what else is attached. Look at all the pieces. Where do you think that might go?"

"Which piece would be a good one to take off first?"

"Where do you think would be the best place to start?"

"Let's look in the back and in the front. Does any piece look like it might come off?"

"Where do you think that might go?"

"What other ways can you hold/move the piece to make it fit?"

"Can you think of another way these might fit together?"

SPECIFIC:

"Let's look at the holes [on the handle]. Is one bigger than the other?"

"Why don't you try turning this/taking this off?" (Point to main fastener/other piece.)

"What will happen if you take off this piece?"

"Let's see what this does." (Demonstrate by turning a main fastener or other piece.)

TABLE 36: ASSEMBLY ACTIVITY SCORING CRITERIA

A. SENSE OF RELATIONSHIP OF PARTS TO WHOLE

1. Child does not know how to begin disassembly with main fasteners or doesn't know where to reassemble main fastener, or both. For example, the child may try to put main fasteners in the top or insert them from the wrong side.

2. Child identifies main fasteners and knows how to begin reassembly with main piece, but initially may have some difficulty with other portions of the disassembly or reassembly. For example, at first, child may put pieces on backwards or in the wrong place.

3. Child takes the grinder apart easily, reassembles it with little trouble, and recognizes where pieces (such as the handle) should go.

B. PROBLEM SOLVING

1. Child tries to force pieces where they don't fit; frequently gives up and goes to another part of the task when unsuccessful. Upon finding that she has left out or misplaced pieces, child does not know what to do with them.

2. Child may try to force some pieces, but eventually tries alternatives. Upon finding that she has left out or misplaced pieces, child has some idea of how to correct mistakes.

3. Child proceeds without errors or recognizes and corrects errors easily.

C. ATTENTION TO DETAIL

1. Child leaves out one or more pieces and fails to make corrections if the handle does not turn smoothly or the grinder rattles or wobbles.

2. Child attaches all pieces but fails to make corrections if the handle does not turn smoothly. Faulty operation may be due either to child failing to attach pieces firmly or to child screwing the pieces on so tightly that the handle does not turn easily.

3. Child takes apart and puts together all pieces; all pieces are attached firmly and the handle turns smoothly.

D. FINE MOTOR SKILLS

1. Child has difficulty manipulating the grinding mechanism and may have some trouble fitting it through the body of the grinder. Child also may have trouble holding onto the grinding mechanism or the handle.

2. Child may have difficulty handling screws or attaching them. Child also may have trouble holding the grinder together while putting pieces on.

3. Child handles all parts of the grinder well; holds grinding mechanism in place while putting "cover" and handle on, but may need help with screws that are on too tight.

TABLE 37: ASSEMBLY ACTIVITY OBSERVATION SHEET

Child:_____   Observer:_____
Age:_____   Date:_____

	Object 1	Object 2	Total for Each Category
Sense of Parts/Whole	1 2 3	1 2 3	___
Problem Solving	1 2 3	1 2 3	___
Attention to Detail	1 2 3	1 2 3	___
Fine Motor Skills	1 2 3	1 2 3	___
Total for Each Object	___	___	**Total Score** ___

Comments/Scaffolding:

TABLE 38: ASSEMBLY ACTIVITY SUMMARY SHEET

Child (age)	OBJECT 1					OBJECT 2					TOTAL	Comments
	Parts/whole	Prob. solving	Attn. to detail	Fine motor	Subtotal	Parts/whole	Prob. solving	Attn. to detail	Fine motor	Subtotal		

CHAPTER 5
SOCIAL DOMAIN

—INTRODUCTION

The social domain is a prominent one for children, parents, and teachers. Like language, the social domain stands out because of its pervasiveness: Each of us is constantly interacting with others at home, work, and play. With regard to children, most researchers and educators define this domain in terms of social development or learning how to get along with others: sharing, taking turns, controlling aggression, and the like. However, we have expanded these more familiar definitions to include understanding of oneself and of other people and their interactions. We look at social competence as it is displayed either during *interactions* with others or through *analytic reflection*.

Social awareness originates in the bonds between an infant and her primary caretakers. By age 2, the child is becoming aware of her separate identity. By age three, she enjoys watching and playing near other children, and participates in simple group activities. Between the ages of two and five, the child continues to develop the ability to differentiate herself more clearly from others and begins to display a sense of autonomy and initiative (Erikson, 1963).

For the preschooler, particularly in the United States, peer relations become more important as the focus of the child's attention gradually shifts from adults to agemates. Learning to get along with other children is a central part of the preschool experience. Children are eager to interact with others, but because of the relative egocentrism of this age, they may find it difficult to take into account anyone else's feelings or point of view. In general, the more time a child spends with others, the more reciprocal her interactions become. She begins to share materials, to take turns (with some adult guidance), and to assume a variety of roles in dramatic play. Cooperative, organized play becomes more frequent as children engage in joint and group efforts directed toward a common goal or product.

Ordinarily, measures of social competence are either tests of social-cognitive abilities or observations of social interaction. We used both techniques in order to tap the full range of social abilities. First, we designed an activity that would help children to reflect on their everyday activities and to exhibit their social understanding of themselves and others. Second, we developed an observational framework for teachers to identify children who regularly assume one of four social roles: *facilitator, leader, team player,* or *independent player*.

Social competence yields a wide range of potential roles or end states. Effective therapists display their social skills through analyzing the thoughts, feelings, and actions of other people; outstanding leaders, negotiators, and caretakers demonstrate their abilities in interactions with others. All these professionals need other people in order to exhibit their skills; social abilities are not readily assessed in structured tasks with carefully controlled variables. Instead, we needed assessment vehicles that would examine a child's ability to interact in and understand a world where relationships constantly evolve and groups and context continually change. We chose to develop a framework for observing children in their own environment.

Part of this framework is a list of observable behaviors that teachers can use to monitor a child's interactions with peers over time. Emerging patterns of behavior can be used to determine whether a child fills, or is trying to fill, a particular social role in the classroom. However, some children who are shy or hesitant in their relationships with others may still be socially aware. To elicit children's understanding of themselves and of others, we designed an activity that uses a model of the classroom. This model allows teachers to assess whether a child's reflections mirror, extend, or contradict the nature of her interactions in the classroom.

❑ CLASSROOM MODEL

—Purpose and Activity Description

The purpose of the Classroom Model Activity is to assess children's abilities to observe, reflect on, and analyze social events and experiences in their classroom. The assessment is conducted with a scaled-down replica of the classroom complete with a set of wooden figures resembling the children and teachers. In much the same way that children approach a three-dimensional doll house with toy figures and miniature furniture, children can arrange the figures in the classroom model to concretize their understanding of their peers, teachers, and social experiences. One part of the assessment asks children to place themselves and others at their favorite activities. Another investigates children's awareness of social roles. Because linguistic competence varies greatly among preschool children, the Classroom Model is designed to tap social analytic skills without placing excessive verbal demands on the child. Children can either manipulate or point to the figures in response to many of the questions.

The approach we use differs from other social reasoning measures in that it allows teachers to capitalize on the actual experiences and people in children's daily lives. Often, social measures use short stories or pictures depicting generic situations that children may or may not have encountered. Or, they frequently include imaginary characters outside the children's own social world. By drawing directly from children's social experiences, the Classroom Model Activity provides a level of validity that may be lacking in other approaches.

The Classroom Model allows children to reflect upon a range of social themes without being judged by their peers. The questions addressing knowledge of self, others, and relationships purposely focus on the activity dimension of children's behavior and interactions as the most relevant criterion for this age group. For example, most 4-year-olds tend to depict a friend as "somebody I like to play with." However, some children also may exhibit a rudimentary understanding of the reciprocal nature of friendship. The questions allow children to articulate further their understanding of the various ingredients of different social roles, to the extent of their verbal abilities.

Four- and 5-year-old children are experimenting, and may change their minds often about playmates and favorite activities. Still, by midyear, there is usually a stable and predictable social environment in the classroom. Children have become acclimated to the routines of the school day, and show preferences for certain children and types of activities. At this point, teachers can create a social map of the classroom delineating each child's preferences, and identifying the salient friendships, activity areas, and social roles. The map is used in scoring the children's responses to questions in the assessment.

—Materials and Set-Up

In order to make concrete the social world of the preschool classroom, we created a scaled-down, three-dimensional replica of the classroom with small wooden figures of each person. (See illustration that follows.) The model is set on a 2' by 3' wooden board. It replicates the Spectrum classroom exactly, with the different play areas, observation booth, doors, and windows. The model and furniture can be made out of such materials as pine wood, tagboard, foamcore board, cardboard boxes, and small pieces of cloth. We identified play areas by finding or creating tiny replicas for each activity: miniature paintings for the art table, tiny blocks for the block area, and so on. Although we matched the furniture, fabrics, and colors as closely as possible to the actual classroom set-up, this level of precision is not necessary.

We represented every child and adult in the classroom by gluing a photograph to the front of a

CLASSROOM MODEL

WOODEN FIGURES

2" or 3" wooden figure, then coating the figure with shellac for protection. We attached magnets to the backs of the figures and provided a large magnetic board so that children could play with the figures outside of the classroom model. We also photographed the materials for each of the Spectrum assessment activities and arranged the photos on colored posterboard for a "self-assessment" conducted at the beginning of the activity. (See Question 2 in Table 39, p. 135.)

The assessment is conducted either in a separate room or in a relatively isolated, quiet area of the classroom. The child sits in front of the classroom model with the magnetic board to one side with all the figures lined up on it. The teacher sits on the other side of the model with a list of questions and a pencil. Taping the session facilitates scoring.

—Procedure and Script

Introduce the Classroom Model as a formal activity after midyear. By this time, teachers will be familiar enough with the children to construct a reliable social map (see Table 41). The activity can be introduced at group time as follows: "Today children will have a chance to play with the little classroom one at a time. You will be able to use all the little figures of the children and teachers."

To individual children, you can introduce the activity as "the little classroom," or you might want to ask them what they think the model is. To make sure that they understand the location of each of the different activity areas, go over the different sections of the model. Tell them that figures representing all of the children and all of the teachers are on the magnetic board, and ask them if they can find themselves. Then, follow the questions on Table 39, writing each child's responses in the appropriate spaces.

Feel free to make the questions more concrete and contextualized, depending on the nature of your particular classroom. If your writing seems to distract the child, you can use a tape recorder instead. However, if the child is pointing to and placing the figures in different areas without talking, remember to verbalize her actions yourself, for example, "Oh, you placed Julie at blocks."

Question 2 is designed to help you gain a sense for a child's own understanding of her strengths, interests, and areas of difficulty. Show the child the photographs

of all of the Spectrum activities that she has participated in to date, reviewing them together before posing the questions listed.

For Question 3, probe once after the child places one or two figures at each area: "Is there anyone else who plays at _____?" Before Questions 4 and 5, have the child help you return all of the figures to the magnetic board. For Question 4, you do not need to ask the questions regarding where children play if they already have given you that information in Question 3. If a child wants to play in her own way with the model, explain that she can have a chance to do that in a little while, after you have asked the questions.

Some of the questions in Table 39 will need to be eliminated, modified, or replaced in order to reflect accurately an individual classroom. Suggestions for additions or substitutions for Questions 5 through 11 include:

"If children are writing letters at the writing table, and they don't know how to do a letter, which child knows how to help them write letters?"
"Show me the child who notices if somebody is sad."
"Show me the child in your class who has lots of different ideas."
"Show me the child who always brings in things for show and tell."
"Show me someone in your class who always brings in different creatures to share with the kids."
"Who always swings high on the swings?"
"Show me which child always likes to climb up high."
The aim of the questions for this activity is to identify the children who are keen observers of the class, as well as to probe for a deeper understanding of social roles and dynamics.

—Scoring

The majority of children's responses are scored according to the social map of classroom dynamics (see Table 41). Fill out the social map immediately prior to the introduction of the Classroom Model Activity to insure that it reflects children's most recent preferences for friends and activity areas. If a class is team-taught, it may be helpful for both teachers to collaborate in creating the map. In addition to ranking three choices for each child, note if a child does not exhibit a clear preference for either friends or activities. For the purposes of the map, *friend* is defined as the child with whom one spends the greatest amount of time. The map includes space in which to list the most salient friendships and connections between children and activities, as well as the classroom caretakers (children who try to help others when they need it), "bosses" (children who are always telling other children what to do), and leaders (effective organizers of activities). Each list is ranked from most to least salient. Because each classroom will have its own social makeup, the questions for the activity and social map will vary.

The scoring procedure for this activity involves recording the child's responses on the Classroom Model Observation Sheet (Table 39), with a back-up tape recording if necessary. The activity assesses the child's ability to place herself and others in the appropriate activity areas, awareness of friendships among her peers, and recognition of different styles of interaction.

Children's responses can be divided into three categories. Questions 1 and 2 elicit a child's self-understanding; Questions 3 – 6 elicit a child's understanding of her peers; and Questions 7 – 11 elicit a child's understanding of social roles. Refer to Table 40 for the point allotments for each question.

Questions 1 and 3–6 can be scored with the help of the social map. The scoring for these questions is based on a correspondence between the teacher's and the child's responses. Questions 1 and 2 draw upon self-knowledge. Award 2 points for a matching answer to Question 1. For Question 2, allot 2 points if the child's responses reveal a sense of self-understanding, for example, "I like art the most, but I can't draw that good." For Question 3, award 1 point for each response that corresponds to the names listed on the social map (the maximum score for this question is 6 points). For Question 4, score only the child's responses for special friends, since play areas were already scored in Question 3. Award 1 point for each matching answer for each part of Question 4 (the highest score attainable in this question is 6 points). You can consider the child's response a "match" if she matches any of the names listed on the social map. Award 2 points each for correct answers to Questions 5 and 6.

Questions 7 – 11 assess a child's understanding of social roles. If a child says "I don't know" or gives a nonsensical answer, do not award any points. Award 1 point for an answer with no reason given. Award 2 points for responses with reasons that can be considered

typical for 4-year-olds. Finally, responses with explanations that indicate an unusual sensitivity to social dynamics or self-awareness are awarded 3 points. Also, sometimes, the most revealing information about children's social sensitivity is not contained in their direct responses to questions, but in their more informal comments and elaborations, or role-playing.

Typical responses to Question 7 probing children's understanding of friendship ("What makes _____ a *special* friend of yours?") include "because he plays with me all the time" or "because she likes to play with me." Since most 4-year-olds define a friend as a peer with whom one plays, such a response would receive 2 points. However, some children may exhibit a deeper understanding of the reciprocal nature of friendship: "Mark is a friend of mine, but I am not sure that he thinks of me as one of his friends." This response would merit 3 points, as would the response "She is my favorite, favorite, favorite friend that I know for a long time. She likes to help me with something. If I am hurt, instead of me [going] to the teacher, she goes to the teacher for me."

For Question 8, award 1 point for a "yes" or "no" answer with no reason, and 2 points for responses such as "No, because we fought." A 3-point response might be "Yes, because we are back together later on." On Question 9, the most typical response is for a child to name a friend, but some children may demonstrate a greater sensitivity to the characteristic helping behavior of a friend: "My best friend would [help] . . . and she says, 'don't get concerned.' " This response would receive 3 points.

Questions 10 and 11 address two kinds of leadership roles. A common response for what makes a person bossy is "because he hits." An example of a 3-point response is "because Fred is always telling kids in blocks what to do." A more subtle 3-point response is "Billy *thinks* he's the boss." This child demonstrates an awareness of the discrepancy between Billy's view of himself and his peers' view of him. For Question 11, a typical response is for the child to pick herself as teacher for the day. An example of a 3-point response is picking a classmate because of such leadership qualities as knowing a lot about the classroom.

—Preliminary Results: 1985–1987

Children's responses on the Classroom Model indicated a range of knowledge about self and others. A child's awareness of where she spends time and with whom did not necessarily correlate with an awareness of the friendships and activities of other classmates. Whereas some children were aware of the social dynamics only in the areas with which they were most familiar, others demonstrated an understanding of the social network of the entire classroom. Most of the children successfully identified the most salient friendships and were aware of the children who played most frequently in the specific activity areas. Interestingly, the children whom the teachers perceived as leaders or as playing other dominant roles in the classroom were not the ones who stood out on this activity. Several children surprised us because of their unusual understanding of themselves and others despite their younger age or quiet demeanor.

On the more open-ended questions, children's responses varied greatly. When asked, for example, to articulate why a particular child is bossy, explanations ranged from "because he hits" to much less common answers such as "because they don't like other children to do what they want to do at school." When asked to explain why someone is a special friend, many children responded "because he plays with me" or "she likes me." However, one child elaborated with the thoughtful response mentioned earlier: "She likes to help me with something. If I am hurt, instead of me [going] to the teacher, she would go to the teacher for me." When asked to choose a child who could be the teacher at meeting time for a day, the majority of children chose themselves. But the explanations varied from "because I want to be that" to "because I know how to take care of babies" and "because we're not bossy." One child chose "Timmy because he's 5."

The child who showed the greatest strength was a boy usually on the periphery of activities, alone much of the time, and often involved in his own fantasy play. Not only was he able and eager to place all of the children in the areas of the classroom where they liked to play, but he also accurately grouped friends together, noticing those children who play alone and those with many playmates. As this child articulated his knowledge of his peers, he showed unusual sensitivity and interest in them. For example, when asked which child he might choose to be "teacher for the day," his answer showed an awareness of his own limitations, as well as his appreciation of the strengths of a fellow classmate: "I would choose Sara because most of the things I don't know, she knows. And she knows the things I know. That means she knows more." In describing other children, he said, "Susie is kind of shy" and "Billy *thinks* he's the boss."

In sharp contrast, another child who appeared to be a leader among the girls was very interested in placing the children in the classroom model, but revealed little understanding of groupings of friends other than her own. She also was unaware of the interests of other children in the class. A third child, a leader in several areas, displayed the kind of interest in social dynamics that we expected of a child with leadership traits. She played with the model on her own and spent a long time discussing the different children: "I like Scott because he likes to play dress-up" and "I don't like Marcia because she's too bossy." This child also enjoyed telling stories using the model and the wooden figures to create hypothetical social situations.

Because the Classroom Model gives children a chance to reenact social experiences, it can yield interesting and instructive information about the different ways in which these experiences are perceived. Some children were most interested in using the model for dramatic play and storytelling, acting out situations using dialogue and narration. Some children showed more interest in the teacher figures than in the figures of their peers, and repeatedly asked when the teachers could be used. Some focused only on the figures, and played with them outside of the model itself. One little boy focused almost exclusively on his male classmates, placing only boys at the different play areas. Many children were fascinated with the details of how the model was made.

TABLE 39: CLASSROOM MODEL OBSERVATION SHEET

Child _____   Observer _____
Age _____   Date _____

1. Please show me where you spend *most of your time* playing in the classroom.

    Is that your favorite activity? Why?

    What if that place were already full of children—show me where you would go.

2. Here are some pictures of the different games that you played with _____.

    Which one do you think you were the best at?

    Why?

    Which one was hardest for you to do?

    Why?

    Which one of the games was your favorite?

3. Let's put other children where they like to play . . . show me someone in your class who *always* plays at:

    Blocks _____
    Dramatic Play _____
    Art _____
    Water Table _____
    Writing Table _____

      [If child volunteers only one or two people, ask, "Is there anyone else?"]

    At this point, ask child to help you return figures to magnet board before asking next question.

4. Let's see if some other children in your class have a special friend . . .

      a. Does _____ have a special friend(s)? Who is that? [Show me where they like to play together.]

      b. What about _____? Does he have a special friend? Who is that? [And where do they play?]

      c. Does _____ have a special friend? Who is that? [Where do they like to play?]

      d. I wonder if _____ has a special friend? Who is that? [Where do they like to play?]

      e. Are there *any other* children who also have a special friend? Show me who they are.

Again ask child to help you return figures to magnet board before asking next question.

5. Show me someone in your class who watches what other children are doing a lot of the time.

6. Please show me someone in your class who likes to play alone most of all.

7. Tell me, who is your *very special* friend? What makes _____ a special friend of yours?

8. Suppose you and _____ were fighting about a toy. Would you still be friends?

    Why (not)?

9. Show me the child in your class who helps children when they need it.

    Why did you choose that child?

10. Is there a child in your class who seems bossy to you? What makes him/her so bossy?

11. Imagine the teachers said one day that it is a child's turn to be the teacher at meeting time.

    Which child would you want to be teacher for the day?

    Can you put him/her where your teacher sits at meeting? Why did you pick _____?

TABLE 40: CLASSROOM MODEL SUMMARY SHEET

	Child (age)		
Understanding Self	Q1 2 pts.		
	Q2 2 pts.		
	Subtotal—Self		
Understanding Others	Q3 (1 pt./matching ans.) (max = 6 pts.)		
	Q4 (1 pt./matching ans.) (max = 6 pts.)		
	Q5 2 pts.		
	Q6 2 pts.		
	Subtotal—Others		
Understanding Social Roles	Q7	1 pt. = Answer w/no reason	
	Q8	2 pts. = Typical response	
	Q9	3 pts. = Unusual response	
	Q10		
	Q11		
	Subtotal—Social Roles		
	TOTAL		
	Comments		

TABLE 41: SOCIAL MAP

Teacher/Class _____   Date _____

Child		*Special Friend	**Activity Area
_____	1.		
	2.		
	3.		
_____	1.		
	2.		
	3.		
_____	1.		
	2.		
	3.		
_____	1.		
	2.		
	3.		
_____	1.		
	2.		
	3.		
_____	1.		
	2.		
	3.		

*children in class with whom child plays most often, in order of frequency
**areas in classroom where child plays most often, in order of frequency

QUESTION 3 (SEE TABLE 39)

Children (child) who always play(s) at:

Blocks _____

Dramatic Play _____

Art _____

Water Table _____

Writing Table _____

QUESTION 4

Most salient friendships:

1.   3.

2.   4.

Others:

QUESTION 5

Children who spend a lot of time watching what other children are doing:

1.   3.

2.

QUESTION 6

Children who prefer to play alone most of the time:

1.   3.

2.

QUESTION 9

Children who help other children (caretakers):

1.   3.

2.

QUESTION 10

Children who often tell other children what to do (bosses):

1.   3.

2.

QUESTION 11

Children who effectively organize activities (leaders):

1.   3.

2.

—Purpose and Activity Description

The purpose of the Peer Interaction Checklist is threefold:

1. to provide a tool that can be used to analyze peer interactions;
2. to describe a range of typical types of peer interactions among children of this age;
3. to identify children who show strength in this area by consistently assuming a social role that is valued in our culture.

To conduct the assessment, teachers use a checklist describing a wide range of actions and responses that typically characterize preschool children's interactions with their peers. Although many children at this age experience significant shifts in ability and interest in relating to peers, it is still possible to discern consistent patterns of behavior in individual children.

In fact, we found that as early as 3 and 4 years old, children showed signs of assuming social roles considered desirable in our culture, although few children were able to sustain these roles across different activities and with different peers. For example, certain children frequently would comfort a classmate who was crying, or convince other children to join in a game.

Based on our observations of preschool children at play, we found that these emerging behaviors could be described by four social roles that also are valued in adult society: leader, facilitator, independent player, and team player. We included an intermediate category, *transitional child*, to help teachers identify children who are struggling to find a role and who may need some social support.

We have described each role by means of a general definition and a list of characteristic behaviors (see Table 44, pp. 147–148). These behaviors, which make up the Peer Interaction Checklist, were selected because they *differentiate* among children of this age. Those behaviors that describe the social development of most children of this age (e.g., sharing materials and space with other children, understanding turn-taking) are not included on the checklist.

Because a child's behavior may vary depending on the type of activity in which she is engaged and the children with whom she is interacting, assessment of the child's social interaction should not be limited to a single observation period. When completing the Peer Interaction Checklist, teachers should draw on multiple observations and accumulated knowledge about a child.

The approach we use differs from other measures of children's interaction with peers in that it involves attention both to specific behaviors (e.g., a child's response to conflicts with peers) and to more general patterns (e.g., a child's expertise as a facilitator). Often, discussions of children's interactions with peers focus on global qualities, such as "bossy" or "quiet." Operating on this level, teachers may overlook important exceptions to such tendencies or fail to recognize a child's emerging capabilities. On the other hand, if teachers are aware only of particular behaviors, they may lose sight of the existence of meaningful patterns and roles.

—Procedure and Scoring

The assessment procedure for the Peer Interaction Checklist consists of four basic steps:

1. either on your own or with other teachers, fill out an interaction checklist for each child;
2. use a summary sheet to determine if the behaviors correspond to one of the social roles;
3. decide whether the child has generally positive interactions, and whether she is successful in carrying out the identified role;
4. conduct additional formal or informal observations to confirm your findings.

The formal assessment should be conducted both at midyear and at the year's end. If you are a member of a teaching team, either you can complete the checklists, interpret them independently, and then discuss your findings with other team members; or you can work together and collaborate as a team throughout the assessment process. In either case, the discussion promoted by this framework is an important component of the process.

Prepare for the assessment by reviewing the behaviors on the Peer Interaction Checklist (see Table 42). When familiar with the behaviors, complete a checklist for each child in your classroom during your planning time. Check the items that are most descriptive of each child's behavior during peer interactions in the classroom. In most cases, checking seven to nine behaviors will accurately capture a child's mode of relating to peers. All children display many of the behaviors identified in this checklist at some time. Check only those that *distinguish* a particular child (see

Table 45 for further observation tips).

If using the checklist prompts you to recall observations or adopt certain teaching strategies (e.g., helping a child pursue her own ideas about using materials by asking what her plans are before the child enters into an activity), note these in the Comments section that follows the list of behaviors. Also note in this section any relevant behaviors that are not included in the checklist.

When you have completed the checklist, prepare a summary sheet for each child (see Table 43). On this page, specific behaviors are categorized according to valued social roles. (If more than one teacher completes a checklist for each child, the summary sheet can be divided into columns so that teachers' assessments can be listed side by side. This formatting makes it easier for the team to identify and discuss agreements and disagreements about a child's behavior.)

To determine whether or not one of the roles fits the pattern of a child's behaviors, consult the definitions and behavioral characteristics of the social roles (see Table 44) and review the child's individual summary sheet. A child who consistently assumes one of these roles exhibits the characteristic behaviors across settings and regardless of peers involved. Generally speaking, if a child consistently displays four out of the six behaviors characteristic of a role, then the role accurately identifies that child's mode of interacting with peers. If a child displays behaviors across several or all of the roles, then that child's interaction with peers is not consolidated in terms of a single role. It is also important to consider the scatter of behaviors across all roles. For some children, a wide scatter may indicate a transition in orientation to peers.

If a child's interaction with peers does not reflect a single role, it may be possible to identify meaningful role combinations. For example, a child who displays transitional behaviors as well as those characteristic of a leader may be in the process of developing skills as a leader. A child whose behaviors are concentrated in the leader and facilitator roles may be very involved with peers and may be able to assume both of these roles quite skillfully. For every child, the total number of behaviors checked may provide relevant information about relationships with peers. A child who has a large total number may be more interested in all dimensions of interaction than a child who displays a few of the behaviors. You also may find that a child who

consistently assumes a role uses particular behaviors characteristic of other roles to accomplish her goals. For example, a child who plays the role of leader may sometimes respond to other children's leads in order to sustain their interest in the activity she initiated.

If you determine that a child's pattern of behavior fits a particular social role, you next must evaluate whether the child is using that role in a way that is constructive and valued in the classroom. The questions on the individual summary sheet will help you make that determination. Are the child's interactions generally positive? Is this child usually successful in carrying out this role? If the answer is yes to these questions, the child may have a strength in the social domain.

In order to confirm these interpretations, keep these questions in mind as you observe and interact with these children over the next few days. Do these children actually serve as leaders? Are they successful facilitators? Are they effective independent players? Are they struggling to find a role? Note how other children respond to their efforts. If there is time, you may want to focus your observations on one or two of these children and fill out the checklist again immediately after class. This will give you more information for answering the questions.

After reviewing the individual summary sheets and conducting further observations to confirm strengths in this area, you may want to compose a narrative summary that describes each child's interaction with peers (see Table 46 for sample narratives). When composing the summary, you may find it helpful to consider two or three examples of a child's typical behavior with peers and to focus the summary on these observations. When communicating with parents, try to avoid using labels and focus instead on the interactional patterns and examples from your observations of the child in the classroom.

—Using Information From Peer Interaction Observations

For children who are not successful in their roles or who are struggling to find a role, it may be helpful to arrange situations that will increase their chances to participate in successful interactions. For example, children often are able to interact more positively with and direct other children when they are involved in activities at which they excel or in which they have some experience or interest. Information from the other Spectrum assessments may help you to identify such activities.

You then can make these activities available to the child and encourage her to work in that area with a peer. Selecting a competent and friendly peer, and asking the child to explain how to carry out the activity, is one way to implement this plan.

To help you make such identifications, note the activity and the other peers involved each time you observe the child acting as a leader, facilitator, or positive team or independent player. Alternatively, keep a record of those situations and those peers with whom the child experiences difficulty. Finally, filling out the interaction checklist and summary sheet a number of times during the year for children who appear to be having problems can help you to document their progress and evaluate the success of your efforts.

—Preliminary Results: 1987–1988

Of the 20 children in the 1987–88 preschool class, the two Spectrum teachers identified 2 as leaders, 1 as a facilitator, and 2 as independent players. In addition, 7 children exhibited transitional behavior and another 8 did not consistently take on any of the social roles. The teachers felt that one child, the facilitator, demonstrated strength in the social domain because of positive and successful interactions with peers. The behavior of the leaders, on the other hand, often was interpreted as "bossy" by their classmates.

Teachers found that they did not always initially agree on whether or not specific behaviors on the checklist were characteristic of a child's peer interactions. The discussion that followed this discovery of differing perceptions prompted teachers to articulate more clearly their informal assessments of a child. The teachers also said that use of the checklist helped them make more systematic assessments.

—Further Suggestions for the Domain
Model Activities

We recommend building a classroom model because it can be used in many ways in many domains. The model can be played with by individual children or used in small groups or in activities structured by the teacher. Children can reenact actual situations in the classroom. Teachers can present different social situations, providing children with the opportunity to reflect on them, express their feelings, and propose possible resolutions for them.

Thus, the model can serve as a window for observing the ways in which children think about stressful events such as starting as a new member of the class, being excluded from a group of peers, trying to enter activities, making friends, and handling social conflicts. As with the storyboard, children also may use the model on their own to tell stories that may reveal their concerns and desires.

Just as children can build their own storyboards in the art area, they also can construct their own classroom models or dioramas. The teachers at the Eliot-Pearson Children's School in Medford, Massachusetts, created a scaled-down model of the school playground that enabled children to work on issues related to their outside time. You can also observe whether children who are put off by the fantasy component of the Storyboard Activity are more interested in storytelling when using the reality-based classroom model.

The classroom model also lends itself to examining abilities in the spatial domain. Children can be asked to place furniture in the model to correspond to its placement in the classroom. Some children will make random placements, whereas others will correctly place the more salient items but not attend to such details as whether an item is placed at the correct angle. Children with unusual spatial abilities will accurately and precisely place all of the furniture, examining the classroom itself when necessary to make sure that each item is accurately placed in the model. Such performance is particularly impressive if the model is placed at a different angle from the child's view of the classroom.

Group Time and Classroom Activities

At the beginning of the school year, you can sing songs that include children's names to help children develop a sense of belonging to the group. As the year progresses, inviting children to take a turn at leading the group time can give them a special opportunity to share with others. They can sing a song, tell a story, or show a special toy or object from home.

You can use group time activities to promote discussions of books, movies, or classroom situations that present opportunities for social problem solving. You might want to use books and movies in which conflicts arise, but solutions are left up to the audience. For a more physical activity, you can take large building blocks to the playground to encourage children to organize and lead "construction crews." Other activities that involve cooperation and caretaking include having partners each paint one side of a clear plexiglass sheet, or participating with a friend in a long-term project such as growing a plant or caring for an animal.

The Social Center

Another possibility is to establish a social center in the classroom where the classroom model, a photo album, and a message board are kept. This center can be a quiet area where children can reflect on their social experiences in the classroom. Children can use the model either in tasks structured by the teacher or for free exploration.

You can ask children to help you place photographs of school events and classroom activities in a classroom portfolio. Children can use these photographs as reminders for recording and reflecting on their experiences. They also may use these photographs as reference points for sending their parents short notes about what they have been doing at school.

Professional Roles

Explorations of adult professional roles can stimulate and support children in their interactions and lead to a better understanding of the social world outside the classroom. You can invite parents or other members of the community to describe their work and bring in materials for the dramatic play area, or you can take field trips to places of interest.

TABLE 42: PEER INTERACTION CHECKLIST

Observer _____   Date _____

Child _____   Age _____

HOW TO USE THE CHECKLIST

Complete a checklist for each child in your classroom. After you review the items in the list, check those that best characterize each child's behavior during peer interaction in your classroom. In most cases, checking *seven to nine behaviors* will accurately capture a child's mode of relating to peers. All children display many of the behaviors identified in this checklist at some time. Remember to check only those that are most *distinctive* about a particular child. If use of the checklist prompts thoughts about the child's relation with peers, record them in the Comments section at the end.

CHECKLIST

1. _____ makes connections to the activities of other children through imitation or verbal checking (e.g., "What are you doing? I'm doing . . ." "Let's do this, OK?")

2. _____ mediates when conflicts occur during play

3. _____ initiates activities in which other children then participate

4. _____ takes initiative to lead but is not usually successful

5. _____ usually responds to other children's leads rather than initiating activities

6. _____ spends a lot of time observing the play of other children

7. _____ willing to accept compromises or leaves area when conflicts occur during play

8. _____ is more interested in own activity than in what other children are doing

9. _____ often invites other children to join in play

10. _____ tends to direct action of other children

11. _____ tends to continue a play activity as long as others remain involved

12. _____ usually does not respond to other children's requests when doing so interferes with own activity

13. _____ often extends and elaborates other children's ideas

14. _____ often assigns roles to children

15. _____ makes some effort to control what other children do

16. _____ follows other children when they move to different play areas, entering into interactions smoothly

17. _____ is persistent in carrying out own ideas

18. _____ directly requests and receives assistance from other children

19. _____ often is sought out by other children

20. _____ when playing, focuses primarily on materials

21. _____ expresses concern about whether or not he or she is being accepted by other children

22. _____ cooperates with other children

23. _____ often gives feedback to children about what they are doing (e.g., "Not like that . . . let me show you.")

24. _____ frequently plays independently
25. _____ shares information and skills with other children (e.g., shows another child how to play a game)
26. _____ usually talks more than other children during play
27. _____ provides nurturance or assistance when other children need help or attention
28. _____ choice of play area reflects interest in activity rather than presence of preferred peers
29. _____ often has difficulty complying with other children's requests

COMMENTS:

TABLE 43: PEER INTERACTION CHECKLIST

Individual Summary Sheet

Observer _____   Date _____

Child _____   Age _____

Team Player Role: Checklist Items   1,   5,   7,   11,   16,   19

Facilitator Role: Checklist Items   2,   9,   13,   22,   25,   27

Leader Role: Checklist Items   3,   10,   14,   18,   23,   26

Independent Player Role: Checklist Items   8,   12,   17,   20,   24,   28

Transitional Child Role: Checklist Items   4,   6,   15,   21,   29

QUESTIONS:

1. Are the child's interactions generally positive?

2. Is the child usually successful in carrying out this role?

3. How do other children respond to the child's efforts?

TABLE 44: CHARACTERISTIC ROLE DEFINITIONS AND BEHAVIORS

TEAM PLAYER ROLE

Definition: The primary characteristic identifying this role is the child's willingness to cooperate with others and participate in social activities.

Characteristic Behaviors

—makes connections to the activities of other children through imitation or verbal checking

(e.g., "What are you doing now? I'm doing . . ." "Let's do this, O.K.?")

—usually responds to other children's leads rather than initiating activities

—willing to accept compromises or leaves area when conflicts occur during play

—tends to continue a play activity as long as others remain involved

—follows other children when they move to different play areas, entering into interactions smoothly

—often is sought out by other children

FACILITATOR ROLE

Definition: The child who assumes this role effectively shares ideas, information, and skills with other children.

Characteristic Behaviors

—mediates when conflicts occur during play

—often invites other children to join in play

—often extends and elaborates other children's ideas

—cooperates with other children

—shares information and skills with other children

—provides nurturance or assistance when other children need help or attention

LEADER ROLE

Definition: The child who plays the role of leader frequently is involved in attempts to organize other children.

Characteristic Behaviors

—initiates activities in which other children then participate

—tends to direct action of other children

—often assigns roles to other children

—directly requests and receives assistance from other children

—often gives feedback to children about what they are doing (e.g., "Not like that. . . let me show you.")

—usually talks more than other children during play

INDEPENDENT PLAYER ROLE

Definition: The child who displays this role typically chooses to focus on the use of materials rather than on interactions with peers.

Characteristic Behaviors

—is more interested in own activity than in what other children are doing

—usually does not respond to other children's requests when doing so interferes with own activity

—is persistent in carrying out own ideas

—when playing, focuses primarily on materials

—frequently plays independently

—choice of play area reflects interest in activity rather than presence of preferred peers

TRANSITIONAL CHILD ROLE

Definition: The transitional child appears to be making an effort to construct a classroom role for herself.

Characteristic Behaviors

—takes initiative to lead but is not usually successful

—spends quite a bit of time observing the play of other children

—makes some effort to control what other children do

—expresses concern about whether or not he or she is being accepted by other children

—often has difficulty complying with other children's requests

TABLE 45: TIPS FOR OBSERVATION

There is much to observe in any preschool classroom, particularly with regard to social interactions. In order to make the observation process more efficient, it may be helpful to focus your observations on those areas and events in which children are most likely to take on a social role. For example, indoor activity time (during which children make their own choices about where to play and how long to play) typically offers more information about peer interaction than group time does. The dramatic play and block areas in particular offer many opportunities for children to organize and direct the play of their peers. By watching cooperative play, you can see which children are capable of sharing information and skills with other children, as well as extending and elaborating their ideas. As you focus your observations, you will become more aware of the situations that are most likely to support particular behaviors.

Leaders can be found in social activities such as fantasy play and block building. They tend to suggest the theme for play, assign the roles, or explain how the activity is carried out. During games that involve rules and turn-taking, children who act as leaders tend to oversee and direct the conduct of the game. Some leaders are more successful than others. Their tone may range from bossy to encouraging. Some leaders are direct; they tell other children where to go and what to play. Others may be able to organize activities simply through the force of their ideas; they make suggestions that are so appealing that other children clamor to join in. Despite their different styles and attitudes, however, all leaders participate in initiating and organizing activities.

Facilitators often reveal themselves in activities where materials and resources need to be shared. For example, block building usually requires children who are willing to work together to share space and blocks. Playdough also needs to be divided fairly and children often have to take turns using implements. Consequently, play in these areas may progress more smoothly when a facilitator is involved. Facilitators can also be identified when other children are in distress. They may gather around, ask what the matter is, or offer to help when a peer needs assistance. Some facilitators may be particularly concerned with fairness and with insuring that group play is equitable and orderly (mediators), whereas others may be more concerned with individual children and their needs (caretakers).

With regard to the *independent player*, it is important to distinguish between children who play alone because they do not have adequate interactive skills and those who choose to play independently because they are primarily interested in what they can do with materials. Both children and teachers recognize that some children prefer to engage in self-directed activity by themselves. A child who assumes the independent player role may do so through a clear sense of what she is capable of and what she enjoys doing alone.

Team players are likely to be found in group activities, either as active participants or observers. On the playground, they may seem to follow other children around; in the classroom, they often select the same activity as a particular peer and may refuse to choose activities for themselves. In interactions, they are often quiet and take direction from others. While this role may not seem to describe a strength, there are some children who are very successful team players. They often are sought out by others or have formed close friendships with particular peers. In addition, rather than being on the fringes of group activity, they are often in the center of it, ready and willing to be a partner in any escapade.

TABLE 46: SAMPLE NARRATIVE SUMMARIES

BILLY
(A CHILD WHO DISPLAYS STRENGTH AS A LEADER)

Billy has assumed the role of leader for most of the year. He is confident, persistent, and takes great enjoyment in carrying out his ideas. Almost every morning, he runs out onto the playground and directly into a group activity. He immediately yells to the children who often play "ghostbusters" with him, "Hey, you got a ghost call!" When he decides to play with the big blocks, he searches for recruits to help him build a boat, rocket ship, or some other vehicle. Even when he plays on his own, other children often notice and then join in his activities. When he breaks up pieces of ice he has gathered and puts the pieces into a large bucket, children who have been playing nearby begin to collect their own ice. He advises them about the proper size of their pieces and then leads them to a table where he directs what he calls an ice factory. He picks out pieces of ice and puts them in a vise which he uses to crush them further. After he has crushed a number of pieces, he lets another child take a turn while he becomes "ice catcher."

Occasionally, Billy's ideas and directions bring him into conflicts with others. He likes to see things done "his way." Several times he has tried to support his position by claiming that he is the "leader of the fours." When play is particularly loud and exciting, he is likely to stick to his own ideas. However, when play is relatively calm, he is more likely to pick up and elaborate on the ideas of others. When Michael found a small hole on the playground that he referred to as a trap, Billy suggested that they could catch ghosts in it and gathered some leaves and grass in order to camouflage it. Despite his enjoyment of social activities, Billy also plays on his own comfortably and in a focused manner. He does not depend on others for ideas, but often turns others' ideas into group activities.

BOBBY
(A CHILD WHO DISPLAYS STRENGTH AS A FACILITATOR)

Bobby plays easily and happily with all of his classmates. He is tolerant, willing to compromise, and sensitive to others' concerns. He walks up to other children to ask with assurance, "Can I play with you?" He clearly invites others to join his activities. When he tires of an activity, he informs his playmates and usually asks if they would like to move on as well. He is flexible enough to modify his plans and find a mutually interesting activity, but does not simply give in and ignore his own preferences. In disputes, Bobby is often the one who finds solutions. When Micky takes one of the arch blocks that Bobby is using, Bobby demands that he give it back. But he also finds another block just like the one Micky took and happily gives it to him. When there are more children than tape dispensers at the writing table so that a struggle for control ensues, Bobby suggests, "Why not everybody share?" He then oversees the distribution, pointing out where the dispensers should be placed so that they are within everybody's reach.

In addition to his ability to compromise, Bobby shows his concern for others through his empathy and support when his peers are distressed. When Sam falls and hurts his knee, Bobby reaches down and rubs his own knee. "I hurt my knee too," he explains. When Susan shows Chris where she burned herself, Bobby gets up to look at it too. He asks her how it feels, and then tells her about a time when he burned himself. If a wrong is committed against one of his playmates, Bobby usually will stand up for the injured.

During a dice game, Tom begins to cry because Andy refuses to let him take his turn. Bobby insists that Andy give Tom the dice and the game continues. Possibly because of this ability to support his friends and facilitate their interactions, Bobby is one of the most sought-after playmates in the class.

SHIRA
(A CHILD WHO DISPLAYS STRENGTH AS AN INDEPENDENT PLAYER)

Although Shira has many friends, she often prefers to play by herself. She is very self-assured and is not concerned with finding playmates. Although at times she can be observed sitting by herself, she doesn't seem left out. When she does play with others, she often focuses on the materials rather than the social activity swirling around her. On one occasion, she and three other girls were wandering around the playground. Suddenly, Shira announced, "I'm going to play here." She picked up a stick and began scratching through the pebbles. "I'm looking for mica," she explained. She displayed the pieces she had found. The other three girls also picked through the pebbles, but their presence didn't seem to make any difference to Shira.

Shira has many inventive play ideas. It is difficult to capture her attention before she completes an activity to her satisfaction. While she is playing by herself, she often will ignore other children's requests and sometimes will simply say no when others ask if they can join her. Whereas many children at the writing table talk about and examine each other's pictures, Shira usually looks at her own page. She draws princesses and horses while the girls around her all draw rainbows. When not focused completely on her own activities, Shira is able to build upon and use the ideas of those around her. One day she and several other girls build "swimming pools" with the blocks. Shira gathers pieces of blue plastic from the art table to serve as water; she also brings over small figures of bears to "go swimming." When Samantha sets up a row of colored blocks with a nut on top of each, Shira suggests, "Let's have a tea party!" She transforms the blocks and nuts into tables and cups. Perhaps because of her inventiveness and self-assurance—despite her primary interest in materials—many children look to Shira for ideas and companionship.

CHAPTER 6
VISUAL ARTS DOMAIN

—INTRODUCTION

> *Once I drew like Raphael, but it has taken me a whole*
> *lifetime to learn to draw like children.*
>
> —Picasso

The capacity to create lines and shapes that resemble actual objects is a symbolic competence that humans alone possess. Although the arts often are seen as a matter of "feeling" or "inspiration," they actually involve a wide range of cognitive abilities and skills. Over the past few decades, researchers have learned a great deal about the stages of artistic development (Gardner, 1980; Gardner, 1990). The one-year-old child makes a lot of marks, but is even more interested in the act of holding the marker in her hand and moving it around. Between the ages of 18 months and 2 years, the child begins to see the marker as a tool for exploring her environment, though the focus is still more on the physical movements than on the marks on the page. The *scribbling stage* occurs between the ages of 2 and 4, when the random marks that a child makes gradually become more organized and controlled (Lowenfeld & Brittain, 1982).

By the age of 3 or 4, most children have moved into the *preschematic stage.* They are able to create recognizable representations of objects in their environment, such as the well-known tadpole person (Kellogg, 1969). Objects are understood only as they relate to the child; thus they may be variable in size and randomly placed on the page. Form typically takes precedence over color, and color rarely has any relationship to the object being represented. For example, colors may be chosen because one dish of paint was thicker than another, or because no one else had used it yet. Individual differences can be discerned in that some children are more interested in patterns and configurations, whereas others are more concerned with illustrating stories. Four-year-olds are generally more interested in exploring the special qualities of line, shape, and color than the motor actions that preoccupied them at 2 and 3. However, for the young child, the *process* of creation is often more important than the actual product. Children enjoy physically manipulating materials through which they can communicate and express ideas about themselves and their world.

Art areas in most preschool classrooms include a range of activities, from easel painting and finger painting to collage and clay sculptures. Many preschool teachers consider art to be a key area in their classroom, in part because of the rich opportunities it provides young children for self-expression and discovery. Children at this age do not have the language skills to talk through complex and abstract issues such as the nature of the self or world, or conflicting impulses of good and evil. Means of expression such as drawing, telling fairy tales, and dramatic play allow children to grapple with such concepts.

Typical assessments in this domain have included copying geometric and block designs (Wechsler, 1967) and drawing a person (Harris, 1963). However, many important components such as expressiveness, inventiveness, and embellishment have been left unexamined in these assessments. Traditional assessments are further limited by the constraints of a one-time sampling. In contrast, the Spectrum assessment involves collecting children's art throughout the year, and examining this body of work for three main components: level of representation, degree of exploration, and level of artistry.

—CONCEPTUALIZING THE ART ACTIVITIES

The end states that have guided our analysis of the visual arts domain include painters, sculptors, and architects. Although chess masters, engineers, cartographers, mathematicians, and scientists also rely upon spatial ability, the Spectrum assessment focuses on those roles central to the realm of visual arts. Ability in this area involves the capacity to perceive the visual world accurately; sensitivity to composition, balance, and other aspects of visual or spatial displays; and the capacity to represent spatial information in graphic form. Painting, drawing, and sculpture involve both sensitive observations of the visual-spatial world and the ability to refashion that world in a work of art. Of course, fine motor skills also play a role in the development of artistic ability.

Early signs of ability in the visual arts include interest in visual patterns, noticing similarities in disparate objects, noticing and exploring interesting visual forms, unusual attention to detail, and precocious representation ability (Winner & Pariser, 1985). Such ability might show up in different areas of the classroom. For example, a child's sense of design might reveal itself in the blocks area when she builds a curved block structure. Or the child may be especially interested in the visual patterns and textures in her environment.

The Spectrum art assessment is based on the teacher's yearlong art curriculum, supplemented by four structured activities. Because children's artwork changes over time and cannot be evaluated adequately from a single sample, children's art products are collected for review both at the middle and end of the year. Teachers are encouraged to provide a range of art activities in their curriculum, including drawing with pencil, crayon, markers and chalk; painting with different paints (tempera and watercolor) and on different surfaces; and creating three-dimensional pieces (collages, sculpture, woodworking, dioramas). Some children will be more capable with markers than paint; others will be more facile using clay than wire. Some may prefer fluid, free flowing materials such as paint to more controlled and precise media such as markers. By exposing children to different media and becoming sensitive to the distinguishing features of children's artwork, teachers will be able to gain a more informed picture of each child.

The four structured assessment activities enable teachers to look at specific abilities. Three structured drawing activities elicit examples of children's schemas for animals and people, as well as giving children the chance to incorporate elements of novelty into their schema (via an imaginary animal drawing). A three-dimensional task allows teachers to look at a child's ability to organize such elements as design and pattern in space; her awareness of how different materials such as wood scraps and wire can be integrated into a unified whole; and her sensitivity to the inherent properties of different kinds of media.

❏ ART PORTFOLIO

—Purpose and Activity Description

The portfolio, including structured activities as well as the other work produced by the child at school, is the primary vehicle for assessment in the visual arts domain. Teachers need to look at many samples, collected over time, to assess accurately young children's artistic abilities. Even within a week, children may experiment with different formulas for drawing a topic of interest (Kellogg, 1969). Thus one drawing of a person does not necessarily represent a child's ability to depict human beings. A child may take one step forward and two steps back before advancing in a particular area. To make sure we captured the full range of the child's work, we decided to collect all art.

The portfolio also helps teachers identify unique interests and style. Some children are more comfortable with reality-based drawing, whereas others prefer to work primarily from their imaginations. In representation, some children may exhibit preferences for narrative or depicting a story; portraying scenes, such as a farmyard; or drawing particular objects and figures, such as houses and animals. Other children may prefer to work on and elaborate a particular schema, like vehicles, people, or animals. Of course, such preferences may reflect messages from parents, teachers, or peers, and thus can be broadened sometimes by introducing the child to new ideas.

Before attempting to assess children's artwork, teachers should expose children to the different media and dimensions of visual arts. Children should have the opportunity to do representational as well as design or abstract work. They should explore such dimensions as the function of color and different kinds of lines, shapes, and patterns. Rather than their only working on art products in a vacuum, children should be given the opportunity to produce art for specific purposes, such as decorating a birthday card or illustrating a story, poem, or concept (such as changing seasons or city life).

The Spectrum art activities ensure that children complete a range of art projects they might not otherwise attempt. Children's portfolios, containing both free exploration and assigned activities, are assessed in terms of three categories. *Level of representation* refers to the ability to create recognizable symbols for common objects such as people, vegetation, houses, animals, and vehicles, as well as the capacity to integrate these elements spatially into a larger design (Feinburg, 1987). *Degree of exploration* refers to the extent to which flexibility, generativity, inventiveness, and variations are reflected in the child's designs, representational drawing, and in the use of art materials (Feinburg, 1988, personal communication, May 15, 1990; Gardner, 1980; Goodman, 1988; Strauss, 1978). Finally, *level of artistry* refers to the capacity to utilize the various elements of art such as line, shape, and color to depict emotions, produce certain effects, and decorate the artwork (Feinburg, 1988, personal communication, May 15, 1990; Gardner, 1980; Goodman, 1968, 1988; Winner, 1982).

—Materials and Set-Up

The four structured Spectrum activities require four or five sets of nonpermanent, nontoxic markers, good quality white paper (11" by 14") and materials for a three-dimensional project, such as clay, plasticine, pipecleaners, popsicle sticks, toothpicks, and paste. The rest of the artwork used comes from the teacher's own visual arts curriculum. Suggestions for activities (based on Pitcher, Feinburg, & Alexander, 1989) include the following:

1. **Crayon:** rubbings, melted crayons, etchings, different-sized crayons (have children use sides as well as ends). Have children use single-color crayons or different-colored paper.

2. **Tempera paint:** roller painting, straw painting, sponge painting, textured painting, fancy paper painting, color mixing, soap painting, string painting, painting with different-sized brushes, painting on different surfaces — wood, clay, shells, paper bags, egg cartons, stones, etc. Also use finger paint and water color. (Note: Easels are recommended, but not necessary.)

3. **Collages:** *textured* materials such as felt, burlap, cloth, feathers, shells, cotton, velvet, seeds, fur scraps, corrugated paper, etc.; *shapes* such as buttons, straws, paper clips, cork, toothpicks, string, yarn, macaroni, spaghetti, beads, bottle caps, etc.; *patterned* materials such as wallpaper samples and gift wrapping; *transparent and semitransparent* materials such as net sacks, doilies, lace, thin tissue paper, and colored cellophane; *sparkling or shiny* materials like sequins, glitter, and aluminum foil; and *scattering* materials such as sand, sawdust, and salt.

4. **Paper:** Use to make different kinds of shapes, strips, masks, mobiles, puppets, and flowers (tissue paper). Make available different sizes and kinds of paper.

5. **Chalk:** Use with wet and dry paper. Use for color mixing.

6. **Cutting and tearing, pasting, taping:** Cut and tear different kinds of paper. Paste macaroni, dried beans, paper, sand, and pebbles on paper.

7. **Materials for three-dimensional work:** clay (stored in airtight, watertight containers), plasticine, playdough, wire, Styrofoam, small boxes, mobiles, wood scraps, toothpicks, popsicle sticks, pipe cleaners, paste, and various recycled materials.

—Procedure

At the beginning of the year, help children to construct a large art portfolio for collecting their artwork each semester. Children can decorate the portfolios as they wish. The portfolios should include drawings, paintings, collages, and three-dimensional pieces (or photographs of them if storage presents a problem). Throughout the year, try to insure that the child's name and date are written on each piece. You might also give parents a letter at the beginning of the year informing them that children's artwork will be collected in classroom portfolios that will be sent home at the end of each semester. Of course, some children may want to take particular pieces home with them during the semester, in which case you can ask parents to save them in a folder at home. At the end of each semester, you might want to have a show-and-tell, when children show one of their pieces to the class.

In general, try to provide children with a range of art activities, including design, representational work, and both two- and three-dimensional projects. The four structured activities should be introduced one at a time every 6 to 8 weeks, and all children should be encouraged to complete them. This will give you a sense for what each child is capable of at a particular point in time, as well as a chance to see how children's products differ when they are presented with the same task. You can conduct the structured activities either with individual children, in small groups, or with the whole class.

• Activity 1: Draw an Animal

Before you conduct this activity, use a group time to discuss with children the different kinds of animals that live on a farm. You also might want to sing "Old MacDonald." (Other appropriate themes for this activity include animals children would most like to have for a pet, animals they might see on a jungle trip, or animals they would like to have in a "classroom zoo." You might tell a story about a zoo visit or an adventure trip to the jungle to help motivate children and elicit ideas.)

For the assessment, ask children to think of an animal that they might see on Old MacDonald's farm and then draw that animal. Tell them that each child will be making a drawing of an animal that will be put in a folder, and when the folder is full, the class will make its own MacDonald's farm. Give each child a piece of good quality white paper (11" by 14") and an assortment of markers of different widths and colors. (These materials also will be used for Activities 2 and 3.) Allow up to 20 minutes for children to complete their work, warning them a few minutes before time is up. Make sure to put children's names and the date on the

back of the drawings. You also can jot down any observations you made, such as which hand a child used, and whether she was particularly focused, worked for a long time, or revised her drawing.

After the activity is completed, make a book of children's drawings or display the animals on a wall. Perhaps children can describe what their animals do on the farm.

• Activity 2: Draw a Person

As part of a unit on oneself or one's family, ask children to draw a picture of themselves with their family. The portraits eventually can become part of a "Book About Me" that also lists children's likes and dislikes, friends, pets, favorite things, and so on. Give each child the same set of materials as in Activity 1, allowing 20 to 30 minutes for completion. Let children know you will be keeping their drawings.

• Activity 3: Draw an Imaginary Animal

Pass out paper and markers to the children. Tell them: "I am going to tell you a story about a strange creature, and it is your job to draw a picture of that creature. You can take as much time as you want, and you can tell me when you are finished. I will be saving the pictures that kids make here. Here is the story:

"Three children were going home from school one day when they suddenly saw the strangest creature. It was like no other animal they had ever seen. It did not look like a dog, or cat, or elephant, or anything they had ever heard of. It didn't move like any animal or person they knew, and it even sounded very strange when it made a noise."

Record the amount of time children spend on the activity and any other observations on the back of the drawings.

• Activity 4: Create a Sculpture

There are many different materials that can be used for this activity. You can choose from clay, plasticine, playdough, Styrofoam and toothpicks, wood scraps, pipe cleaners, or popsicle sticks and paste. Limit the kinds of materials that are available to children. First, allow children to make whatever they wish. Later on, you can suggest different ideas: "make something an animal or person could live in," "Make something that moves," or "make something that is happy, sad, angry, or showing another emotion" (Pitcher, Feinburg, & Alexander, 1989).

• *Other Suggested Structured Activities* (based on Pitcher, Feinburg, & Alexander, 1989)

In general, children are more likely to produce drawings that exhibit creativity, embellishment, and attempts at representation if you give them a task with a strong stimulus rather than asking them to draw spontaneously. Therefore, we include suggestions for more open-ended projects you may wish to try.

Collage: This is an organizational task involving shape and color. Provide children with different shapes, sizes, and colors of paper, cloth, and textured materials, such as colored cellophane. Give children strong glue, scissors, and background paper. First, ask children to select and arrange materials without any particular focus. Later suggest ideas such as "a place where they'd like to live," "a make-believe animal," "a happy or sad feeling." Look for whether children exhibit a sense of design.

Beautiful Junk: This is a three-dimensional construction task. Supply children with empty boxes, paper towel tubes, old ribbons, corrugated paper, egg cartons, kitchen salvage, bottle caps, straws, and other recycled materials. Give children white glue, scissors, and a paper punch. Tell them they can make whatever they want. After they've finished one creation, offer suggestions such as "Build a simple machine, vehicle, or house for people or animals."

Drawings:

1. Give children time to explore an interesting object in the classroom. Choose an object with some novelty, but familiar enough to children that they do not get too distracted by the object itself. Possibilities include a green pepper, cube, realistic stuffed animal (perhaps borrowed from a museum), telephone, chair, guitar or other musical instrument, simple bicycle (without training wheels) or tricycle, exotic flowers (birds of paradise), or crayfish. After they have studied and touched it, ask children to draw the object while looking at it often to check their work. Children can also be asked to draw the object from different perspectives.

2. Have children create drawings that incorporate elements of movement, such as drawings of themselves and their friends on the playground, or of circus people performing various stunts.

3. Ask children to draw pictures to accompany a story such as the adventures of Pinocchio.

4. Give children basic shapes (such as a square and triangle "house" shape) to decorate in their own way.

5. After a field trip to a farm, museum, or aquarium, ask children to draw pictures of what they saw.

—Scoring

The scoring system for the Art Portfolio is based on the visual arts scoring criteria developed for the Spectrum Field Inventory (Chen & Feinburg, 1990). Although the scoring criteria refer primarily to two-dimensional drawings, they can be adapted for use with paintings and three-dimensional work as well. Table 47 (pp. 159–161) defines the main scoring categories, and describes the three scoring levels for each component. Observation and summary sheets are included in Tables 48 and 49. Space is also provided to note whether children indicate a preference for certain types of media and whether the child seems to be right handed, left handed, or switches from one hand to another. In Tables 50 and 51 we have included an earlier version of the scoring system that is less rigorous but may be easier to use.

A total of nine elements are used in scoring the portfolios (see Table 48). The elements are scored as follows: 1 = low, 2 = average, and 3 = high ability. Although each element is scored separately, the elements are only meaningful with reference to the general categories of representation, exploration, and artistry. Children's artwork should not be scored as individual pieces, but as a whole. If the level of work seems inconsistent, the score should be based on the operational or dominant level of the majority of the child's products (although the fact that the work is inconsistent is itself worth noting). We suggest that the portfolio be reviewed midyear and at the end of the school year. You might ask the parents of children who have sparse portfolios whether their child does any art at home.

—Preliminary Results: 1986–1988

The children's art portfolios were reviewed twice during the year, in December and April. Two children were identified as exhibiting outstanding ability in the visual arts. The first child focused primarily on representational drawing using markers. His command of detail, perspective, and composition was striking. His drawings depicted a wide variety of objects and scenes. Some of the drawings included figures in profile or partially obstructed objects, and revealed a nascent sense of perspective. He also was able to convey a sense of motion through his use of line.

The second boy worked comfortably and effectively with a wide range of materials. He was extremely curious about how materials could be used alone and in combination (in collages and sculptures). His drawings and paintings displayed an unusual sense of composition, balance, color, and detail. For example, one of his drawings depicted a highly detailed underwater scene, including several kinds of fish, an underwater vehicle, and a whale spouting water. The drawing covered the entire page. His sculptures and three-dimensional constructions revealed an awareness of the different angles for viewing an object.

Some of the children exhibited distinctive ability only in particular components. For example, one child, whose work was primarily exploratory, used color in a distinctive manner. She used the spectrum of colors in every one of her drawings and paintings, but in a slightly different way each time. She selected color deliberately for the purposes of design or representation, and frequently experimented with mixing her own colors for special paintings.

Most of the rest of the children produced art that was either characteristic for their age, or that was primarily exploratory (e.g., paint-mixing on paper, or large scribbles). Much of this latter work focused more on how the materials could be used than on producing a particular product. Many of the children exhibited preferences for specific kinds of media. In general, boys seemed to be more drawn to collage and assemblage than to painting and drawing, whereas girls tended to exhibit the opposite pattern. One boy seemed to be most interested in crafts — making various three-dimensional products and maps. Another boy did his strongest representational work in clay. A third child, a girl, focused on tiny drawings that were narrative, decorative, and highly detailed. Two children almost never worked at the art table, so that the structured activities provided the only opportunity to assess their artistic capability.

TABLE 47: VISUAL ARTS SCORING CRITERIA

© 1990 Chen & Feinburg

LEVEL OF REPRESENTATION: The ability to create recognizable symbols for common objects (e.g., people, vegetation, houses, animals) as well as the capacity to coordinate these elements spatially into a unified whole (Feinburg, 1987).*

Elements	Level 1	Level 2	Level 3
Basic Forms	Vertical, diagonal, and horizontal lines exist in isolation. Drawings that include structures are covered by scribbling, and scribbling is random.	Certain geometric forms (circles, rectangles, triangles) are coupled with a proclivity to combine these marks into more intricate patterns.	Contours are present. Geometry is not the primary mechanism to constitute the drawing. Profiles and side views may be included.
	Objects such as person or house are incomplete (e.g., tadpoles missing salient parts).	Major features of objects are included (e.g., arms, legs and eyes for a person; ears, eyes and a mouth for a dog; simple squares for windows).	Distinguishable detailed features are included (e.g., fingers, eyebrows, shoes, and clothing for a person; cross squares for windows).
Color	Sizes of units are not consistent either within or among objects (e.g., head is bigger than body for a person, baby is larger than the mother).	Proportions used are essentially consistent with reality within, but not among, objects and figures.	Proportions are close to reality and consistent both within and among objects and figures (e.g., hands are smaller than feet; people are smaller than houses).
	Colors are used randomly, with no relation to objects being portrayed in drawings.	Multiple colors are used with at least a couple of examples of realistic or true representational color.	Multiple colors are used in drawing and they are placed deliberately in most drawings (e.g., yellow sun, blue sky, or green grass). Very few drawings are presented with unrealistic colors.
Spatial Integration	Elements float ambiguously in space. Objects, figures, and features are upside down, tilted, and stray, appearing scattered around the page.	There is a crude acknowledgment of baseline. Objects and figures are often not related to one another or are limited to a specific area on the paper (e.g., one corner or center of page).	Elements reveal a clear sense of baseline (e.g., land and sky). Objects are shown in relation to one another and to the page as a whole. A clear sense of top, bottom, inside, and outside is evident.

* Most elements described on this page are adopted from Feinburg (1987).

159

VISUAL ARTS SCORING CRITERIA

DEGREE OF EXPLORATION: The extent to which flexibility, generativity, inventiveness, and variations are reflected in the child's designs, representational drawings, and in the use of art materials (Feinburg, 1988; Feinburg, personal communication, May 15, 1990; Gardner, 1980; Goodman, 1988; Strauss, 1978).

Elements	Level 1	Level 2	Level 3
Color	Each single drawing is primarily monochromatic. Colors are used consistently from drawing to drawing with little change.	Multiple colors are used; simply playing with color is the dominant pattern.	Multiple colors are used effectively to depict moods or atmospheres. Contrasting and mixing of colors is apparent. Drawings appear colorful and flavorful.
Variations	Patterns and designs are repeated with little or no changes. Very limited scheme is presented in drawings.	A number of schemes in drawings (e.g., dots, lines, circles, ovals, and letterlike forms) may be interwoven or appear in collected drawings.	Lines and shapes are used to generate a wide variety of forms in designs (e.g., open and closed, explosive and controlled).
	Representational forms are presented with little or no variation over time (e.g., drawing the same house in the same way time after time).	Representational drawings are presented with a moderate range of patterns, objects, or themes.	Representational drawings are presented with noticeable variation in forms or themes.
Dynamics	Lines, shapes, and forms are consistently depicted in a very rigid way; drawings rely exclusively on basic geometric forms with little use of diagonals, fragmentation, or stray lines. Drawings appear static and repetitive.	Lines, shapes, and forms are used playfully or vigorously in representational drawings and designs. Drawings appear smooth and free, flowing spontaneously.	Lines, forms, and colors evoke vivid motion with rhythm, balance, and harmony; dynamic tension may be exhibited.

VISUAL ARTS SCORING CRITERIA

LEVEL OF ARTISTRY: The capacity to utilize the various elements of art (e.g., line, color, shape) to depict emotions, produce certain effects, and embellish the drawings (Feinburg, 1988; Feinburg, personal communication, May 15, 1990; Gardner, 1980; Goodman, 1968, 1988; Winner, 1982).

Elements	Level 1	Level 2	Level 3
Expressivity	Little emotion is evident in drawings (e.g., person does not show any facial expression). Drawings hardly evoke any emotional response or reaction.	The capacity to evoke feeling or mood through lines and shapes is evident, though some degree of ambiguity exists.	Strong mood is conveyed through literal representation (e.g., smiling sun, crying face) and abstract features (e.g., dark colors or drooping lines can express sadness). Drawing appears "lively," "sad," or "powerful."
Repleteness	Variations in line (if any) prove immaterial to the impact of the drawings.	Variations in line are used to contribute certain effect on designs as well as depict certain one or two particular elements in representational drawings (e.g., hair or eyes).	Lines of varied thickness are used to texturize several elements in the drawing. A certain effect (e.g., shading or shadow) may be produced.
Aesthetic Sensibility	No sense of beauty is evident; little deliberate decoration and elaboration in drawings are exhibited. Multiple colors may be used, but they are not utilized to enhance the drawing; they are primarily functional (e.g., rainbow).	Color is chosen deliberately for the purpose of decoration, though the decoration can be exaggerated or possibly cartoonish (e.g., extra circle in the face for make-up). Individual shapes reveal some sense of beauty and harmony.	Concern with decoration is evident; patterns or repetitions are presented with rhythm and embellishment and forms are filled in carefully and deliberately placed. Drawings are colorful, balanced, and rhythmic; show an individual participating in a meaningful way in the process of aesthetic self-expression.

TABLE 48: VISUAL ARTS OBSERVATION SHEET

Child: _____   Age: from _____ to _____

Observer: _____   Date: collected from _____ to _____

Preferred Medium: _____   Handedness:_____

Number of Drawings: _____

Number of Paintings: _____

Number of Three-Dimensional Products: _____

SCORE FOR LEVEL OF REPRESENTATION: _____   **NOTES/EXAMPLES:**

3	3	3
2	2	2
1	1	1
Basic Form	Color	Spatial Integration

SCORE FOR DEGREE OF EXPLORATION: _____   **NOTES/EXAMPLES:**

3	3	3
2	2	2
1	1	1
Color	Variations	Dynamics

SCORE FOR LEVEL OF ARTISTRY: _____   **NOTES/EXAMPLES:**

3	3	3
2	2	2
1	1	1
Expressivity	Repleteness	Aesthetic Sensibility

GENERAL COMMENTS:

Child (age)		Representation	Exploration	Artistry		
	Basic Forms					
	Color	Representation				
	Spatial Integration					
	Subtotal					
	Color		Exploration			
	Variations					
	Dynamics					
	Subtotal					
	Expressivity			Artistry		
	Repleteness					
	Aesthetic Sensibility					
	Subtotal					
	TOTAL					
	Preferred Medium					

TABLE 49: VISUAL ARTS SUMMARY SHEET

163

TABLE 50: ALTERNATE VISUAL ARTS SCORING CRITERIA

The purpose of the following categories is to help you record your overall impressions of children's collected artwork.

Consistency: Extent to which collected artwork exhibits a consistent use of skills, style, or both; includes exhibiting a style, composition, or design so distinctive that an observer can identify which child is the artist.

Imagination: Capacity to be fluent and flexible in generating new forms and combinations of forms; generative and inventive in approach; original.

Variety: Repertoire of schemas available to child — in design, representation, type of media explored, or some of these; use of different subject matter, styles, or both.

Sense of Completeness: Extent to which pieces look finished; the whole picture (not just individual parts) is treated with sensitivity to balance and cohesiveness, awareness of how parts interrelate.

PART II: FEATURES

Each of the following features is described in terms of the artwork considered characteristic or distinctive for a 4-year-old child. Refer to these descriptions as you fill out the observation sheet (Table 51).

1. Use of Lines/Shapes

Characteristic: Child uses a few different kinds of lines (e.g., straight, jagged, curved) and constructs some discrete forms (e.g., circles, rectangles). Some shapes and lines are joined to form simple patterns and objects.

Distinctive: A rich variety of schemata is used consistently (e.g., different kinds of lines, shapes, dots, cross-hatching). These may be used together or separately for design and representational purposes. Combinations of lines, shapes, or both are effective in forming more complex patterns and more distinguishable representations.

2. Use of Color

Characteristic: Child shows a preference for some colors and begins to explore color mixing. Colors may not relate to object(s) being portrayed in representations, and may be used randomly in design.

Distinctive: Paintings and drawings show some understanding of the role that color can play in design and representation. Color may be used effectively in depicting moods and atmospheres, or for representation or fantasy. Child is able to use knowledge of color mixing to create colors that she wishes to work with, and may request particular colors for her work.

3. Composition

Characteristic: Child may explore a few different compositional patterns, but variety and exploration are limited. Objects, figures, and features vary in size, and are scattered around the page or floating in space. Objects may be related to one another, but not to the page as a whole. Figures are often limited to a specific area on the page (e.g., one corner). Generally, objects are worked on in isolation and are portrayed in space as the child understands them in relation to herself.

Distinctive: Ability to use grid-spatial treatment (e.g., baseline, sky, above, next to) in representation and design. A variety of compositional patterns is explored. Objects are shown in relation to one another and to the page as a whole. Work may exhibit a sense of perspective, and may even include some occlusion, three-dimensionality, profile, and overlapping.

4. Use of Detail

Characteristic: Some objects may be identifiable, but most are undetailed and simplistically rendered. Major features may be omitted in representations. Features portrayed tend to be those most salient to the child. Designs and patterns are simple and broadly drawn.

Distinctive: Representations have distinguishable, detailed features. Most major features and more subtle features (e.g., fingers with fingernails, face with eyes, nose, mouth, ears, eyelashes, and eyebrows) are included. Designs are embellished through use of a variety of lines, shapes, patterns.

5. Expressiveness

Characteristic: Child's work is sketchy and straightforward with little sense of mood conveyed.

Distinctive: Child is able to depict mood, atmosphere, movement, or some of these through her use of line, color, and composition. Paintings and drawings are flavorful, visually striking.

6. Representation

(Note: The following descriptions incorporate many of the features listed above.)

Characteristic: Representations tend to be of single objects or small groups of objects, e.g., people, animals, vehicles. Objects portrayed are identifiable, but simplistic and undetailed. Figures and features most salient to the child are portrayed. Major features may be omitted (e.g., hair, nose on a person). Proportions tend to be inconsistent with reality; those things most important to the child are made largest. Colors may not correspond to objects depicted.

Distinctive: Representations are clear and detailed and may include more than one person, animal, or object at a time. Distinguishing features (e.g., hump on a camel's back, elephant's trunk) and more subtle details are incorporated as well as major features. Proportions more closely resemble reality. Colors realistically reflect objects being portrayed.

TABLE 51: ALTERNATE VISUAL ARTS OBSERVATION SHEET
Drawings and Paintings

Child: _____   Age: From _____ to _____

Observer: _____   Date: Collected from _____ to _____

Preferred Medium: _____   Handedness: _____

Number of Drawings: _____
Number of Paintings: _____
Number of Three-Dimensional: _____

PART I: GENERAL CATEGORIES

Begin by looking through the child's collected paintings and drawings. Based on your overall impression of the collection, indicate the level at which each of the following characteristics can be seen in the child's artwork.

	Distinctive	Present	Limited
Consistency	_____	_____	_____
Imagination	_____	_____	_____
Variety	_____	_____	_____
Sense of Completeness	_____	_____	_____

COMMENTS/EXAMPLES:

PART II: FEATURES

For each of the following features, check whether you consider the child's work to be "characteristic" or "distinctive," according to the standards in Table 50. Include examples and descriptions for each feature. Conclude with a brief overview of what you find most characteristic or striking about the collection of artwork.

Examples/Descriptions:

1. Use of Lines and Shapes
        Characteristic: ___
        Distinctive: ___

2. Use of Color
        Characteristic: ___
        Distinctive: ___

3. Composition
        Characteristic: ___
        Distinctive: ___

4. Use of Detail
        Characteristic: ___
        Distinctive: ___

5. Expressiveness
        Characteristic: ___
        Distinctive: ___

6. Representation
        Characteristic: ___
        Distinctive: ___

OVERVIEW:

Include observations of any striking differences between the child's paintings and drawings. For example, are drawings more detailed? Are paintings more colorful? Also, include any observations of children's three-dimensional work.

COMMENTS ON STRUCTURED ACTIVITIES:

CHAPTER 7
MUSIC DOMAIN

—INTRODUCTION

Individuals experience the music domain in a variety of ways: through singing, playing an instrument, listening to performances and recordings, and dancing. From an early age, children hear music at home and on the radio or TV. Even infants have a rudimentary sense of music. Their babbling includes melodic experimentation and they respond to different rhythmic and tonal patterns (Davidson & Scripp, 1991; Hargreaves, 1986; Sloboda, 1985). Young children sing and chant spontaneously as they play, creating simple songs to accompany their activities. They also often respond to music with their bodies, keeping time with a beat or expressing a song through movement.

In Western culture, music ability traditionally has not been considered an intellectual ability; rather, it has been thought of as a "talent" or "skill" (Bamberger, 1991; Blacking, 1974; Davidson & Torff, 1993). For the majority of individuals, there is little musical development after the school years begin, since such training is not emphasized in the typical academic curriculum. Formal instruction often is reserved for a relatively small number of voluntary participants. Parental support and guidance, as well as the self-discipline to spend long hours practicing, are important components of further development in the field.

Although relatively little research has been conducted on the development of musical competence in young children, we do have preliminary information about the characteristics of the preschool child's experience with music (e.g., Hargreaves, 1986). Most children start singing by creating spontaneous songs or repeating small bits of familiar tunes. By age 3 or 4, the spontaneous songs generally have disappeared and been replaced by the traditional songs of the culture. Also by this age, most children can reproduce the basic outlines of a song —they can capture general relationships such as whether the phrases are fast or slow, rising or falling, or include large or small gaps between pitches. Although they cannot match pitches precisely or maintain a key with complete accuracy, they have largely mastered the text, phrase boundaries and contours (the rising and falling direction), and the surface rhythm and underlying pulse (the metronomic beat organizing the rhythmic structures of a song) (Davidson, McKernon, & Gardner, 1981).

In the preschool setting, children typically learn songs with their teachers at group meetings. Some classrooms provide musical instruments such as a piano, bells, or Autoharp to accompany the singing. It is relatively easy for the teacher to discover the child who is an enthusiastic singer. This child usually overpowers the other children with her strong voice while her body is involved actively in the process of singing. It is more challenging to recognize the child who is sensitive to the rhythmic pattern of a song or the child who sings a song from start to finish in the same key in which she began.

Traditional measures of musicality have focused primarily on the child's ability to perceive differences in rhythm and pitch (Deutsch, 1983; Dowling & Harwood, 1986). There are three major tests of musicality other than the now outdated Seashore Measures of Musical Talent (commonly considered the grandfather of such tests): the Gordon Primary Measures of Musical Audiation, the Bentley Measures of Musical Abilities, and the Wing Standardized Tests of Musical Intelligence. The Gordon covers ages 5 to 8 and 9 to adult. It includes 30 to 40 items that require the subject to determine whether tonal and rhythmic pairs and patterns are the same. The Bentley is for ages 8 to 14 and includes pitch discrimination, tonal and rhythmic memory, and chord analysis. The Wing test is the most comprehensive, measuring aural acuity and appreciation of rhythm, harmony, intensity, and phrasing. However, it is intended for use with individuals aged 14 and above. (See Shuter-Dyson & Gabriel, 1981 for a more detailed description of the available tests.)

Most of the music tests are aimed at populations aged 8 or 9 years to adulthood. Schools specializing in music training generally do not use formal tests for admitting students, but conduct a more informal assessment including activities such as clapping hands and playing singing games. Schools often consider, as well, the parents' ambitions and desires for their children to be exposed to music.

—CONCEPTUALIZING THE MUSIC ACTIVITIES

The two main components of Western music are pitch and rhythm. Expressiveness is also an important element, since communicating emotions is an essential aspect of music's power. There have been two main approaches to the psychological investigation of music: "top-down" and "bottom-up" (Gardner, 1983). The bottom-up approach examines the different ways in which individuals process the basic components of music, such as simple rhythmic and tonal patterns, without the contextual information of the complete piece (Deutsch, 1983; Dowling & Harwood, 1986). The top-down approach focuses on detecting the individual's perception of the more global properties of music such as tempo, dynamics, texture, tonal quality,

and mood (e.g., Bamberger, 1991; Davidson & Scripp, 1991; Serafine, 1988; Sloboda, 1988). The Spectrum activities take a middle-ground approach of eliciting children's musical production abilities in curriculum- and age-appropriate contexts (the Birthday Song), as well as assessing their sensitivity to such purely musical elements as pitch discrimination (the Music Perception Activity).

The end states that guided our thinking about significant musical roles include the singer, the instrumentalist, the composer, and the music critic. Singer and instrumentalist seemed to be the most useful end states for looking at 4-year-olds, since some abilities required by the latter two roles tend to emerge at later ages. Ability in music can emerge early in a child's development. The Suzuki Talent Education Program begins training young performers in violin as early as age 3.

In a longitudinal study of musical giftedness, researchers Lyle Davidson and Larry Scripp found that musically precocious children demonstrate a number of distinctive characteristics (Davidson & Scripp, 1994). They remember tonal and rhythmic patterns virtually spontaneously and learn new material at a far faster rate than do their peers. One 3-year-old child was able to sing an entire song in key starting from a single pitch, with or without a piano accompaniment. She could maintain both pitch and rhythm stability regardless of changes in the text, and corrected the wrong ending to a song she was singing from recall. She even sang several parts in vibrato.

While the child just mentioned came from a rich musical background, a child from a less musical background demonstrated equally striking but different abilities. Before she was 5 1/2, she revealed a beginning understanding of musical principles when she was asked to invent two of her own songs. Her first song lent itself to conventional harmonizing and used parallel structure in the first two phrases. The second tune captured the improvisational style typical of jazz. She clearly understood the function of phrasing and cadences and organized the pitches around tonal centers. Such precocity doubtless will be recognizable in a class no matter what the teacher provides as curriculum or uses as means of assessment. Our activities, however, are designed to pick out the different sensitivities and strengths presented by children with a wide range of musical ability.

❑ SINGING ACTIVITY

—Purpose and Activity Description

A competent singer demonstrates accurate pitch, maintains a steady tempo, and is able to stay in the same key. At the preschool level, however, many young singers make up their own words, drift from one tempo into another, and find it a challenge to finish the song in the same key in which they began. By listening to a child sing just one song, we could learn a good deal about her attention to lyrics, rhythm, and pitch. However, we wished to explore a more complete repertoire of abilities involved in musical production. Thus, we designed a production activity with four parts.

We conducted the first three assessments in one session and conducted the fourth assessment later with those children who demonstrated unusual musical strength.

Part I: Favorite Song

The teacher starts the session by asking the child to sing her favorite song. The element of choice enables some children to pick a song that is more musically sophisticated than "Happy Birthday" and that lends itself to more expressive coloring or greater variation in theme, dynamics, or pacing.

The teacher records her overall impressions of the child's performance, including the level of difficulty of the song and the enthusiasm that the child brings to the task.

Part II: Birthday Song

In this part of the activity, the child sings "Happy Birthday" by herself from start to finish, and then sings it responsively, alternating phrases with the teacher. "Happy Birthday" was purposefully chosen to control for differences in starting knowledge, since most children are familiar with the tune.

The child's performance is evaluated phrase by phrase, and scored on four measures of rhythm and three measures of pitch. The responsive singing part of the activity allows the teacher to assess how well the child can follow the musical pattern that the teacher has established in the first phrase of the song. This exercise measures a child's ability to come in on key as well as her ability to maintain the song's rhythm, pitch, and contour patterns.

Some children are reluctant to enter an activity that requires singing because it makes them feel more exposed than speaking. The teacher needs to be sensitive to each child's level of comfort with these activities. The birthday scenario and song have the advantage of being familiar to most, if not all, 4-year-olds. Most children enjoy the discussion of how old they are and eagerly announce how old they will be on their next birthday. A playdough birthday cake gives them something to manipulate and adds a bit of playfulness to the activity. After the assessment, many children create their own playdough cakes and sing "Happy Birthday" to their peers and teacher in the course of other classroom activities.

Part III: Music Memory

Finally, the child is asked to sing a new song that she learned in class four or five sessions prior to the assessment. The teacher should choose a song that is unfamiliar to the children, perhaps even making one up herself. The song also should contain a minimal level of musical complexity and follow the general canons of Western music.

Children will vary in their ability to reproduce the words, correct number of phrases, contour, and rhythm of the new song. The teacher may provide scaffolding to aid children's recollection.

Part IV: Novel Song

If the child performs particularly well during the first session, additional sessions are held in which the child is taught a new and more musically complex song. This allows the teacher to evaluate the accuracy and speed with which the child learns a new tune. We chose a song titled "Animal Song," composed by Lyle Davidson, because it offers a number of musical challenges. It begins in a major mode, shifting midway to a minor mode. The song also contains an octave jump from a middle B to a high B. Teachers may choose another song to teach the child, but it must be sufficiently demanding to challenge children's abilities.

In assessing performance, teachers can look either at global properties such as text, rhythm, and rising and falling contours, or at more detailed nuances such as matching a particularly challenging pitch value or observing the key change in the middle of the song. Children also may exhibit differences in expressiveness.

The materials for the Singing Activity are very simple: a playdough cake in a tin jello mold and six brightly colored birthday candles. You can use a tape recorder to record children's songs so that you can assess them later. Conduct the assessment either in a quiet, comfortable corner of the classroom away from the main activity areas or in a small nearby room if available. Make the setting as comfortable as possible, perhaps by sitting on cushions on the floor or at a small table. If you do not feel that you can sing "Happy Birthday" accurately, you can find a recording of the song and play it during the assessment.

—Procedure and Script

When children have a free-choice time, introduce the Singing Activity as follows: "Today _____ [adult's name] will play some singing games [or the 'Happy Birthday' game] with you. One person at a time can have a turn to go with _____ [adult's name] to play the game."

Part I: Favorite Song

Once the child is comfortable, you might want to acknowledge the tape recorder and perhaps chat a bit about how it works. Depending on whether or not each child has an individual tape, you might say, " I have a special tape and it has your name on it"; or, "Here is a special tape that children sing on. Let's put it in and turn it on. Later we can play it back and hear how you sound."

To start the session, you might ask, "Would you please sing one of your favorite songs for me? Then we will rewind the tape and hear what it sounds like." Or, you might ease the child into the activity by saying, "We're going to be playing a birthday game with this cake, and we're going to be singing 'Happy Birthday.' " But before we do that, I want to ask you if you have a *favorite* song, a song that you really like that you want to sing into the tape recorder. Then we can listen to it and hear how it sounds." (Turn on the tape recorder at this point and leave it on for the duration of the session.) The advantage of using the latter introduction is that the child may find it easier to sing a tune she likes if attention is focused on the birthday script instead of on her. The wording of instructions does make a difference in how children respond and its effect should not be underestimated.

If a child is still reluctant to start singing, you can encourage her by asking again, "Do you have a song that you really like?" or, "Are there any songs you've been singing at home?" Sometimes, it is better not to pose a question, but to say, "Let's start with your favorite song. You can sing it to me. It can be one you've been singing at home or at school." Further support such as "I'm ready," "You can start," or, "OK, you can sing it now" also can be provided, but if a child remains reticent, move to the next part of the activity. If the child chants or speaks her way through the song, you might say, "This time you sang it in your talking voice. Now you can try it in your *singing* voice."

Part II: Birthday Song

Birthday Game: You can introduce the next part of the assessment by saying, "Now we're going to play our birthday game. Here's a cake, but it's not a real cake. What do you think it's made of? . . . Now we're going to pretend it's my birthday and then it can be your birthday. First, you can decorate the cake with candles for my birthday and I won't look." Give the child no more than six candles to arrange (too many candles become a distraction). Turn around or close your eyes and say, "When the cake is ready, you'll tell me and you'll sing the 'Happy Birthday' song to me. Then I can make a wish and I'll blow out the candles."

If the child seems to avoid singing, you can offer to sing the song first, saying "Next, it will be your turn." Another scaffold might be, "How about if I sing it first so you can remember how it goes, and then you can sing it." If the child is singing too softly or quickly, ask "Could you sing it a little bit louder [or more slowly] so that the tape recorder can hear?"

Responsive Singing: You can lead into the next part of the activity by saying, "Now I want a chance to sing a little bit too, so we'll take turns this time." Or you might say, "Now it's going to be your birthday and I'll decorate the cake for you. This time we'll play a taking-turns game with 'Happy Birthday.' " Then model the singing of each phrase: "First, *I'll* sing the first part 'Happy Birthday to you,' and then *you'll* sing the next part, 'Happy Birthday to you,' and then *I'll* sing 'Happy Birthday dear _____ [child's name],' and then *you'll* sing 'Happy Birthday to you.' So we'll take turns singing, but it'll be your birthday." Decorate the cake with candles for the child, and then start singing the first phrase. Sing the phrase in a middle range so the child can reach all of the notes.

If the child does not understand the concept of responsive singing, explain the turn-taking procedure again. While some preschoolers grasp this concept immediately, others need some practice. You also can model responsive singing with the class as a group with songs such as "Pussy Cat, Pussy Cat, Where Have You Been?" If, after singing the first phrase, the child remains silent, you can whisper, "Now it's your turn," and look at her expectantly. Once the child has sung the last phrase, it is her turn to make a wish and blow out the candles.

Part III: Music Memory

Preparation: About 4 weeks prior to the assessment, teach the children a new song either at group time or in their regular singing sessions. The song should be simple, repetitive, and short with a distinct melody covering a range of no more than five or six notes. Some folk songs in a minor melody, such as Bela Bartok's "The Turkey," would be good choices. The song used in the Spectrum assessment was "Up in the Air" (see Table 52, p. 175). It has accompanying arm and body motions that help children to become involved in the song and to remember the words.

Teach the song to the children in a way that feels comfortable to you. Slowing the pace, clearly enunciating, and presenting a few lines at a time are some techniques you might try. It may be helpful to sing the song first by yourself, although children can join in right away if they wish. The arm movements can be incorporated into the song from the beginning.

The children start with their arms at their sides. As they sing the first phrase, "up, up, up in the air," the children raise their arms towards the sky. In the next phrase, "little birds fly, up in the air," the children flap their arms up and down like the wings of birds. In the last two phrases, "up, up, up, up" and "little birds fly, high up in the air," the children raise their arms slowly up to the sky and then flap them up and down. Children can be challenged to stand on their tiptoes in order to reach the sky better.

To ensure that children have an opportunity to learn the song, the teaching sessions should take place over three meetings, preferably once a week for 3 consecutive weeks. One week after the last lesson, ask children individually to reproduce the song during the assessment session.

Assessment Session: After you have completed the responsive singing of "Happy Birthday," say to the child; "There's one more thing about singing I wanted to ask. Remember a song that I taught you during singing time a while ago? We did something like this." Stand up and start raising your hands. "Do you remember a song when I did this? Please sing it for me so I can remember how it goes." If this does not help the child, you can repeat the arm motion while saying (not singing) "It went 'up, up, up . . .'" As a final cue, *sing* the words "up, up, up . . ." while moving your arms and ask if the child remembers anything at all about the song or how it went, and then, "anything else?" Children may remember different aspects of the song: words, motions, or melody. If the child just offers single words such as *birds* or *fly,* you can prompt by saying, "You remember some of the words. Do you also remember how the song went?"

To close the session, ask the child what she would like to hear on the tape recorder. Rewind the tape and play either a part or all of the singing (but remember to advance the tape for the next child). Then you can chat a bit with the child and ask for help taking the candles out of the cake and getting the playdough ready for the next child. Children enjoy the process of covering up the candle holes by pinching together the playdough.

Part IV: Novel Song

A second session can be held with children who exhibited strengths in music during the first session. In a comfortable setting, tell the child: "Today I am going to teach you a new song called 'Animal Song.' I am going to sing it all the way through once. Then we are going to sing the song in small parts. I will do it first, and you can be my echo and repeat after me." Present the song as follows (see Table 53):

1. Sing the entire song once.
2. Sing each phrase four times and ask the child to echo each phrase each time.
3. Sing the song together with the child.
4. Ask the child to sing the song through on her own.

In a few weeks, hold a third session to give the child another opportunity to learn the same song. First, establish how much the child has retained from the previous session. Then, using the same teaching procedure, teach the child the song a second time. One month later, hold another session to determine how well the child is able to recall the various elements of the song. Ask the child, "Do you remember a song called 'Animal Song' that we sang together some time ago?" Provide scaffolding as needed (see Music Memory assessment).

—Scoring

To score the children's performance on the Singing Activity, follow the guidelines in Tables 54 and 55. The Favorite Song is scored informally and on the basis of overall impressions. Try to keep in mind the child's attention to rhythm and pitch as well as the song's musical challenge. Record your comments on Table 55 for Favorite Song and for Music Memory, which also is scored descriptively. Note the number and order of phrases that the child remembers, whether she reproduces the general contour of the phrases, and whether melody or text is more prominent in her recall. The level of scaffolding required also should be noted.

The Birthday Song can be scored in one of two ways. You can use Table 54 to score the song phrase by phrase. The four rhythm measures total a possible 16 points and the three pitch measures a possible 8 points. The responsive phrases are scored similarly, looking in particular at the child's ability to come in on key and her pace of delivery. Or you can use Tables 56 and 57 to record your impressions of the song as a whole. Use Table 58 to summarize the performance of each child, but ignore the column labeled "general" if you have scored the song phrase by phrase. If you do not have a sense of key, you can have someone else score the song, or you can match the fifth note and the final note of the piece (both of which are the tonic) to a tuning fork or keyboard.

If you wish to explore the strengths of musically precocious children using "Animal Song," you can score the performance informally using the following guidelines. First, you can look at the rate at which the child learns the range of musical features presented by the song. Does the child demonstrate an overall feel for the song, attending to both pitch and rhythm? Does the child include all parts of the song or does she pick up on the contour of a particular phrase and repeat it a number of times? Does she attend to the repeating elements in the song? Are the phrases in the correct order?

In the area of rhythm, you can examine whether the child demonstrates a consistent sense of the rhythmic structure of the song. Does she sing the long and short notes accurately? Is she sensitive to the length of a pause? Finally, you can analyze the child's command of pitch. Does the child observe the key change in the middle of the song? Can she reproduce the correct jump from one note to another and end up in the right place? The scoring system for "Happy Birthday" can serve as a guideline for generating appropriate scoring criteria.

—Preliminary Results: 1985–1987

In each segment of the activity, children exhibited a better command of rhythm than of pitch. The Favorite Song yielded a variety of tunes both familiar and original. One child's creation contained a strong rhythmic element: "Punch, punch, I was eating my lunch. Boom, boom, boom, boom, boom, boom." Another original song was inspired by the necklace the teacher was wearing that day: "Necklace is one of my favorite song/When I did it it's lots of fun/I just find it on and on/When it's on the necklace breaks." Many children did not produce a favorite song.

On "Happy Birthday," most children knew all of the words and demonstrated a solid grasp of the rhythm. A smaller group was sensitive to pitch distinctions, but most did not exhibit a stable sense of key. On both the full and responsive versions, a number of children confused the contours of the first and second phrases.

On the recall of "Up in the Air," most children remembered the melody. Many could recall the words or at least the "bird" theme. One child remembered the melody, but added her own text. The children's ordering of phrases was usually accurate.

The few children who stood out musically and were taught "Animal Song" remembered a surprising amount of the song. They mastered global properties such as text, rhythm, and rising and falling contours. They repeated challenging pitch values and intervals and accurately reproduced the octave jump at the beginning of the song. On the other hand, they had trouble making the key change in the middle, and their delivery did not always capture the more expressive elements in the song.

TABLE 52

Up in the Air

by Raymond Abrashkin

Up, up, up in the air,

lit - tle birds fly, up in the air,

Up, up, up, up,

lit - tle birds fly, high up in the air.

TABLE 53

Animal Song

Traditional children's verse

Music by Lyle Davidson

TABLE 54: BIRTHDAY SONG SCORING INFORMATION

There are four phrases in "Happy Birthday." The first phrase is "Happy birthday to you"; the second phrase is "Happy birthday to you"; the third phrase is "Happy birthday dear teacher"; and the fourth phrase is "Happy birthday to you." Each phrase is scored on four categories of rhythm and three categories of pitch. The scoring categories are defined below. If in doubt, give the higher score.

HAPPY BIRTHDAY TO YOU
by Mildred J. Hill and Patty S. Hill

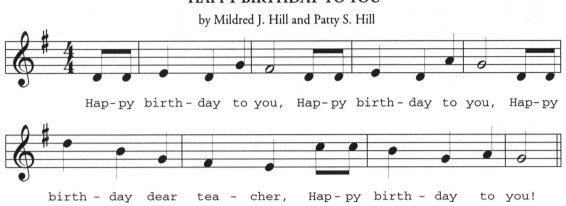

RHYTHM

1. Number of Units

   This measure refers to the number of notes that the child includes in the phrase. For example, in the first phrase of "Happy Birthday" there are six notes. Score (1) if the child produces six notes. Score (0) if she produces more or less than six notes.

2. Grouping

   This measure reflects the child's attempt to make distinctions between long and short durational patterns. Grouping is indicated by either long or short notes, pauses, and accents. For example, score (1) if the child can convey the difference in timing between the short notes in "Hap-py" versus the longer lasting notes in "you." Score (0) if no distinction is apparent where changes in pattern take place.

3. Pulse

This measure focuses on the child's ability to keep a regular underlying unit of time. Credit is given even if the tempo is not exactly that of "Happy Birthday," as long as the tempo is regular and consistent all the way through the phrase. It might be helpful to tap the beat that the child starts with, to make it easier to establish if that tempo is maintained. Score (0) if the child alternates among several different units of time.

4. Clarity

Clarity refers to the ability to project an accurate sense of rhythm. Credit is given if the child attacks notes on the appropriate beat. Mark (0) if she appears vague about the rhythm or makes up her own rhythm as she goes along.

PITCH

1. Contour

Contour refers to the up and down motion of the melody. In this category the child gets a score of (1) if the general direction of the phrase is appropriate (even if the individual notes are not). In the first phrase of "Happy Birthday" the movement is from lower to higher. Give the child (1) if she adheres to this pitch pattern and score (0) if she moves in the opposite direction, that is from higher to lower.

2. <u>Key</u>

This measure assesses the child's ability to remain in the same key from phrase to phrase. It might be helpful to sing along with the child as you score this particular category in order to distinguish if the child's later phrases remain in the same key in which she began. Give the child a score of (1) if she remains in the same key from one phrase to the next. Score (0) if she drifts from one key into another from one phrase to the next.

3. <u>Interval</u>

This measure assesses the child's ability to make a jump from one note to another and end up in the right place, not higher and not lower. In the first phrase of "Happy Birthday," such a jump occurs between "day" and "to." In the second phrase, the jump again occurs between "day" and "to." In the third phrase, the greatest leap happens between "happy" and "birth," and finally in the fourth phrase between "birth" and "day." Score (1) if the child can jump the correct distances in all the intervals. Score (0) if she ends up higher or lower in one or more intervals.

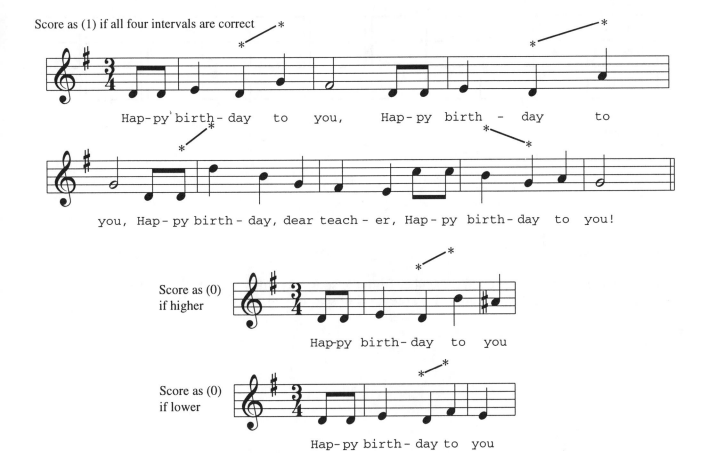

TABLE 55: SINGING ACTIVITY OBSERVATION SHEET

Child _____ Age _____ Date _____ Observer _____

I. Favorite Song:

Song Chosen:_____

Comments: (Note attention to rhythm, pitch, level of musical challenge, etc.)

II. Birthday Song:

	Number of Units	Grouping	Pulse	Clarity	Rhythm Subtotal	Contour	Key	Interval	Pitch Subtotal	TOTAL
Phrase 1							/////	/////		
Phrase 2								/////		
Phrase 3								/////		
Phrase 4										

Responsive Singing

Phrase 2								/////		
Phrase 4										
TOTAL										

Comments:

III. Music Memory:

Comments: (What does the child remember from the song? Words? Tune? Number and order of phrases? Contour? Also note level of scaffolding.)

TABLE 56: ALTERNATE SCORING OF BIRTHDAY SONG

This alternate scoring system is a less detailed method of capturing a child's performance in the Birthday Song exercise. The observation sheet (Table 57) is completed immediately after the child has finished the singing task; the observer/scorer records her general sense of the child's singing ability based on the performance as a whole, and records any incidental information that surfaces during the activity.

The categories of skill assessed in the alternate scoring system are the same as those analyzed in Table 54. In addition, the alternate version includes two other scoring categories: (a) a general sense of the child's performance, and (b) expressiveness. Because the alternate scoring system does not require analysis of each individual phrase in the song, the criteria for the categories of skill are slightly different from those listed in Table 54. The following is a list of the categories of skill and their definitions as they are used in the alternate scoring system.

RHYTHM

1. *Number of Units:* The number of notes that the child includes in the song. Observer should listen for omission of notes in song; it is unnecessary to record where notes are omitted.

2. *Grouping:* Distinction between long and short durational patterns. Grouping is indicated by either long and short notes or pauses and accents. For example, a distinction should be clear between the short notes in *ha-ppy* versus the longer lasting note in *you*. Observer should listen for overall consistency of grouping in child's singing.

3. *Pulse:* The underlying unit of time or tempo. Credit should be given even if the tempo is not *exactly* that of the Birthday Song, as long as child maintains a regular and consistent tempo throughout song.

4. *Clarity:* An accurate performance of the song's rhythm. Credit is given if the child attacks notes on the appropriate beat.

PITCH

1. *Contour:* The up-and-down motion of the melody. Observer should listen for reproduction of general contour of the phrases in the child's singing.

2. *Distinction Between Phrases:* A distinguishable difference between phrases. For example, in "Happy Birthday" there is a slight difference between the first and second phrases—children often sing these two phrases identically. Observer should listen for distinction of phrases in child's singing.

3. *Interval:* The jump from one note to another, ending up in the right place—not higher and not lower. For example, in the first and second phrases of "Happy Birthday" such a jump occurs between *day* and *to*; in the fourth phrase, a jump occurs between *birth* and *day*. The greatest leap in the song occurs in the third phrase between *happy* and *birth*. Observer should listen for a general sense of child's ability to leap successfully from one note to the next; also, observer should record if the child has difficulty with all interval leaps in the song or only with the widest interval in the third phrase.

4. *Proper Pitch (in Tune):* Singing the correct notes. Observer should score the child on whether she sings most of the song in tune.

GENERAL MUSICAL ABILITY

1. *Exceptional Production:* Entire song is both in tune and rhythmically correct.

2. *Expressiveness:* Song is rendered in a manner that reflects mood or feeling. Observer should listen for accented words and lowering or raising of voice for emphasis.

TABLE 57: ALTERNATE BIRTHDAY SONG OBSERVATION SHEET

Child _____   Age _____   Observer _____

Song _____   Date _____

Yes = 2 points
No   = 0 points
N/A = if singing is inaudible or child does not participate in activity

	Yes	No	Score
1. RHYTHM			
Child includes the correct number of notes (number of units)	____	____	____
Child makes a distinction between long and short notes (grouping)	____	____	____
Child keeps a regular and consistent tempo throughout song (pulse)	____	____	____
Child sings notes on appropriate beat (clarity)	____	____	____
Rhythm Subtotal			____
2. PITCH			
Child's general direction of phrases is appropriate (contour)	____	____	____
Child makes a distinction between the different phrases of the song	____	____	____
Child is able consistently to jump from one note to another and end up in the right place (interval)	____	____	____
Child sings most of the song in tune	____	____	____
Pitch Subtotal			____
3. GENERAL			
Child sings the song exceptionally well, is in tune and rhythmically correct	____	____	____
Child is expressive; accenting words, reflecting a mood in her rendition, or both	____	____	____
General Subtotal			____
TOTAL			____

COMMENTS:

TABLE 58: ALTERNATE BIRTHDAY SONG SUMMARY SHEET

Child (age)	RHYTHM					PITCH					GENERAL			TOTAL
	Number of Units Grouping	Pulse	Clarity	Sub-total		Contour	Distinct Phrases	Interval	In Tune	Sub-total	Exceptional	Expressive	Sub-total	

MUSIC PERCEPTION ACTIVITY

—Purpose and Activity Description

The purpose of the Music Perception Activity is to assess a child's ability to make musical discriminations. Because singing is not necessarily an accurate indicator of a child's ability to discriminate pitch (for example, she may be able to perceive she is off key without being able to produce the correct notes), this activity provides an important supplement to children's performances in the production activity.

The perception activity is divided into five parts: *Song Recognition* (recognizing excerpts from well-known tunes); *Error Recognition* (identifying incorrect versions of a familiar tune); *Play and Match* (matching pitches using a set of three Montessori bells); *Listen and Match* (discriminating pitches on the bells heard from behind a screen); and *Free Play* (free play on the bells). The activity uses Montessori bells because the bells look identical, but produce different tones. Thus, with the usual visual cues absent, children are forced to rely solely on auditory discrimination when trying to match pitches. The bells also provide children with a performance-based mode of response, which may be the most effective way of gaining access to children's musical sensitivities (Webster & Schlentrich, 1982).

A review of the literature suggests that problems in terminology might confound determination of a child's conceptual understanding of music. Children are able to discriminate pitches before they can describe what they hear (Flowers, 1985). Young children's difficulty in using the terminology of *high/low* and *up/down* has been well documented. Although they do understand the difference between *loud* and *soft*, and *fast* and *slow*, and can apply these words correctly to music, children describe pitch differences more easily and consistently in terms of *light/dark*, *small/big*, and *light/heavy* than *high/low*. In order to avoid such confounding terminology, we ask children in the Spectrum activity to identify pitches on the Montessori bells as *same* or *different*.

In the first part of the activity (Song Recognition), it is important to choose tunes that are equally familiar to all of the children. Teachers might want to use the song selected for the Music Memory part of the Singing Activity, or new songs that have been taught to the children during class time or used in the creative movement sessions.

In Error Recognition, the song used must be one that is clearly familiar to children of this age group. We used "Row, Row, Row Your Boat" in the 1987–1988 Spectrum class because it is a well-known song in Western culture (every child in the class was able to identify it correctly). It also has clear scalar and triad features that make it simple enough for young children to learn, although it does entail some musical complexity.

When we presented the three variations of the song, we progressed from the most to the least salient errors. See Table 60 (p. 191) for one possible version of this task. The first variation changes the last note in the first measure from an E to an E-flat, shifting the mode of the piece from major to minor. In the second variation, the wide intervals in the third measure are compressed by playing a descending diatonic scale. Finally, the third variation contains the most subtle error: The second measure begins by shifting to an F instead of an E, thereby creating interval distortion within the key.

In the two pitch-matching sections, the child is presented with a set of bells and asked whether pitches sound the same or different. In general, the sets of pitches are ordered from easiest to most difficult to perceive. To avoid the potentially confounding variables of memory or organizational ability, children never have more than three bells from which to choose. In Listen and Match, the teacher's bells are hidden behind a screen so that the child can focus solely on the sounds being produced.

In Free Play, the child is encouraged to play freely with the bells. This play allows the adult to gather some descriptive information about the child's ways of approaching the task and her interest in it, but it is not formally scored. Like the Assembly Activity, this activity also involves a fine motor component in striking the bells. Children differ both in terms of how delicately they hit the bell and whether they can position the mallet to achieve a clear tone.

—Materials and Set-Up

The materials for this activity include a set of Montessori bells, two identical mallets, a cardboard screen, two specially prepared music tapes, two tape recorders (you may wish to tape-record the activity so that you can refer back when scoring children's responses), and a tray. If the bell stands are different colors, we recommend sanding them down and painting them the same color to eliminate any visual cues. Or, if the bells are too expensive, you can adapt the activity and use cheaper materials such as xylophones or bottles filled with different amounts of water. Just make sure that the visual cues are hidden, for example, by a cardboard screen.

Prepare the music tapes in advance, preferably by playing the tunes on the piano. The tape for Song Recognition consists of the first four phrases of three songs that are very familiar to the children, with a short pause in between each phrase. The tape for Error Recognition consists of correct and incorrect versions of a familiar song, with short pauses between the versions (see Table 60). The tape should be recorded as follows:

1. Correct version
2. Incorrect version 1
3. Incorrect version 2
4. Correct version
5. Incorrect version 3

Conduct the assessment in a relatively secluded area of the classroom both to avoid distracting other children, and to prevent other children from overhearing their classmates identify the tunes in Song Recognition.

—Procedure and Script

At group time, introduce the activity as follows: "Today we have a new music game in the classroom. Children can play with some special bells that sound like this. [*Play three bells and explain that they must be treated with care.*] One child at a time will have a turn to play with _____ [*adult's name*]."

Song Recognition

Although you will not need the bells right away, the session will proceed more smoothly if you set them up before the child arrives. Arrange the bells on a tray next to you in three rows as follows:

C D E F G
C D E F G
A A B B C'

(C' is the C above middle C.) Cover the bells with a cloth so that they will not distract children during the first part of the activity.

To begin the session, ask the child to sit in front of you. Tell her, "There are two parts in the game that we are going to play. First, there's a listening part and then there's a playing part. For the first part, I am going to play a song, and I want you to tell me if you know what

song it is. Listen very carefully, and tell me what the song is as soon as you know it." Play the first phrase of Melody 1 on your prerecorded tape. Stop the tape and ask the child if she knows what the song is. Make a note if the child recognizes the song immediately, even before you ask for her answer. Mark on the score sheet (Table 59) the phrase at which the child identifies the tune. If she does not know what it is, play the second phrase, stop the tape, and ask again. If she is still unable to identify the tune, rewind the tape and play the first two phrases again. If she cannot identify the tune at this point, play the last two phrases. If the child cannot identify the song after all four phrases have been played, tell her what it is and proceed to the next song. Whenever the child makes an identification, whether or not it is correct, record her response and move on to the next melody. Repeat this procedure with the next two songs.

Error Recognition

To introduce the next exercise, say, "Now the tape recorder is going to play another song and I want you to tell me what song it is." Play the first correct version of "Row, Row, Row Your Boat." If the child does not recognize the song, rewind the tape and play it again. If the child still does not identify the song, sing the words for her. If she is not familiar with the song, do not continue with this part of the activity. If she makes the correct identification, say, "Let's see how well you know this song. I am going to play it a few times and I want you to listen very carefully, because *sometimes there may be something that sounds wrong in the song.* If you hear something that sounds wrong or different in the song, tell me as soon as you hear it. Now, remember to listen very carefully to the *whole* song, because there may be something wrong at the beginning *or* at the end."

After each version, ask the child, "How did that sound? Was there anything wrong or was it OK?" Be careful to use the same phrasing after each version to avoid giving the child cues about the right answer. Some children immediately will recognize a tune as incorrect. If a child gets distracted while listening to the tape, or says that she doesn't know, replay the version a second time and record it on the score sheet. If she still does not know, do not give her credit for that version. Some children will simply say either that all of the versions are correct, or that all are incorrect. Note on the score sheet whether you think the child seems to be using this strategy. Also, notice how quickly the child is able to identify the wrong notes. Always play through the entire melody regardless of when the child makes her identification.

Play and Match

Begin this part of the activity by giving the child a set of five bells arranged in a scale from C to G, from the child's left to right. Tell her, "Here are some bells that we are going to use to play a game. These bells are special because they *look the same*, but they *sound different*. Let's try playing them." Show the child how to produce the clearest sound by lightly hitting the widest part of the bell. Also ask the child what the bells sound like to her.

To introduce the exercise, give these instructions: "Now we are going to play a game with the bells. I am going to give you one bell. You need to find another bell that sounds just like it." Give the child a mallet and a D bell. "This bell is going to be your bell. Here are two other bells (C' and D), and I want you to tell me which one of these bells sounds just like your bell does." Point to each bell as you refer to them. Play the child's bell

first. Then say, "Does *this* bell sound like your bell [*play C' bell*] or does *this* bell [*play second D bell*] sound like your bell?" If the child does not know which two are the matching bells, tell her which two you think sound alike.

Now, put the three bells back on the tray, and give the child a C bell. Place an F and a C bell in front of her bell and ask her, "Which one of these bells sounds like your bell?" Remind the child always to play her bell first, and then each of the other two. If the child only plays one of the new bells, suggest that she also play the second bell: "Let's check the other bell to make sure." If the child gets distracted by other activities in the classroom or does not seem to be listening to what she is doing, suggest that she play the bells one more time. In general, let the child play the bells as much as she needs to try to find the matching bell. Repeat this procedure for the other three sets of bells. Use the following order for the matches:

(To model) Match D with D or C' (not scored)
1. Match C with C or F (interval of fourth)
2. Match F with F or G (interval of second)
3. Match D with D or A (interval of fifth)
4. Match A with A or C' (interval of third)

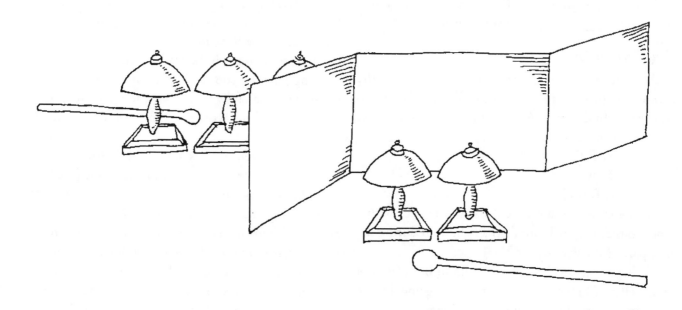

Listen and Match

Put the bells back on the tray and place the small screen between you and the child so that she cannot see your bells. Give the child a D, G, and C' bell (in that order) and place a G and D bell behind the screen. Say, "Now I am going to play a bell behind the screen, and I want you to play your bells like this [*lightly tap each bell*] to find which one of your bells sounds just like the one I am going to play." Play the G bell once. Try to play your bell with the same amount of force each time so that the child does not focus on loudness as a variable.

Each time the child hits one of her bells, play the target bell again. Encourage the child to try all three, rather than stopping after the first or second bell. Next play the D bell, and ask the child to tell you which one of her bells sounds like the one you just played.

Now remove the G and C' bells and replace them with the C and E bells arranged in front of her as D, E, C. Replace your bells with a C and E. Repeat the above procedure, first with the E bell and then with the C bell.

It is important to keep in mind that children will interpret the word *same* differently. For example, children might be listening to how hard the bell is struck or looking at your stroke. Some children might also focus on the timbre (the bells all "sound like bells" or "they all sound sweet"). There is no way to ensure that a child is listening to the tone alone, but you may want to ask children, "In what way do the bells sound the 'same?'" This knowledge may help clue you in to the reasons for some of the child's inaccurate responses.

Free Play

Add the F and G bells to the child's set of three, and order them in a scale from C to G. Tell the child, "Now you can play whatever you like on the bells. You can try to play a song like this [*play the first four phrases or so of "Mary Had A Little Lamb"*] or you can move them around. Although this part of the activity is not scored, observe and record how the child plays with the bells. Does she try to play a recognizable song or create her own melody? Note whether she includes a beginning, an end to her song, or both. Also, notice whether she experiments with tones of varying loudness. Does she play each bell only once or many times? Does she linger on different bells? Record any spontaneous comments about how the bells sound, as well as the child's level of interest.

—Scoring

Use Table 59 to keep track of correct and incorrect answers as you conduct the activity, but award the correct number of points for each section later. Transfer the scores to the summary sheet in Table 61 and mark with an asterisk if you have important comments that cannot fit on the table. If you taped the activity, use the tapes as a back-up when scoring.

—Preliminary Results: 1987–1988

One of the 18 children who participated in this activity earned 48 points, a perfect score. Three children received scores of 44 points or more. These children made their identifications accurately and quickly. The majority of the class fell within the range of 25 to 35 points.

Song Recognition produced a diversity of responses: Most children were able to identify at least one tune during the first or second phrase, and approximately half of the children identified all three tunes by the fourth phrase. Some children were able to identify the tunes almost immediately, after only the first few notes were played.

The Error Recognition task was easier for children to complete. One child was even able to distinguish among the degrees of error, describing the different variations as "a little the same," "a lot different," and "a very lot different." Only two children were unable to identify any of the versions correctly.

Most of the children were able with relative ease to match pitches on Play and Match. Again, only two children were unable to match more than one pair of pitches. Listen and Match proved more difficult, probably because of the problem-solving aspect of figuring out how to compare the sounds of more than two bells. One child was unable to differentiate any of the tones, maintaining that all of the bells sounded the same. Two children who were especially sensitive to the volume at which the bells were played also commented on the differences in tone produced by the plastic and wooden mallets.

Many children were intrigued by the appearance of the bells. (In fact, this activity also can shed light on a child's approach to scientific reasoning.) One boy initiated a discussion about what could account for the differences in tone when all the bells looked identical. He speculated that the bells might be made out of different metals. He was also interested in how the bells produced their sounds: he noticed that the bells "shook" when you hit them, and that when he stopped the shaking with his finger, the sound stopped. Another boy thought that the location of his hand on the mallet could produce different sounds.

During Free Play, some children attempted to play familiar tunes. Although they did not play the correct notes, they were able to maintain the correct rhythm. Whereas some children timidly touched each bell once, or played an entire tune on the same bell, others would experiment with loudness and rhythm, playing different bells a number of times and exploring various arrangements of the bells. Some children sang along with their tunes.

The Montessori bells lend themselves to a variety of uses, especially for children who are ready for further challenge. Children can be asked to create a scale, play a simple tune such as "Mary Had A Little Lamb," or complete a tune started by the adult. Of course, children also will have many creative ideas of their own.

—Further Suggestions for the Domain

Enriching the classroom musically can help you notice which children are attracted to different music materials. You can put more music into your curriculum by providing both exotic and familiar instruments (e.g., piano, Montessori bells, xylopipes, keyboard); setting up a tape recorder for listening to and recording children's songs; and playing movement and rhythm records, such as those by Ella Jenkins.

The following are some other suggestions for music activities are:

1. Look at a wordless or a simple rhyming book with the child. Make up your own song about the pictures, then ask the child to make up another one (e.g., if the book involves farm animals, you can sing about the rooster and she can sing about the lamb). Or you could suggest, "Instead of reading this book, pretend we sing it. What do you think it would sound like?"

2. Sing or play a melody with the phrases out of order. Ask the child what sounds different. Ask the child to put the song back in order.

3. Present a song and ask for variations: Children can focus on just tapping out the rhythm, or humming just the melody or general contour of the song.

4. Play a song the child knows, leaving out some notes, and ask her to fill in the missing notes.

5. Place stickers with numbers on 10 keys of the piano, and cover the other keys. Tell children they can put their names to music. They can choose any note they wish, recording the sequence by writing down the numbers. Then invite other children to come and play their names.

6. Observe children's sensitivity to contrasts in different kinds of music: fast/slow, loud/soft, high/low.

7. Take the children to a live performance or invite a performer to the classroom. Tape it if possible. Ask the children to draw, sing, reenact, or describe to you in words what they remembered or liked about the performance.

8. Teach a song such as "Hickory, Dickory, Dock" with weighted notes and pauses. Observe whether a child captures the more expressive, performance-related aspects of the song.

9. Play different kinds of music. Ask children to close their eyes and listen quietly. Then ask children to draw how the music makes them feel.

TABLE 59: MUSIC PERCEPTION OBSERVATION SHEET

Child _____   Observer_____
Age _____   Date_____

Part I. Song Recognition

Check at which point child recognizes song.

4 pts. =   recognizes song in first phrase
3 pts. =   recognizes song in second phrase
2 pts. =   recognizes song after hearing first two phrases twice
1 pt.   =   recognizes song after hearing all four phrases

Recognizes in: 1st phrase   2nd phrase   1st and 2nd phrases twice   4th phrase

Melody 1

Melody 2

Melody 3

Subtotal: [ ]

Part II. Error Recognition   **Comments:**

Place a check next to each version that child
accurately identifies as correct or incorrect (3 pts. each)

_____   Incorrect version 1
         (E-flat in first measure)

_____   Incorrect version 2
         (change in triplets in third measure)

_____   Correct version

_____   Incorrect version 3
         (mistake in second measure—starts on F instead of E)

Subtotal: [ ]

Part III. Play and Match   **Comments:**

Check if child identifies matching pair (3 pts. each)

First pair
(C, C)
Second pair
(F, F)
Third pair
(D, D)
Fourth pair
(A, A)

Subtotal: ☐

Part IV. Listen and Match   Comments:

Check if child identifies matching bell (3 pts. each)

(1) (G, G)

(2) (D, D)

(3) (E, E)

(4) (C, C)

Subtotal: ☐

TOTAL: ☐

Part V. Free Play — Comments:

(unscored)

TABLE 60: ROW, ROW, ROW YOUR BOAT
CORRECT AND INCORRECT VERSIONS

Correct Version

Variation #1

Variation #2

Correct Version

Variation #3

✳ Denotes alteration from the correct version

TABLE 61: MUSIC PERCEPTION ACTIVITY SUMMARY SHEET

* = look at Observation Sheet for additional comments

Name (age)	PART I: Song Recognition (0–4 pts./melody)			Subtotal	PART II: Error Recognition (3 pts. each)			Subtotal	PART III: Play/Match (3 pts. each)				Subtotal	PART IV: Listen/Match (3 pts. each)				Subtotal	*	TOTAL
	Melody 1	Melody 2	Melody 3		1	2	Correct Version 3		CC	FF	DD	AA		GG	DD	EE	CC			

CHAPTER 8
WORKING STYLES

—INTRODUCTION

The distinction between competence and performance has been a controversial one in cognitive-developmental research (Kogan, 1983). It is generally accepted that among adults, success requires not only ability in one's domain, but also particular approaches to work, such as concentration, dedication, or sustained effort over time. Even at the preschool level, children may demonstrate significant differences in the way they approach a task. Observing children's *working styles* can provide important information about their ability to perform in different domains and in different types of situations.

Traditionally, researchers have believed that cognitive style cuts across domains (see Messick, 1985). We wanted to determine whether approach to a challenge instead varies from one domain to the next, just as strengths and weaknesses do. We were most interested in the following two questions:

1. Do children use distinctive working styles when solving problems from different domains? If so, what are the differences in approach in the children's areas of strength and weakness?

2. Are some working styles more effective than others in particular domains or across domains?

For the purposes of the Spectrum project, we developed the construct of *working styles* to describe a child's interaction with the tasks and materials from various content areas. These working styles are intended to reflect the *process* dimension of a child's work or play, rather than the type of product that results. They address indices of affect, motivation, and interaction with materials, as well as more standard stylistic features such as tempo of work and orientation toward auditory, visual, or kinesthetic cues.

Table 62 (p. 196) lists 18 distinct stylistic features we identified as that we watched the children complete the Spectrum activities. They reflect a child's approach to various activities at a particular point in time, rather than a set of stable traits. Although we tried to use descriptors that carried neither positive nor negative connotations, some of the terms may seem more evaluative than descriptive. Table 63 presents brief definitions of the working styles. These are not intended to be definitive; rather, they represent observations of children engaged in the Spectrum activities over a 2-year period.

Our goal was to provide teachers with an accessible and straightforward means for recording their observations about a child's stylistic tendencies. These observations could in turn help teachers individualize instruction, for example by highlighting those situations or domains in which a child becomes frustrated most easily and thus might need extra help; loses interest most quickly and thus might benefit from activities that can be completed in a short time; enjoys experimenting and can express her creativity; or requires structure and specific directions to function most effectively.

—Procedure

Although most teachers already are making informal observations of children's working styles, the Working Styles Checklist (Table 62) provides a simple, easy-to-use format for accurate and consistent record-keeping. The checklist is designed as a rough-and-ready means to capture a child's working styles across activities. In the first section, it is not necessary to check one adjective in each pair. You should only check a particular style when it stands out as a distinctive characteristic of a child's approach to an activity.

Realistically, it is not always possible to record children's working styles in much detail; however, the checklist will be most informative if comments and anecdotes are included whenever possible. These comments should describe behaviors that lead you to check a particular style. For example, on the Storyboard Activity, "easily engaged" might be checked with the following comment: "Kim immediately started to tell her own story before I was able to finish my introduction." A general, descriptive phrase such as "Joe proceeded methodically and carefully through each step of the assembly task" often may capture a child's approach more fully than the descriptors listed on the checklist.

For research purposes, we filled out a checklist for every child on every activity. However, you may wish to use the checklist more selectively, either to test a hypothesis about a particular child, or simply to gather more information about a child's performance in different domains. Table 64 helps the teacher compile a portrait of a child's working styles during different activities. Record the total number of times each working style was checked in the bottom row. Researchers can use the same grid to explore how different working styles correspond to particular domains. In that case, write the number of times all the children demonstrated each working style in the designated boxes.

Before you use this assessment in the classroom, you might videotape children during different activities, and then review the tape with your colleagues. You can each fill out a checklist, and compare your observations afterwards, discussing any differences that emerge either in your definitions of the descriptors or in your interpretations of children's behavior.

—Preliminary Results: 1986–88

Based on our work with the 1986–87 and 1987–88 classes, we were able to obtain preliminary answers to our two major questions (the following information was reported originally in Krechevsky & Gardner, 1990). With regard to the domain-specificity of working styles, our results showed that for the majority of children, one or two working styles obtained across domains, but other working styles depended more on the content of the area being explored. Approximately three quarters of the 33 children included in this analysis exhibited general working styles. Even these general working styles could be influenced by the nature of the activity. For example, one child was easily engaged and confident, even in areas of weakness, as long as the task involved a performance aspect.

Not surprisingly, performances in an area of strength were typically characterized by "easily engaged," "confident," and "focused" working styles. In contrast, weak performances were characterized by "distractible," "impulsive," and "reluctant to engage" working styles. "Playful" characterized both strengths and weaknesses. Also, children were most likely to demonstrate reflectiveness and attention to detail in their areas of strength. Three of the five children who exhibited no strengths relative to their peers never reflected on their own work, and eight children only reflected on their work in areas of strength.

Five children demonstrated dramatic variation in working style from one domain to the next. One of these children found it very difficult to remain focused on most of the Spectrum and classroom activities. However, when presented with the materials for the Assembly Activity, she worked in a focused and persistent manner until she had completely taken apart and reassembled the objects. Another child exhibited confidence, attention to detail, seriousness, planning skills, and reflectiveness only in the visual arts and mathematical domains — his areas of strength.

With regard to our question about the effectiveness of working styles across domains, we found that a few working styles did appear to help performance in a broad fashion. One child, for example, worked in a serious and focused manner across domains, two styles that enabled him to complete activities at which he appeared to be struggling as well as those at which he clearly exhibited competence. Other working styles appeared to help the child's performance only in certain domains (e.g., the child's areas of strength); only in certain types of situations (e.g., open-ended vs. structured activities); or to have little correlation to performance. Surprisingly, the styles, "confident" and "shows pride in accomplishment" were not necessarily linked to successful performance. Every child did exhibit confidence in at least one activity, usually in her area of strength. However, one girl, who revealed no strengths relative to her peers, nonetheless demonstrated "pride in accomplishment" on more tasks than any other child. Another child who did not exhibit any strengths relative to her peers never showed any tentativeness, whereas all but three of the other children were "tentative" in their approach at least once. In this case, her apparent confidence may have prevented her from grappling with the more challenging aspects of the activities.

Other working styles were linked to successful performance in specific types of situations, rather than in specific domains. One boy, for example, demonstrated great experimental ability during his explorations in the classroom, constantly formulating and testing hypotheses to find out more about the world around him. But his desire to bring his own ideas to each task actually inhibited his performance on the more structured Spectrum activities. Although his ideas were often compelling, his unwillingness to attend to the task frequently caused him to perform poorly. During the Music Perception Activity, he was most interested in how the metal bells, which looked exactly the same, could produce different sounds. Instead of matching the bells by tone as instructed, he examined differences in their vibrations after hitting them with his mallet. He also invented new rules for the Dinosaur Game, and tried to fashion tools out of the parts of the two food grinders in the Assembly Activity. Because he was so interested in exploring his own ideas, he often resisted exploring the ideas of others. When he had trouble with an activity, he would become frustrated and turn to his sense of humor to distract the adult from the task at hand.

In a similar fashion, working styles that aided performance on the Spectrum activities might not aid performance in other contexts. One boy became so immersed in the materials that he required very little direction to complete the activities. Unfortunately, his intense focus on materials to the exclusion of other people — whether child or adult — could present problems for his future scholastic performance.

TABLE 62: WORKING STYLES CHECKLIST

Child _____   Observer _____

Activity _____   Date   _____

Please mark which working styles are *distinctive* during your observation. Mark only when obvious; one from each pair *need not be checked.* Please include comments and anecdotes whenever possible and write a general, overall phrase that best describes how the child approaches the activity. Star (*) any outstanding working style.

Child is   **Comments**

easily engaged in activity _____

reluctant to engage in activity _____

confident _____

tentative _____

playful _____

serious _____

focused _____

distractible _____

persistent _____

frustrated by activity _____

impulsive _____

reflective _____

apt to work slowly _____

apt to work quickly _____

conversational _____

quiet _____

---

responds to visual ___ auditory ___ kinesthetic ___ cues

demonstrates planful approach _____

brings personal strength to activity _____

finds humor in content area _____

uses materials in unexpected ways _____

shows pride in accomplishment _____

attends to detail; is observant _____

is curious about materials _____

shows concern over "correct" answer _____

focuses on interaction with adult _____

TABLE 63: DEFINITIONS OF WORKING STYLES

The following list of working styles was designed to describe the process by which the child approaches and performs Spectrum activities. No positive or negative connotations are intended by these descriptions. The styles refer to the child's relationship with the materials and activities.

EASILY ENGAGED:

Child enters activity eagerly, responsively; child attends and adapts to format and content of activity. Note if the child begins by herself, possibly even before the adult explains what the activity will be.

RELUCTANT TO ENGAGE:

Child shows resistance to structure of activity; may require coaxing or restructuring of activity format by adult; child may impose own agenda in order to deflect goals of activity.

CONFIDENT:

Child seems at ease with materials and her ability; child makes moves, offers answers or opinions readily and in a self-assured manner. Note: Confidence occasionally can be high regardless of actual success or ability in the domain.

TENTATIVE:

Child is hesitant well into activity; may seem unsure of how to use materials, even after explanation; resists offering answers or persists in seeking approval or reassurance from adult; child is wary of making "wrong" move.

(E.g., after each move child makes on the Dinosaur Game, she looks to adult for reassurance.)

PLAYFUL:

Child delights in materials or activity; child easily uses materials, frequently making spontaneous comments or playful extensions of the activity.

(E.g., child talks to the pieces of the grinder, telling them to stay on, move, etc.)

SERIOUS:

Child's approach to activity is straightforward, businesslike; child does not engage in game casually but instead approaches materials in an "all work, no play" manner; child can be serious and show enjoyment in task, materials.

FOCUSED:

Child demonstrates an intensity in the activity or in use of materials; child attends to her work despite surrounding distractions (this goes beyond straightforward interest; focus indicates an unusual attention and singularity of purpose on part of child).

DISTRACTIBLE:

Child has difficulty screening out surrounding classroom activity; child may seem to fade in and out of attending to task.

(E.g., while at storyboard, child keeps looking over at another area where her friends are playing.)

PERSISTENT:

Child sticks with activity tenaciously, responds to challenges with equanimity and continues despite difficulties; child also can be persistent without the presence of any particular difficulties.

(E.g., child keeps trying different ways to get pieces together even when it requires repeated trial and error during the Assembly Activity.)

FRUSTRATED BY ACTIVITY:

Child has difficulty getting around challenging or frustrating parts of activity; child may turn quickly to adult for solutions to problems; child may express reluctance to continue with task.

(E.g., when child is unable to keep track of the number of people getting on and off the bus during the Bus Game, she asks to leave.)

IMPULSIVE:

Child's work lacks a sense of continuity; child works so quickly that she is careless.

(E.g., during Treasure Hunt Game, child pulls tops off cups to discover treasures before making predictions.)

REFLECTIVE:

Child comments on or evaluates her work, giving it either a positive or negative review; child takes a step back from the actual process of work or play to assess how her performance matches her expectations, hopes, etc.

(E.g., after singing a song, child says, "It's all mixed up. I can't do it the right way," or "That wasn't quite right. Let me try it again.")

APT TO WORK SLOWLY:

Child takes or needs plenty of time to prepare and execute her work; child works slowly yet methodically on a given activity.

APT TO WORK QUICKLY:

Child's pace is quicker than most children's; child enters into activity immediately and moves through it.

CONVERSATIONAL:

Child chats with adult as she works on activity; initiates discussion related or unrelated to the activity (but not as an avoidance of the activity).

QUIET:

Child says very little while working, talks only when required by the activity (lack of talk is not necessarily due to discomfort or tentativeness).

RESPONDS TO VISUAL, AUDITORY, OR KINESTHETIC CUES:

Child exhibits a need or preference for entering into a task through visual stimuli (looking carefully at materials); auditory stimuli (hearing directions, music); or kinesthetic stimuli (feeling materials or using movement to assist understanding).

DEMONSTRATES PLANFUL APPROACH:

Child exhibits strategic use of materials or information; child states her objectives and then proceeds to fulfill them, frequently describing her progress.

(E.g., during the Bus Game, child makes separate rows of chips and spaces them; child systematically tests bells for pairs during Music Perception Activity; or child explains what her story will be about while setting up the storyboard.)

BRINGS PERSONAL STRENGTH TO TASK:

Child uses her own proclivities as a means of engaging in or interpreting given activity.

(E.g., child explores manual dexterity with dice, sings through numerical calculations, or transforms Bus Game into narrative task about the people who are riding the bus.)

FINDS HUMOR IN CONTENT AREA:

Child discovers a humorous element in the content area or activity; child is able to take a step back from activity as it has been defined to find a silly, ironic, or unexpected facet.

(E.g., during Storyboard Activity, child tells slapstick story with guards backing into each other, etc.; during Classroom Model Activity, child laughs and comments that "we're like giants compared to this!")

USES MATERIALS IN UNEXPECTED WAYS:

Child redefines materials and activities in quirky, novel, or imaginative ways. Note if and how unexpected use affects child's process or product.

(E.g., during Assembly Activity, child balances pieces of grinder on table or creates metaphoric descriptions of pieces such as comparing a screw to a pair of pants walking; child uses prop box as sailboat during Storyboard Activity.)

SHOWS PRIDE IN ACCOMPLISHMENT:

Child shows pleasure in her success with a material or activity.

(E.g., after child has calculated correctly throughout the Bus Game, she leaves smiling and tells classmate or teacher how well she did; child gets excited when she "breaks the code" of the Treasure Hunt Game and claps each time she finds the desired treasure.)

ATTENDS TO DETAIL; IS OBSERVANT:

Child notices subtle aspects of materials or activity.

(E.g., child comments on the stickers underneath the bells; child notes that the ladder to the dramatic play loft is missing in the classroom model.)

IS CURIOUS ABOUT MATERIALS:

Child asks many questions about what things are and how and why they were made in particular ways.

(E.g., during Storyboard Activity, child asks what cave is made out of, where the trees came from, how the arch was made.)

SHOWS CONCERN OVER "CORRECT" ANSWER:

Child often asks adult if what she is doing is right; child may ask if other children got it right; child shows pleasure when she is "correct" and displeasure when "incorrect."

FOCUSES ON INTERACTION WITH ADULT:

Child is more interested in being with the adult than with the materials; she continually seeks interaction with the adult through conversation, eye contact, sitting on adult's lap, and so on. Even when involved in the activity, she attempts to maintain some kind of interaction with the adult.

TABLE 64: WORKING STYLES SUMMARY SHEET

Child _____ Age _____ Date _____

Spectrum Activity / WORKING STYLE	Obstacle Course	Creative Movement	Storyboard	Reporting	Dinosaur Game	Bus Game	Discovery Area	Treasure Hunt	Sink and Float	Assembly Activity	Classroom Model	Peer Interaction	Art	Singing	Music Perception	Total
Easily engaged in activity																
Reluctant to engage in activity																
Confident																
Tentative																
Playful																
Serious																
Focused																
Distractible																
Persistent																
Frustrated by task																
Impulsive																
Reflective																
Works slowly																
Works quickly																
Conversational																
Quiet																
Responds to visual cues																
Responds to auditory cues																
Responds to kinesthetic cues																
Planful																
Brings personal strength																
Humor																
Uses materials in unexpected ways																
Pride in accomplishment																
Attends to detail																
Curious about materials																
Concern with "correct" answer																
Interaction with adult																

REFERENCES

Adams, M. L. (1993). *Empirical investigation of domain-specific theories of pre-school children's cognitive abilities.* Unpublished doctoral dissertation. Tufts University, Medford, MA.

Bamberger, J. (1991). *The mind behind the musical ear.* Cambridge: Harvard University Press.

Blacking, J. (1974). *How musical is man?* Seattle: University of Washington Press.

Britton, J. (1982). Spectator role and the beginnings of writing. In M. Nystrand (Ed.), *What writers know* (pp. 149–169). New York: Academic Press.

Case, R. (1985). *Intellectual development: Birth to adulthood.* Orlando: Academic Press.

Chen, J. Q., & Feinburg, S. (1990). *Spectrum field inventory: Visual arts scoring criteria.* Unpublished scoring system.

Chick, Chick, Chick. (1975). Los Angeles: Churchill Films.

Consuegra, G. (1986). Identifying the gifted in science and mathematics. *School Science and Mathematics, 82,* 183–188.

Davidson, L., McKernon, K., & Gardner, H. (1981). The acquisition of song: A developmental approach. *Documentary report of the Ann Arbor symposium: Application of psychology to the teaching and learning of music.* Reston, VA: Music Educators National Conference.

Davidson, L., & Scripp, L. (1991). Surveying the coordinates of cognitive skills in music. In R. Colwell (Ed.), *Handbook of research on music teaching and learning* (pp. 392–413). New York: Schirmer.

Davidson, L., & Scripp, L. (1994). Conditions of musical giftedness in the pre- and elementary school years. In R. F. Subotnik & K. D. Arnold (Eds.), *Beyond Terman: Longitudinal studies in contemporary gifted education* (pp. 155–185). Norwood, NJ: Ablex.

Davidson, L., & Torff, B. (1993). Situated cognition in music. *World of Music, 34*(3),120–139.

Deutsch, D. (Ed.). (1983). *Psychology of music.* New York: Academic Press.

Dowling, W., & Harwood, D. (1986). *Music cognition.* New York: Academic Press.

Elementary Science Study Unit. (1986). *Sink or float.* Hudson, NH: Delta Education.

Erikson, E. H. (1963). *Childhood and society.* New York: Norton.

Feinburg, S. G. (1987, Fall). Children's awareness of two aspects of competence in drawing: Level of representation and level of spatial integration. *Visual Arts Research, 13,* 80–93.

Feinburg, S. G. (1988). *Criteria for scoring in the visual arts.* Unpublished writing consultation for Project Spectrum.

Feldman, D. H. (1980). *Beyond universals in cognitive development.* Norwood, NJ: Ablex.

Feldman, D. H. (1985). The concept of nonuniversal developmental domains: Implications for artistic development. *Visual Arts Research, 11,* 82–89.

Feldman, D. H. (1986). How development works. In I. Levin (Ed.), *Stage and structure: Reopening the debate* (pp. 284–306). Norwood, NJ: Ablex.

Feldman, D. H. (1987). Developmental psychology and art education: Two fields at the crossroads. *Journal of Aesthetic Education, 21,* 243–259.

Feldman, D. H. (1994). *Beyond universals in cognitive development* (2nd ed.). Norwood, NJ: Ablex.

Flowers, P. J. (1985). Which note is lighter? *Music Education Journal, 71(8),* 44–76.

Folio, M., & Fewell, R. (1974). *Peabody developmental motor scales and activity cards.* Allen, TX: DLM Teaching Resources.

Gallahue, D. L. (1982). *Developmental movement experiences for children.* New York: Wiley.

Gardner, H. (1980). *Artful scribbles: The significance of children's drawings.* New York: Basic Books.

Gardner, H. (1983). *Frames of mind: The theory of multiple intelligences.* New York: Basic Books.

Gardner, H. (1987a). Symposium on the theory of multiple intelligences. In D. M. Perkins, J. Lochhead, & J. C. Bishop (Eds.), *Thinking: The second international conference* (pp. 77–101). Hillsdale, NJ: Erlbaum.

Gardner, H. (1987b). Beyond the IQ: Education and human development. *Harvard Educational Review, 57*(2), 187–193.

Gardner, H. (1990). *Art education and human development.* Los Angeles: Getty Center for Education in the Arts.

Gardner, H. (1993). *Multiple intelligences: The theory in practice.* New York: Basic Books.

Gardner, H. (1998). Are there additional intelligences? In Jeff Kane (Ed.), *Education, information, and transformation.* Englewood, NJ: Prentice Hall.

Gardner, H., & Hatch, T. (1989). Multiple intelligences go to school: Educational implications of the theory of multiple intelligences. *Educational Researcher, 18*(8), 4–10.

Gelman, R., & Gallistel, C.R. (1986). *The child's understanding of number.* Cambridge: Harvard University Press.

Ginsburg, H., & Opper, S. (1979). *Piaget's theory of intellectual development: An introduction* (2nd ed.). Englewood Cliffs, NJ: Prentice Hall.

Glazer, T. (1983). *Music for ones and twos: Songs and games for the very young child.* New York: Doubleday.

Goodman, N. (1968). *Languages of art.* Indianapolis: Bobbs-Merrill.

Goodman, N. (1988). *Reconceptions in philosophy and other arts and sciences* (2nd ed.). London: Routledge.

Haines, J., Ames, L. B., & Gillespie, C. (1980). *Gesell preschool test.* Flemington, NJ: Programs for Education.

Hargreaves, D. (1986). *The developmental psychology of music.* Cambridge: Cambridge University Press.

Harris, D. B. (1963). *Children's drawings as measures of intellectual maturity: A revision and extension of the Goodenough Draw-a-Man Test.* New York: Harcourt, Brace & World.

Heath, S. B. (1982). What no bedtime story means: Narrative skills at home and school. *Language in Society, II,* 49–76.

Hughes, M. (1981). Can preschool children add and subtract? *Educational Psychology, 3,* 207–219.

Kellogg, R. (1969). *Analyzing children's art.* Palo Alto, CA: National Press Books.

Kogan, N. (1983). Stylistic variation in childhood and adolescence: Creativity, metaphor, and cognitive style. In P. H. Mussen (Ed.), *Handbook of child psychology* (4th ed.) (pp. 630–706). New York: John Wiley.

Krechevsky, M., & Gardner, H. (1990). The emergence and nurturance of multiple intelligences: The Project Spectrum approach. In M. J. A. Howe (Ed.), *Encouraging the development of exceptional skills and talents* (pp. 222–245). Leicester,UK: British Psychological Society.

Laban, R. (1960). *The mastery of movement* (2nd ed.). London: MacDonald & Evans.

Lowenfeld, V., & Brittain, W. (1982). *Creative and mental growth* (7th ed.). New York: Macmillan.

McCarthy, D. A. (1972). *McCarthy's scales of children's abilities.* New York: Psychological Corporation.

McGraw-Hill. (1968). *Elementary science study: Light and shadows.* St. Louis: Author.

Messick, S. (1985). Structural relationships across cognition, personality, and style. In R. E. Snow & M. J. Farr (Eds.), *Aptitude, learning, and instruction: Vol. 3. Cognitive and affective process analysis* (pp. 35–75). Hillsdale, NJ: Erlbaum.

Mukarovsky, J. (1964). Standard language and poetic language. In P. L. Garvin (Ed.), *A Prague school reader on esthetics, literary structure, and style* (pp. 19–35). Washington, DC: Georgetown University Press.

Nelson, K. E. (1973). Structure and strategy in learning to talk. *Monographs of the Society for Research in Child Development, 38* (2, Ser. No. 149).

Nelson, K. E. (1975). Individual differences in early semantic and syntax development. In D. Aaronson & R. W. Rieber (Eds.), *Annals of the New York Academy of Science, 263*, 132–139.

Olson, D. (1977). From utterance to text: The basis of language in speech and writing. *Harvard Educational Review, 47*, 257–82.

Piaget, J. (1952). *The child's conception of number.* New York: Humanities Press.

Pitcher, E. V., Feinburg, S.G., & Alexander, D. A. (1989). *Helping young children learn* (5th ed.). Columbus, OH: Merrill.

Serafine, M. (1988). *Music as cognition.* New York: Columbia University Press.

Shatz, M., & Gelman, R. (1973). The development of communication skills: Modifications in the speech of young children as a function of listener. *Monographs of the Society for Research in Child Development, 38* (5, Ser. No. 152).

Shuter-Dyson, R., & Gabriel, C. (1981). *The psychology of musical ability* (2nd ed.). London & New York: Methuen.

Sloboda, J. (1985). *The musical mind.* Oxford: Clarendon Press.

Sloboda, J. (Ed.) (1988). *Generative processes in music.* Oxford: Clarendon Press.

Snow, C. (1991). The theoretical basis of the home-school study of language and literacy development. *Journal of Research in Childhood Education, 6*, 5–10.

Strauss, M. (1978). *Understanding children's drawings: The path to manhood.* (ERIC Document Reproduction Service No. ED 250 061)

Vygotsky, L. S. (1978). *Mind in society.* Cambridge: Harvard University Press.

Walters, J. (1982). *The origins of counting in children.* Unpublished doctoral dissertation. Harvard Graduate School of Education, Cambridge, MA.

Webster, P .R., & Schlentrich, K. (1982). Discrimination of pitch direction by preschool children with verbal and nonverbal tasks. *Journal of Research in Music Education, 30*, 151–161.

Wechsler, D. (1967). *Wechsler Preschool and Primary Scale of Intelligence.* New York: Psychological Corporation.

Wertsch, J.V. (1985). *Vygotsky and the social formation of mind.* Cambridge: Harvard University Press.

Williams, R. A., Rockwell, R.E., & Sherwood, E.A. (1987). *Mudpies to magnets: A preschool science curriculum.* Mt. Rainier, MD: Gryphon House.

Winner, E. (1982). *Invented worlds: The psychology of the arts.* Cambridge: Harvard University Press.

Winner, E., & Pariser, D. (1985, December). Giftedness in the visual arts. Social Science Research Council, *Items, 39*, 4, 65–69.

Wolf, D. (1985). Ways of telling: Text repertoires in elementary school children. *Journal of Education, 167*(1), 71–87.

Wolf, D., & Hicks, D. (1989). The voices within narratives: The development of intertextuality in young children's stories. *Discourse Processes, 12*(3), 329–351.

APPENDIXES

Appendix A.   Spectrum Parent Questionnaire

Appendix B.   Sample Calendar for Spectrum Class

Appendix C.   Sample Spectrum Profiles

Appendix D.   Sample Parent Letter

Appendix E.   Spectrum Profile Parent Response Form

Appendix F.   Description of Spectrum Activities

Appendix G.   Project Spectrum Parent Activities Manual

Appendix H.   Related Articles

Appendix I.   Other Materials Available From Project Spectrum

Appendix J.   Spectrum Network

Appendix K.   Handbook Evaluation Form

APPENDIX A: SPECTRUM PARENT QUESTIONNAIRE

Child's name: _____   Date: _____

Name of parent(s)
completing this form: _____

We are interested in learning about the kind of abilities and interests your child demonstrates at home, because they may or may not surface in school or during the Spectrum activities. Please take a few minutes to answer the following questions.

1. List the two general areas in which your child shows the most *ability*. Please select from:
> Language
> Logic and Mathematics
> Spatial Understanding (this includes the visual arts, construction, and geography)
> Music
> Interpersonal Understanding (this includes interactions with and knowledge of others)
> Intrapersonal Understanding (this includes a knowledge of one's own abilities and a strong awareness of personal interests, likes, and dislikes)

Why did you pick those two areas?

If possible, please provide specific examples of occasions when your child uses those ability.

2. From the same group of general areas, list one or two in which your child shows the least ability.

Why did you pick this (these) area(s)? Where appropriate, please provide examples.

3. List up to three activities in which your child shows the most *interest*. Number them only if you feel there is a clear difference in the amount of interest that your child shows in each activity. These may or may not be activities in which your child has a strong ability.

4. Are there particular activities or issues that your child often talks about after school? What does your child say?

5. Has there been a particular event or curricular subject that has especially excited your child?

6. Are there particular activities or subjects that your child has especially disliked or avoided?

7. Are there any events outside of school that may have influenced your child's school experience?

8. What things do you know about your child that we might never see in school?

9. In which areas would you like to see your child improve the most?

APPENDIX B: SAMPLE CALENDAR FOR SPECTRUM CLASS

Month	Domain	Assessment	Related Activities	Additional Information
September	Art Science		Begin art portfolios for each child Introduce Discovery Area (ongoing)	
October	Math Movement	Dinosaur Game (7–8 days)	Leave Dinosaur Game in classroom Introduce weekly Creative Movement sessions (ongoing)	
	Science	Assembly Activity (7–8 days)	Introduce art portfolios for each child	
November	Art Language	Art Activity 1 (animal) Storyboard Activity (7–8 days)	Introduce storytelling Leave Storyboard in classroom Begin Weekend News (ongoing)	
	Music	Teach "Up in Air…" (3 weeks)		Mail parent questionnaires
December	Art Music Social	Art Activity 2 (person) Singing Activity		Fill out Peer Interaction Checklist
January	Language Art	Reporter Activities (movie, 8 days) Art Activity 3 (imaginary animal)	Discuss "reporter" role	Review art portfolios
February	Science Music Social	Treasure Hunt Game (5–6 days) Classroom Model (7–8 days)	Introduce Montessori bells Introduce Classroom Model	Take photos for Classroom Model Fill out Social Map
March	Music	Music Perception Activity (7–8 days)	Leave Classroom Model in classroom	
	Social Art Math	Art Activity 4 (sculpture) Bus Game (Session 1) (5–6 days)		
April	Math Science Movement	Bus Game (Session 2) (7–8 days) Sink and Float (7–8 days) Obstacle Course (outdoors) (5–6 days)	Leave Bus Game in classroom	Fill out Peer Interaction Checklist
May	Social Art			Review art portfolios Spectrum Profiles: Write summary profiles for each child

APPENDIX C: SAMPLE SPECTRUM PROFILES

Spectrum Profile: Cathy

This spring marks the end of Cathy's second year of involvement with Project Spectrum. She has exhibited an unusual competence with and understanding of mechanical objects and an emerging strength in the visual arts.

Cathy took a particularly planful and focused approach to an activity that involved taking apart and reassembling two small food grinders. Cathy's interest and ability in this area were evident last year as well as this year. She displayed excellent fine motor skills and used a trial-and-error approach to help her complete the task. She was able to reflect on the work she was doing and on a number of occasions corrected mistakes she had made without any help or suggestion from an adult. In addition, Cathy shows a great deal of interest and ability in doing puzzles and working with assorted small manipulatives.

Cathy's work in the visual arts has changed considerably since the beginning of the year. Most noticeable has been her increased ability to draw representationally. She draws a variety of objects, people and scenes — all of which are far more detailed and proportioned than they were earlier in the year. Her drawings and paintings also exhibit more of an awareness of composition. Figures are drawn in relation to one another and to the page as a whole. Cathy's artwork also shows a great sensitivity to color. She uses colors deliberately for the purposes of design and representation, and frequently experiments with mixing her own colors for special paintings. Based on the review of her portfolio at the end of the year and her involvement in art activities in the classroom, we feel that Cathy might enjoy the opportunity to explore a variety of visual arts materials. A list of suggested materials is included in the Parent Activities Manual.

Cathy has also demonstrated some skill in number-related activities. For example, while playing the Dinosaur Game she exhibited solid counting skills. She understood the one-to-one correspondence between what was on the die and the number of spaces she could move her game piece. Her ability in this area has improved significantly since last year. While playing the Bus Game, a number activity centered on number calculations, Cathy was asked, "If there are four people on the bus, how many hands will be on the bus?" She correctly answered, "Eight." When asked, "How many hands will be on the bus if one more person gets on?" she quickly answered, "10." She was the only child in the group able to make this calculation mentally.

Cathy enjoyed the storytelling activity both this year and last year. She actively manipulated props on the storyboard and told a lively story about a king and his treasures. Informal observations of Cathy in the classroom also attest to her interest in inventing stories. She frequently plays in the dramatic play area assuming many different character roles and creating different situations in which she and other children can become involved. Cathy might enjoy more opportunities to create stories and participate in dramatic play. Children's plays and drama groups may be of interest to her as well.

During other Spectrum activities, Cathy has been less willing to participate and focus on the task at hand. For example, she has resisted participating in creative movement although this was one of her areas of interest last year. In general, Cathy is able to work seriously and effectively on activities of interest to her but tends to be less willing to engage when an activity is of less interest. Because of this, her level of ability in certain areas has been difficult to determine.

Cathy has had a playful and energetic approach to the Spectrum activities that she has become involved with. She enjoyed the one-to-one interaction with Spectrum staff a great deal. It has been a pleasure working with Cathy for the past 2 years.

Joe has shown a strong ability and interest in many of the Spectrum activities presented to the class this year. He has distinguished himself in the areas of visual arts and numbers.

Joe's efforts in the area of visual arts are impressive for a child his age. What is most striking is his comfort and effectiveness in using a wide variety of media. These include paint, markers, collage, wood, and styrofoam. In drawings, Joe has shown an unusual sensitivity to color, composition and detail. His drawings consist of both complex representations and designs. In one drawing, Joe drew an extremely detailed underwater scene including a half-dozen distinctively different fish, an underwater vehicle, a whale spouting water, and flecks of "super red fish food." In another drawing, he drew a Native American with his donkey after carefully looking at a similar picture on the wall of the classroom. He added stripes of face paint in alternating colors and a large headdress complete with dozens of feathers. Joe's use of space is also very effective. He uses the whole page for his compositions, relating individual parts to one another and to the page as a whole. Joe's three-dimensional sculptures are outstanding as well. He exhibits an understanding and awareness of design and composition "all the way around" his creations. Informal observations of Joe in the classroom have shown that he can spend a long time working on a single painting or drawing and that he enjoys reworking many of them over and over again.

Joe has revealed a strong competence with numbers and number concepts. When playing the Dinosaur Game, a Spectrum activity centered around numbers and number concepts, his counting was a bit inconsistent, but he understood the strategy component of the game. When given the choice of a die that had five out of six signs meaning that he could move his gamepiece forward or a die that had five out of six signs meaning he could move backward, he chose the die that would help him to win and articulated the reason for the choice. He also correctly chose the move that would be most beneficial to him and the move that would be least beneficial to the adult, his opponent in the game.

Whereas earlier in the year Joe appeared to have some difficulty counting accurately, while playing the Bus Game in the spring he exhibited an outstanding facility with numbers for a child his age. He devised a successful method of using different-colored chips to help him keep a running tally of figures entering and exiting a toy bus at a series of station stops. Later in the activity, he was able to calculate in his head the number of figures entering and exiting the bus at the various stops.

Joe has also demonstrated a strong interest in the Discovery Area of the classroom. At the very beginning of the year, Joe spent a lot of time looking at animal bones and trying to figure out how the pieces fit together. This interest has persisted throughout the year. Joe often brings in an assortment of his pets from home to put in the Discovery Area and tell the children about during show and tell. In addition, he made a remarkably accurate sculpture of a bone out of clay. Based on these observations, we feel that Joe might enjoy additional opportunities to explore the natural world. The Children's Museum and the Museum of Science both have excellent displays and resources in this area.

In an activity that involved taking apart and reassembling two small food grinders, Joe showed a competence with and understanding of mechanical objects. He approached the task in a straightforward, serious, and focused manner and completed it with very little help from the adult. Joe was attentive to detail and demonstrated an understanding of the causal connection between the various parts of the objects.

Joe was enthusiastic and energetic in his approach to many of the Spectrum activities. He showed that he was capable of extremely focused work in areas in which he was particularly interested, such as the visual arts and natural science. There were, however, some activities in which Joe chose not to engage. For example, he chose not to participate in the two music activities and the storytelling activity. He expressed an interest in the materials themselves, asking how things were made and where things came from, but did not always show an interest in the structured activities related to the materials.

At first, Joe also was reluctant to participate in creative movement. He had some difficulty with the structure of the movement sessions early in the year. He would usually choose to be in the "audience" rather than participate and would sometimes disrupt the group and express his disdain for the movement activities. As the year progressed, Joe became an active member of the creative movement sessions. He generated some inventive movement ideas for the group and participated willingly in most of the group's activities.

Over time, Joe became more comfortable with the one-to-one format of the Spectrum activities. This enabled him to share his ideas more freely and make apparent the strengths and interests that he had in a variety of areas.

Dear Parents,

We would like to thank you and your child for participating in Project Spectrum this year. The time we have spent with the children in the P.M. Fours has been rich and rewarding.

Our staff members have had many opportunities to work with and learn about your child on an individual basis, particularly in the course of Spectrum activities. As you know, these activities are designed to assess children's strengths in a range of intellectual areas (art, language, math, movement, music, science, and social understanding). Throughout the year, your child chose whether he or she wanted to participate in the activities being offered. Based on your child's participation in these activities, we compiled the Spectrum Profile enclosed in this package. You may wish to read another enclosure, the Description of Spectrum Activities, to understand better what each activity involved and how your child responded.

In the Spectrum Profile, we have described the areas of interest and ability, as well as the areas of relative difficulty, that your child demonstrated during the Spectrum activities. We did not make specific comments about those areas in which your child resembled his or her peers. In these cases you can assume that your child is performing at a level appropriate for his or her age. Since this is only the 2nd year in which the activities have been used in the classroom, we do not have the information needed to compare the children from the Eliot-Pearson community with other children of their age group. Instead, the profile tends to reflect the relative abilities and interests of each child and those cases in which a child demonstrated unusual ability in relation to the class as a whole.

We hope that you can learn from this profile, but also recognize its limitations. Many factors influence a child's performance on activities. Any assessment will miss certain features and none can claim to be definitive. Please regard these comments as one more view of your child, a view that should be balanced by your own observations.

In some cases, the profile includes suggestions for activities that parents can conduct with their children. We have made these suggestions in order to challenge children in an area of strength, support them in an area of weakness, or provide enjoyment in an area in which they demonstrate strong interest. In no way, however, do we suggest that you direct your child to participate in these activities if he or she does not want to do so.

Also included in this package is the Project Spectrum Parent Activities Manual, offering ideas for activities in each Spectrum area. The activities are easy to set up and, for the most part, require no special materials. The manual closes with a list of community resources offering programs and activities for the preschool child.

We eagerly welcome your responses, questions, concerns, and any comments on the information presented in your child's profile. We encourage you to telephone us at 495-4342 between 9 a.m. and 5 p.m. Or, please fill out and return the Parent Response Form in the self-addressed, stamped envelope we have enclosed.

Again, we wish to thank you and your child for participating in Project Spectrum.

With best wishes,

The Project Spectrum Staff

APPENDIX E: SPECTRUM PROFILE PARENT RESPONSE FORM

Child's Name _____   Parent's Name _____

Date _____

What was your overall response to the information presented in your child's Spectrum Profile?

What information in your child's profile surprised you the most?

Was there anything important that you felt was missing from the profile?

Do you plan to do anything differently based on the information in the profile?

Comments:

APPENDIX F: DESCRIPTION OF SPECTRUM ACTIVITIES

MOVEMENT ACTIVITIES

Creative Movement: Children participate in creative movement sessions every 2 weeks throughout the school year. This ongoing curriculum focuses on children's abilities in five areas of dance and creative movement: sensitivity to rhythm, expressiveness, body control, generation of movement ideas, and responsiveness to music. Teachers use a balance of semistructured activities (such as Simon Says) and more open-ended activities (such as interpretive dancing to music). The sessions last approximately 20 minutes.

Obstacle Course: In the spring, an outdoor obstacle course provides children with the opportunity to participate in sequences involving complex and combined movements. The course includes a long jump, a balance beam, an obstacle run, and a hurdle jump. These stations draw upon skills found in many different sports, such as coordination, timing, balance, and power.

LANGUAGE ACTIVITIES

Storyboard Activity: The Storyboard Activity is designed to provide a concrete but open-ended framework in which a child can create stories. Children are asked to tell a story using a storyboard equipped with an ambiguous-looking landscape, foliage, dwellings, and assorted figures, creatures, and props (e.g., king, dragon, and jewel box). The activity measures a range of language skills, including complexity of vocabulary and sentence structure, use of narrative voice and dialogue, thematic coherence, and expressiveness.

Reporter Activities: The Reporter Activities assess a child's ability to describe an event she has experienced. In the first activity, the child watches a movie and then is asked a series of questions about it. Her answers are scored in terms of accuracy of content, complexity of vocabulary, level of detail, and sentence structure. Weekend News assesses similar skills, but is conducted throughout the year. Every week or 2, the children pretend to be reporters and tell what they did over the weekend. Their accounts, which are frequently a combination of real world and fantasy events, are recorded by an adult and collected in a special notebook. The notebook provides multiple samples of a child's reporting skills that can be reviewed throughout the year, and also indicates the level of the child's interest.

MATHEMATICS ACTIVITIES

Dinosaur Game: The Dinosaur Game is designed to measure the child's understanding of number concepts, counting skills, ability to adhere to rules, and use of strategy. The game consists of a game board with a picture of a large dinosaur, wooden dice, and small plastic dinosaurs for game pieces. The object of the game is for the small dinosaurs to escape from the hungry mouth of the large dinosaur. Two players take turns throwing dice to determine the direction and the number of spaces they each can move. At the end of the game, the child is permitted to arrange the dice to her own best advantage, revealing how well she understands the rules.

Bus Game: The purpose of the Bus Game is to assess the child's ability to create a useful notation system, perform mental calculations, and organize number information with one or more variables. The Bus Game consists of a cardboard bus, a game board with four bus stops, figures that get on and off the bus, and two sets of colored chips. In the game, the child is asked to keep track of how many people are riding the bus as it makes a number of stops. Each trip becomes increasingly challenging. For some trips the child uses colored chips to keep count of the passengers, whereas for other trips she is asked to keep count in her head.

SCIENCE ACTIVITIES

Discovery Area: The Discovery Area is a year-round area of the classroom devoted to natural science activities. Activities include caring for small animals, growing plants, and examining a range of natural materials such as rocks and shells. While the Discovery activities are not formally scored, teachers use a checklist to record information about children's observations and their appreciation and understanding of natural phenomena. For example, some children notice similarities and dissimilarities between materials as well as changes over time; others ask questions based on their observations in order to find out more about an item in the area.

Treasure Hunt Game: The Treasure Hunt Game is designed to assess the child's ability to make logical inferences. Before the game starts, different types of "treasure" are hidden under a number of different flags. The object of the game is for the child to figure out the rule governing the placement of the treasures, and use this rule to predict where she will find particular types of objects. The child is given a color-coded box that she may use to keep track of the treasures she finds but is not instructed in how to use it. The way in which the child uses the box to sort the treasures can reflect how well she organizes information and can also help her figure out the rule.

Sink and Float Activity: The Sink and Float Activity is used to assess a child's ability to generate hypotheses based on her observations and to conduct simple experiments. The child is shown a tub of water and an assortment of floating and sinking materials. Then, she is asked to make a series of predictions about the objects and to generate a hypothesis to explain their behavior. The child is also encouraged to try out her own ideas for exploring and experimenting with the materials.

Assembly Activity: The Assembly Activity is designed to measure the child's mechanical ability. The child is presented with two food grinders to take apart and put back together. Successful completion of the activity depends on fine motor skills and visual-spatial abilities as well as a range of observational and problem-solving abilities. This activity, in particular, reveals important cognitive skills that might be overlooked in more traditional programs.

SOCIAL ACTIVITIES

Classroom Model: The purpose of the Classroom Model is to assess the child's ability to observe and analyze social events and experiences in her classroom. The child is presented with a small replica of her classroom, complete with furnishings and wooden figures with photographs of classmates and teachers on them. In much the same way that she would play with a doll house, the child can arrange the figures in the classroom model to reflect her understanding of peers, teachers, and social experiences. The child is asked questions about her own preferences for activities and friendships as well as the preferences and friendships of the child's classmates. Awareness of social roles (e.g., which children act as leaders or facilitators) is probed as well.

Peer Interaction Checklist: Teachers use a checklist to help them observe closely and assess the ways in which children interact with peers. After completing the checklist, teachers determine whether a child consistently assumes any of four distinctive social roles: leader, facilitator, independent player, or team player. Each role is associated with specific types of behavior. For example, a child identified as a facilitator often enjoys sharing information with or helping other children; a child who assumes the role of leader often attempts to organize other children.

VISUAL ARTS ACTIVITIES

Art Portfolios: Throughout the school year, each child's artwork is collected in a portfolio. These portfolios include drawings, paintings, collages, and three-dimensional pieces. Twice a year, teachers can review and assess the contents according to criteria that include the child's use of lines and shapes, color, space, detail, and representation and design. The child's preferred medium is noted also.

Structured Activities: In addition to the portfolios, four structured art activities are introduced to the class each year and assessed on criteria similar to those used in the portfolio assessment. Children are asked to complete three drawings and one three-dimensional task. These activities give every child in the group the chance to respond to the same assignment and interact with the same materials.

MUSIC ACTIVITIES

Singing Activity: The Singing Activity is designed to assess the child's ability to maintain accurate pitch and rhythm while singing, and her ability to recall a song's musical properties. During the activity, the child is asked to sing her favorite song and a popular children's song. The child is also asked to recall a song taught to the class prior to the activity.

Music Perception Activity: The purpose of the Music Perception Activity is to assess a child's ability to discriminate pitch in different situations. In the first part of the activity, the first four phrases of three familiar tunes are played on a tape recorder and the child is asked to identify the tunes as soon as she recognizes them. During the next part of the task, the child listens to different versions of a familiar tune and is asked to identify which are correct and which are incorrect. In the last components of the activity, the child plays two pitch-matching games using Montessori bells, which look identical but produce different tones.

WORKING STYLES

Working Styles Checklist: The Working Styles Checklist helps teachers examine the ways in which a child approaches materials and tasks. Teachers fill out the checklist for each child after she completes each Spectrum activity. Examples of working styles include persistent, playful, focused, reluctant to engage, and eager to transform the task to suit personal interests. The checklist helps teachers identify whether there are particular domains or types of situations in which the child works most effectively. For example, the child may be focused when working on assembly or visual arts projects, but easily distracted in other domains; or, the child may be confident when performing highly structured tasks, but hesitant when asked to make up a story or experiment with materials.

APPENDIX G: PROJECT SPECTRUM PARENT ACTIVITIES MANUAL

Valerie Ramos-Ford

Table of Contents

Introduction 218

I.   Number Activities 219

II.   Science Activities 222

III. Assembly Activities 225

IV.   Music Activities 227

V.   Language Activities 229

VI.   Visual Arts Activities 231

VII. Movement Activities 234

VIII. Social Activities 236

IX.   Project Spectrum Community Resources List 237

Introduction

The Project Spectrum Parent Activities Manual is a collection of games and activities for parents and children to enjoy together. It is divided into several sections that correspond to each of the areas addressed by Project Spectrum. The activities are easy to set up and, for the most part, require readily available materials. At the end of each section, we have included suggestions for additional resources pertaining to each area such as activity books, children's books, tapes, or CDs which may also be of interest to your child.

The Activities Manual is meant to be an introduction to the enormous range of educational materials, resources, and activities that are available for today's young children. We encourage you to explore a wide variety of toys, games, activities, and experiences with your child, not just in the areas in which she shows promise or a natural interest, but in all areas.

We also encourage you to look within your community for programs and activities geared toward preschoolers and their families. Libraries, museums, and community groups are suggestions of places where you might begin your inquiry. The manual closes with a list of community resources in the Boston area. These can serve as an example of what may be available in your own communitiy.

Finally, remember that the emphasis of the activities should be on exploration and fun. They will offer you and your child opportunities to play and learn together. There is no right or wrong way to carry them out, and the ideas your child might offer for changing or elaborating any given activity will likely lead to even more exciting discoveries and experiences!

I. Number Activities

—MAKE A CALENDAR

Materials: 16" by 20" piece of posterboard
Clear contact paper
Markers
Yardstick or ruler
Construction paper
Scissors

Help your child make six evenly spaced vertical lines and six evenly spaced horizontal lines across the poster board to form a basic grid for a calendar. Above the columns, write the days of the week beginning with Sunday. Then cover the posterboard with clear contact paper so that your child can tape things to the calendar and remove them month by month without damaging the posterboard.

Each month, your child can cut shapes out of construction paper, number them, and paste them on the calendar. Children sometimes enjoy making cutouts that reflect a special feature of the upcoming month. For example, hearts might be used in February in honor of Valentine's Day, or umbrellas for the rainy days of April. Your child can also make cutouts for special occasions such as birthdays and holidays. At the beginning of each month, help your child put the first paper cut-out on the correct day of the week. Each morning she can put a numbered cutout on the calendar and count how many days of the month have passed

—MAKE A BOARD GAME

Materials: Large piece of cardboard or posterboard
Markers, crayons, or colored pencils
Dice (or small wooden cubes to make dice) or a spinner
Stickers
Game pieces (small figures, toy cars, etc.)

Board games can help children learn about and practice number skills. Using the supplies listed above, you can help your child create a number game of her own.

The game can be a simple counting game or can include a wider range of number-related concepts. For example, a spinner or a die might have numbers on it which tell how many spaces the player can move her game piece. Another die might have symbols on it that tell the direction in which to move (e.g., + for moving forward and - for moving backward).

—GROWTH CHART

Materials: 5' piece of paper (approx. 6" to 12" wide)
Yardstick
Markers, crayons, and so on
Decorative stickers

Place paper on the floor or any spacious surface. Help your child line up the yardstick along one side of the paper and point out the inch marks. Your child can then make a small line on the paper next to each inch mark. Continue until there are inch marks all the way up the side of the paper. Next, help your child count and number the inch marks from 1 to 60. The basic chart is now complete and your child can decorate it as she chooses. Your child and you can place stickers on the chart to mark her height every few months. Each time a sticker is placed on the chart, encourage your child to figure out how much she has grown since the last time and how many total inches she measures.

—ESTIMATING GAMES

Estimating games can be played with many different materials; here are a few examples.

Materials: Boxes, jars, bowls, or paper cups of different sizes
   Measuring cups
   Balance scale
   An assortment of small objects such as shells, rocks, coins, small toys

Encourage your child to explore the materials in a variety of ways. You can stimulate her ideas and play by asking questions about the materials. For example, you can ask: How many shells can this small cup hold? Now can you guess how many this bigger cup can hold? How many of these cups could hold more than 10 nuts? Fewer than 5? Encourage your child to ask you questions as well, and discover some answers together.

—SORTING/CLASSIFYING GAMES

Sorting and classifying games can be played with many different materials, from baseball cards to seashells. Any of the following household items can be used to set up such an activity.

Materials: Egg cartons
   Muffin pans
   Ice cube trays
   Small boxes
   Baby food jars
   Assorted small objects such as buttons, dried beans, unshelled nuts

Questions: How can you use the egg carton to find out how many of each color button there are in this pile? Which color do you have the most of? What other ways can you think of in which to group the buttons together? Color? Size? Number of holes?

—MAKE A GEOBOARD

Materials: 12" square block of wood (1" to 2" thick)
   36 nails (same size)
   Assorted rubber bands

GeoBoards are an excellent and entertaining way for your child to explore geometric shapes. She can make an endless number of shapes and designs by simply stretching rubber bands over nails hammered into a board.

```
*    *    *    *    *

*    *    *    *    *

*    *    *    *    *

*    *    *    *    *

*    *    *    *    *
```

—FINGER PLAYS AND COUNTING SONGS

There are many finger plays and songs that are centered around counting skills, and many books that parents can use to learn and share these activities with their children.

—COOKING ACTIVITIES

Cooking with children is a wonderful way to practice number concepts such as counting and measuring. Choose recipes that are easy for children to follow, and encourage your child to help with the measuring and counting of ingredients as well as the mixing and preparing.

—ADDITIONAL RESOURCES

Anno, M. *Anno's Counting Book*. Crowell, 1987

Carle, E. *The Hungry Caterpillar*. Putnam, 1984, 1986.

Cave, K. *Out for the Count: A Counting Adventure*. Scribner, 1992.

Coglin, M. L. *One Potato, Two Potato, Three Potato, Four! 165 Chants for Children*. Gryphon House, 1990.

Coyle, R. *My First Cookbook*. Workman, 1985.

Maccarone, G. *Monster Math*. Scholastic, 1995.

II. Science Activities

—GROW A GARDEN

There are many ways for children to learn about how plants grow. Here are a few simple suggestions.

Sprout Jars

Materials: Medium-sized mason jar or shatterproof plastic container
Alfalfa seeds or dried beans
Gauze

Place 1 or 2 teaspoons of alfalfa seeds in the bottom of the jar. Add 2 or 3 teaspoons of water and shake jar gently to moisten seeds. Cover the jar with a piece of gauze and place a rubber band around the mouth of the jar to hold it in place. In about three days, seeds will begin to sprout. Seeds need to be kept moist, not wet. Check daily to see if the seeds are moist. Add a few teaspoons of water at a time as needed. Shake the jar gently to fluff up the sprouts every day. Sprouts can be eaten after a week or so.

Growing Seeds

Materials: Any variety of seeds or dried beans
A few small flower pots
Potting soil
Plastic tray

Fill flower pots halfway with potting soil. Moisten with water and let stand for a few hours. Add a few seeds or beans to each pot, cover with a little soil and water thoroughly. Ideally, the soil should be kept moist, not wet, but allow your child to explore her own ideas about taking care of the plant. By growing seeds or beans in separate pots, she can experiment with how to best care for each pot. For example, one pot could be placed in strong sunlight and another in the dark, or one pot could be kept wet and another dry. By experimenting, your child will learn what factors are most important when growing the seedlings. Growing seeds can begin as an indoor activity and then become an outdoor activity as the plants develop.

Rooting Plants

Materials: Plant cuttings
Clear plastic containers
Water

Help your child place plant cuttings in water in a clear plastic container so that she can watch how root systems develop. When the cutting has a few strong roots, it can be transferred to soil. Eventually, you can take cuttings from the new plant and continue the cycle.

—MAKE A BIRD FEEDER

There are many different ways in which to make bird feeders. The following suggestions are easy for preschoolers.

Milk Container Feeder: Cut large windows in the four sides of a half-gallon milk container. Make two holes through the top of the container and tie a string through each hole. Fill the container with birdseed. Hang it outside a window or wherever you can see the birds while they feed.

Pinecone Feeder: Spread some peanut butter on a large pinecone. Then roll it in birdseed and hang it outside.

Tub Feeder: Make four holes in opposite sides of a plastic tub or small cardboard box. Margarine and yogurt containers work well. Tie a string through each hole and fill the tub with birdseed. Hang outside.

—RUBBINGS

Making rubbings and prints are exciting and colorful ways in which to explore the different patterns and textures of natural objects. A variety of natural items can be used for making rubbings.

Suggested materials: Leaves
Pieces of wood
Shells
Rocks
Crayons or chalk
Paper

Have your child place a piece of paper over a flat piece of wood, leaf, etc. Show her how to rub the broad side of a crayon or piece of chalk back and forth over the paper until the lines and grain of the natural object show up clearly on the paper. Then compare rubbings from different objects.

—FEEL BOXES

Feel boxes are a good way for children to become aware of their sense of touch as a way to find out more about the world. Size, shape, texture, and weight are some of the properties that can be explored.

Materials: Small plastic container (yogurt, margarine)
Stretch sock

Feel Objects: cotton balls, rocks, pinecones, dried beans, shells, feathers, coins, small toys, anything with interesting texture

Place one type of object in the container. Stretch the sock over the container until the container is completely covered. Your child can then put her hand into the sock to feel the object inside and make guesses about what the item is. Ask your child to describe what she feels. For example, is it soft or hard? Rough or smooth? Heavy or light?

—CLASSIFICATION COLLAGE

In this activity, your child learns about classification by placing creatures and objects where they belong: on land, in the water, or in the air.

Materials: Three 8" by 10" pieces of posterboard
Nature and other magazines
Scissors
Markers, crayons

Give your child a variety of old magazines. Ask if she can find and cut out pictures of different people, animals, and vehicles. When your child has a collection of interesting pictures, have her choose one piece of posterboard to be the sky. Ask if any of her cut-out people or things belong in the sky. She can then paste them on the first piece of posterboard. Do the same for land and water. Discuss things that might fit in more than one category (e.g., alligators on land and water).

—WATER PLAY

Water play presents many opportunities for discovery and experimentation. Children can experiment with sinking and floating objects, funnels, sieves, siphons, and other containers and tubes in the kitchen sink, the bathtub, a pool, or a small container of water—anywhere there's water!

Materials: Assorted sinking and floating objects such as marbles, straws, corks, sponges, film canisters, small rocks, Ping- Pong balls

—ADDITIONAL RESOURCES

Alexander, H. *Look Inside Your Brain,* Grosset & Dunlap/Putnam, 1990.

Cole, J. *The Magic Schoolbus* (series of books and videotapes). Scholastic.

Ingoglia, G. *Look Inside a Tree,* Grosset & Dunlap/Putnam, 1989.

Ingoglia, G. *Look Inside Your Body,* Grosset & Dunlap/Putnam, 1989.

Ingoglia, G. *Look Inside The Earth,* Grosset & Dunlap/Putnam, 1991.

Kite, L. P. *Gardening Wizardry for Kids.* Barrons, 1995.

Kohl, M. & Potter, J. *Science Arts: Discovering Science Through Art Activities.* Bright Ring/Gryphon House, 1991.

Milord, S. *The Kids' Nature Book.* Williamson Press, 1989.

Otto, C. *I Can Tell by Touching.* HarperCollins, 1994.

Rockwell, R., Sherwood, E., & Williams, R. *Hug a Tree—and Other Things to Do Outdoors With Children.* Gryphon House, 1983, 1990.

Williams, R., Rockwell, R., & Sherwood, E. *Mudpies to Magnets.* Gryphon House, 1991.

III. Assembly Activities

—MARBLE LABYRINTHS

Materials: Hardwood or other sturdy blocks
Paper towel rolls
Tape
Marbles

You can help your child build her own marble run out of household materials. Use the blocks as the foundation and side supports for the paper towel roll runs. To make horizontal marble runs, cut the cardboard tubes in half so that you can see the marble running through. To create vertical drops, leave the paper towel rolls intact. Cut the rolls into various sizes and help your child tape them to the blocks. You may wish to let your child experiment with just the marbles and blocks first, and introduce the paper towel rolls later.

—SIMPLE HARDWARE

Materials: Springs
Hinges
Latches
Small locks and keys
Nuts and bolts
Screwdriver
Wrench

Let your child explore the materials, describe any uses of the hardware with which she is familiar, and make suggestions about other possible uses. Next, give your child pieces of wood, Styrofoam, or cardboard boxes and let her go to work!

—TAKE APART A MACHINE

Materials: Any old machines that can be taken apart easily; for example:
Flashlights
Mechanical typewriter
Adding machine
Telephone

Children enjoy taking apart and examining a variety of simple machines and household items. Talk with your child about how the various pieces might work together to make the machine work and how you might put everything back together. Ask questions such as "What if we put the pieces together in a different way?" or "What if we leave one piece out?"

—IMAGINARY MACHINES AND INVENTIONS

Give your child with a variety of building toys and materials. Brainstorm with your child about different imaginary machines, vehicles, or other items to create and build. For example, help your child create a washing machine for a mouse, a car for a toad, or an amusement park ride.

Materials: Spools
Pipe cleaners
Thin wire
Magnets
Sturdy paper plates
Small pieces of construction paper

Small boxes of various shapes
Paper towel rolls cut to varying sizes
Tape
Glue
Rubber bands

—MAKE A PUZZLE

Materials: Large piece of paper or posterboard
Markers
Magazines
Cardboard or posterboard
Scissors
Paste

Give your child an assortment of magazines out of which she can cut pictures. When your child finds a picture she likes, she may cut it out and paste it onto a piece of cardboard or posterboard. When the paste dries, cut the picture into a number of pieces in order to make it a puzzle.

—OUTLINE PUZZLES

Materials: Large piece of paper or posterboard
Markers
An assortment of familiar items (keys, paper clips, small toys, blocks, leaves, etc.)

Lay the objects on a large piece of paper or posterboard. Ask your child to outline each object with a magic marker, helping if necessary. Next, remove the items from the paper and place them in a small box or bag. Your child can try to match the items to the outlines on the paper.

—ADDITIONAL ACTIVITIES

A number of commercially available games and building sets allow children to experiment with assembly and the relationship of structure and function. These include Construx, Tinker Toys, K-Nex, Erector sets, and an assortment of plastic gears sets.

—ADDITIONAL RESOURCES

Barton, B. *Building a House*. Greenwillow Books, 1981.
Butterfield, M. *Ships*. Dorling-Kindersley, 1994.
Butterfield, M. *Bulldozers*. Dorling-Kindersley, 1995.
Johnstone, M. *Planes*. Dorling-Kindersley, 1994.
Johnstone, M. *Cars*. Dorling-Kindersley, 1994.

IV. Music Activities

—MAKE PERCUSSION INSTRUMENTS (SHAKERS)
Materials: Any small container with a tight fitting lid (film canisters/yogurt containers with lids)
      Rice
      Paper clips
      Beans
      Other small objects

Have your child fill small containers with different materials (e.g., paper clips, rice, dry pasta). Your child can then use the shakers as simple percussion instruments, playing them along with her favorite music.

For a different experience, ask your child to shake the containers and guess what is inside. She can also put the same materials in pairs of containers and then shake the containers to match the pairs that sound the same. You and your child can make an assortment of other simple instruments using common household items such as empty food containers, rubber bands, wooden blocks, pots and pans.

—WATER BOTTLES
Materials: Assorted bottles
      Mallet
      Water

Your child can explore sound production using bottles filled with different amounts of water. Let your child experiment by gently striking the bottle with a mallet, then adding water or pouring some out and striking the bottle again. Your child can also use different tools to strike the bottles (e.g., a spoon or a pencil), and compare the sounds produced.

—SOUND IDENTIFICATION GAME
Materials: Tape recorder
      Household items and appliances

You and your child can make a tape of familiar sounds (e.g., a telephone ringing, a door closing, water running, a dog barking). Play the tape back and ask your child to identify the sounds. To vary this experience, record family members and friends talking and singing. Ask your child to identify whose voice she hears. She might enjoy making tapes to challenge others with as well.

—NEW WORDS FOR OLD SONGS
You and your child can add new verses to the songs that she is familiar with and enjoys. For example, replace "Old MacDonald" with your child's name and ask what kind of animal she would like to have on her farm. Vary this song further by using the tune to sing about other places, such as a toy store.

—OTHER ACTIVITIES
Look at a wordless book with your child. Make up your own song based on the pictures (e.g., sing about a cow in a picture book of animals). Then invite your child to make up a song (e.g., about the horse). Or you could suggest, "Instead of reading this book, let's sing it. What do you think it would sound like?" Your child might also enjoy playing a guessing game about the songs she knows. Rather than singing the words, take turns humming the tunes and guessing what songs they are.

Music varies in terms of its tempo (fast/slow), dynamics (loud/soft), and pitch (high/low). To enhance your child's sensitivity to these elements, you can play a number of games. Compare running to walking. Help your child to feel the difference in her pulse when she moves quickly and slowly. Create the sounds of a mouse creeping and an elephant stomping. Sing songs in a whisper and a loud voice. Pretend to take an elevator ride. As you go up, make your voice higher; as you go down, make it lower.

—ADDITIONAL RESOURCES

Blood, P., & Patterson, A. (Eds.). *Rise Up Singing: A Group Singing Songbook.* Sing Out Publications, Bethlehem, PA, 1992.

Guilmartin, K. *Music and Your Child: A Guide for Parents and Caregivers* [Tape, songbook, and guide]. Music and Movement Center, Princeton, NJ, 1990.

Raffi. *Singable Songs for the Very Young.* NY: Crown Publishers, 1976.

Raffi. *Singable Songs for the Very Young.* Shoreline: MCA 1976, MCAD #10037.

Raffi. *Baby Beluga,* [Music CD]. Shoreline: MCA 1980, MCAD #10036.

Raffi. *Baby Beluga,* NY: Crown Publishers, 1990.

V. Language Activities

—TALK ABOUT YOUR ARTWORK

Materials: One of your child's drawings, paintings, collages, or sculptures
Construction paper
Markers
Glue

When your child produces a special work of art, ask her to tell you about it. For example, help her to display a special drawing or painting by mounting it on a piece of construction paper that is slightly larger than the drawing itself. Some questions you might ask include: Tell me about this drawing. Is there a story that goes with the picture? Is it a picture of someone or something special to you? Write down what your child tells you on the construction paper. Eventually, she might want to make a book of these drawings.

—MAKE A STORYBOARD

Materials: Large piece of cardboard, posterboard, or felt for the base
Assorted figures and props
Markers, crayons, or some or all of these

Storyboards can be intriguing vehicles through which children can tell stories. A storyboard can include any props that your child wishes to incorporate into her story. Some suggestions include small figures (people, animals, imaginary creatures), trees and bushes, shelters (e.g., houses made out of small boxes), and props that suggest story ideas (e.g., a suitcase, treasure box, magic wand). Your child may decorate the board itself as well by painting or drawing grass, ponds, and other features to create a scene in which their stories can take place.

—NEWS REPORTER

Your child might enjoy pretending to be a news reporter. She could interview family and friends, asking questions such as, What did you do last weekend? What are your favorite foods? What do you like to do? This activity allows children to practice their verbal skills through conversation with family members and friends. Your child might enjoy using props such as a note pad and pencil to "take notes" or may ask you to help write words down. A tape recorder, if available, would enable your child to play back the questions she asked and the answers she received.

—MAKE A PUPPET

Children can easily make their own puppets for storytelling and imaginative play. The following methods use household materials, require little adult supervision, and allow children to create a wide variety of character puppets.

Paper Bag Puppets

Materials: Small paper bags
Construction paper cut-outs
Stickers
Yarn
Glue
Glitter
Markers and crayons

Sock Puppets

Materials: Old socks
Yarn
Felt or fabric scraps
Glue
Buttons

—CHAIN STORIES

A "chain story" is started by one person and continued, in turns, by others. For example, you might begin by saying, "Once there was a large castle in a forest. It belonged to..." Ask your child to tell the next part of the story. Take turns until the story comes to an end. This game can be played with two or more people, and is a good activity for involving older and younger siblings. You can also make props or storytelling figures available to help children stick to the story line. Some children might find it easier to begin this activity using a familiar story line or familiar characters. For example, you might begin the story by saying, "One day while [*child's name*] was walking through the forest, [*she*] found the Three Bears' house. [*She*] opened the door to see who was inside."

—FURTHER SUGGESTIONS

Your child may be interested in illustrating the stories they tell and making them into books. They can then collect the stories to enjoy again and share with others.

If a tape recorder is available, your child might enjoy taping her stories privately, without an audience, to listen to or share with others at a later date.

After your child makes up a story, invite her to act it out. Suggest adding dress-up clothes, puppets, music, creative movement or some of these to the performance.

—ADDITIONAL RESOURCES

Carson, J. *Tell Me About Your Picture: Art Activities to Help Children Communicate.* Dale Seymour Publications, 1992.

Raines, S., & Canady, R. *Story Stretchers: Activities to Expand Children's Favorite Books.* Gryphon House, 1989.

VI. Visual Arts Activities

If you offer your child a variety of materials, she can devise many visual arts activities of her own. The following materials can be fun to have on hand:

> Crayons, markers, chalk, colored pencils
> Watercolors
> Tempera (poster) paint
> Children's scissors
> Glue
> Sponges
> Assorted brushes and rollers
> Assorted paper (construction, tracing, computer)
> String, yarn
> Small pieces of fabric
> Three-dimensional materials (clay, plasticine, styrofoam, wood)
> Playdough
> Smocks (old T-shirts, oil cloth)

—MAKING AN ART PORTFOLIO

Materials: Large piece of oaktag or posterboard (20" by 24")
Paper punch
Yarn or string
Decorative stickers, glitter, and so on

Many children take a great deal of pride in the artwork they produce. By making a portfolio, your child can create her own safe place to keep special drawings, paintings, and collages. Begin by helping your child fold the oaktag or posterboard in half. Punch three holes on each side: one a few inches down from the open end, one a few inches up from the fold, and one in the middle. Tie a piece of string or yarn loosely through each of the six holes to hold the sides of the portfolio together. Your child can then decorate the portfolio as she chooses and begin to collect their special artwork. You may also want to write any description of the artwork your child shares with you and the date it was created on the back.

—ACTIVITIES WITH PAINT

Using paint brushes is only one way in which children enjoy exploring paint. Many children continue to enjoy using their hands even after they have the fine motor skills necessary to use brushes. There are a number of other materials that can be used to apply paint, such as string, sponges, rollers, squeeze bottles, toy vehicles, and even marbles!

—"BUTTERFLY" PAINTINGS

Materials: Two or three colors of tempera paint
Construction paper

Help your child fold a piece of paper down the center by demonstrating how to line up the corners with one another. Make a crease at the fold. Open the paper and lay it flat. Have your child drop small amounts of different colored paint on one side of the crease. Then have her fold the dry side over the painted side and rub. The rubbing will cause the paint inside the sheet of paper to spread and form a mirror image on the dry side of the paper. Open the paper slowly to find a butterfly-type design.

—DIPPING COLORS

Materials: Paper towels
Dluted food coloring
Small containers for colors

Have your child dip corners of paper towels or crumpled paper towels into the different food colors. This is a good way for children to experiment with color mixing and to develop an understanding of the concept of absorbency.

—PRINT MAKING

Children can use a variety of materials as stamps for making prints: wood blocks with a patterned surface, sponges, cookie cutters, plastic toys, shells, and rocks. Let your child dip the "stamp" into a shallow dish of slightly watered-down tempera paint or rub it on an ink pad with washable ink. Then she can stamp the pattern onto construction paper. Although your child usually will have an idea of which colors to choose, she can create interesting effects using light paints on dark paper and vice versa.

—CREATE A SCULPTURE

Materials: Styrofoam, clay, playdough, beeswax
Pipe cleaners
Ice cream sticks
Wood scraps
Assorted decorative materials such as beads, dried beans, buttons

There are many modeling and recycled materials that your child can use to create three-dimensional artwork. For example, she can make sculptures by gluing together scrap wood of different shapes and sizes or incorporating a variety of materials such as pipe cleaners or ice cream sticks into her play with modeling clay or playdough.

—RECIPE FOR PLAYDOUGH

Ingredients: 2 cups cold water
1 cup salt
2 cups flour
4 teaspoons cream of tartar
Food coloring or 1 packet of a powdered flavored drink mix (i.e. Kool-Aid)

Making playdough is an exciting art activity that incorporates simple number concepts such as counting and measuring. Cook and stir the above ingredients over a medium heat for a few minutes until the mixture thickens to the consistency of mashed potatoes. Remove from pot and lay on waxed paper to cool quickly, and cover with a damp cloth. Playdough will stay soft for several weeks if stored in a plastic bag or airtight container. Sculptures will harden if left to air-dry overnight.

Materials to use with playdough: Ice cream sticks
Small plastic figures
Cookie cutters
Garlic presses
Rolling pins

—COLLAGE MATERIALS

Collages are an excellent way for your child to explore the use of space and how different materials can work together. Collages can include any available odds and ends—the more variety, the better. Here are a few suggestions:

- use any color paper with an assortment of geometric shapes of varying size and color.

- use triangular-shaped background and paste smaller triangular pieces onto it.

- use a dark background and paste onto it scraps and shapes of different, lighter shades of the same color.

- use a white background with assorted scraps of tissue paper. Use liquid starch instead of paste and apply it with a soft brush. Tissue paper will become transparent when wet. New colors can be created by laying one color over another.

- three-dimensional collages on paper or cardboard: Paste on household objects such as dried beans, pasta, rice, seeds, beads, wood scraps, fabric scraps, string, yarn, straws, or Styrofoam.

- collage constructions: paste materials onto cardboard boxes of varying sizes, paper towel rolls, or other objects.

(These ideas are adapted from *Creative Art for the Developing Child* by Clare Cherry [1972, 1990].)

—ADDITIONAL RESOURCES

Carlson, L. *Kids Create! Art Activities for 3–9 Year Olds.* Williamson, 1990

Kohl, M. Mudworks: *Creative Clay, Dough, and Modeling Experiences for Children.* Bright Ring/ Gryphon House, 1989.

Lohf, S. *Things I Can Make With Beads.* Chronicle Books, 1990.

Lohf, S. *Things I Can Make With Boxes.* Chronicle Books, 1990.

Lohf, S. *Things I Can Make With Cloth.* Chronicle Books, 1987, 1989.

Lohf, S. *Things I Can Make With Cork.* Chronicle Books, 1990.

Press, J. *The Little Hands Art Book.* Williamson, Charlotte, VT, 1994.

Wilmes, L., & Wilmes, D. *Exploring Art.* Building Blocks. Gryphon House, 1986.

VII. Movement Activities

—SIMON SAYS

You and your child can create many variations of this traditional game. You might want to begin with a simple version that includes moving major body parts. Whoever takes the role of Simon might say, "Simon says, 'Move your head in a circle.' " A more advanced version of the game might include requests for combined movements such as "put your hands on your head and hop on one foot" or "swim with your arms and march with your feet." You might also suggest more creative movement ideas such as "dance like a cat would" or "melt like an ice cube in the sun." Adults and children may take turns being Simon.

—CHARADES

There are a number of simple versions of charades that children can play. The game can help your child to think through and act out creative movement sequences that evoke a mood or image.

Explain the game to your child by saying, "We're going to play a game in which you have to help me guess what something is without using any words." You can begin by asking her to think of an idea to act out. It is best to pick a category for each game or turn. For example, you might begin with animals: "Think of an animal. Now, without speaking any words, move around so that I can guess what kind of animal you're pretending to be." You and your child might also try to act out some of the following:

Things in nature:	tree in the wind, snowflake, a leaf falling
Familiar objects:	ball, bicycle, swing, automobile, boat
Shapes:	square, triangle, letters of the alphabet
Feelings and moods:	happy, sad, angry, surprised, fearful

—DANCING TO DIFFERENT KINDS OF MUSIC

Many children enjoy listening and moving to different kinds of music. Help your child collect her favorite kinds of music for dancing. Introduce her to different styles and tempos of music. Encourage your child to think about the different ways of moving to each. Your child may also enjoy incorporating props such as scarves, ribbons, balls, or hoops into her dancing.

—BALLOON GAME

Have your child try to keep a balloon afloat for as long as possible. Take turns tapping the balloon into the air with your hands rather than catching and throwing it every time it descends. Variations: Keep the balloon afloat for as long as music is playing, then catch it when the music stops. Use body parts other than the hands to keep the balloon afloat: feet, elbows, top of head.

—RELAYS

Relays are an exciting way for children to develop their sense of balance, agility, and overall coordination. They are also good practice for taking turns and working in teams. The only materials you need for relays are a starting line (which can be made with string, chalk, or a line in the dirt) and some simple props such as balls or balloons for variety. If more than one child is participating, you may suggest that they work together to "beat the clock" rather than have them compete against one other. Here are a few suggestions for relays:

Walking relays:	walking backward, forward, sideways
Jumping relays:	feet together, hopping, leaping

| Animal relays: | move like a crab, a frog, a cat, and so on |
| Spoon relays: | balance a bead or a small ball on a large kitchen spoon and walk as fast as you can |

—MIRROR GAME

Have your child pretend to be a mirror. Explain that when you look in a mirror, the mirror reflects back exactly what you are doing. Take turns pretending to be the mirror. When your child is pretending to be the mirror, she must make all of the movements that someone else does, as accurately as possible. During the next turn, she may choose to lead the game and have someone copy her movements.

—MS. & MR. OPPOSITES

One person at a time is chosen to lead the game. The game is called Ms. & Mr. Opposites because the person who is following the leader does exactly the opposite of what the leader does. For example, if the leader sits down, Ms. or Mr. Opposite stands up. If the leader runs, the other walks, and so on. It may be difficult at first to think of the opposites for some movements, so you might want to brainstorm with your child ahead of time or cut out several pictures of people doing a variety of different things to use to stimulate some ideas. Take turns with your child leading the game.

—ADDITIONAL RESOURCES

Carr, R. *Be a Frog, a Bird, or a Tree: Creative Yoga Exercises for Children.* Colophon Books/ Doubleday 1989.

Fluegelman, A. *The New Games Book.* Dolphin Books, 1990.

Miller, K. *The Outside Play and Learning Book.* Gryphon House, 1989

Orlick, T. *The Cooperative Sports and Games Book.* Pantheon Books, 1978.

VIII. Social Activities

—A BOOK ABOUT ME

Help your child to make a book about herself. In this book, your child can identify her likes and dislikes, friends, and most recently acquired skills. After you write what your child wants to say about herself, suggest drawing pictures or using family photographs to illustrate the book. Making this book together, and adding to it when your child is interested in doing so, communicates to your child that she is an important person and also gives your child an opportunity to reflect on who she is.

—PERSONAL PHOTOGRAPH ALBUMS

Keeping their own photograph album helps children recall experiences with family and friends. Help your child select special and meaningful photographs for the album. Together you can periodically look through it and talk about the people and places in the pictures. Your child might even try taking her own pictures to include.

—WRITING LETTERS

Helping children write a letter to a grandmother or to a special friend opens up new ways in which to communicate with others. Encouraging your child to express and recognize her feelings is an important part of this process. Ask your child if there is someone special she would like to send a letter to. Your child may choose simply to draw a picture or may ask for your help writing words.

—EXPLORING FEELINGS

When your child comes home from preschool or from playing at a friend's house, invite your child to tell you about her day. When your child has had a difficult day, talking with you about it may help her to understand better what happened. When your child has had a good day, sharing it with you extends her positive experience.

As you read stories to your child or look at pictures, take time to discuss their interpersonal dimensions. Why is Sally crying? What could Cynthia do to help her feel better? What makes you mad? Such conversations help children understand their own feelings, those of others, and their relationship with others. Talking with your child will also help you understand your child's feelings and actions.

—OTHER ACTIVITIES

Children can take great pride in contributing to a group effort. When engaged in a cooperative project, call your child's attention to the contributions she is making. Baking muffins, washing the car, and building castles out of blocks are examples of activities that provide you and your child with opportunities to cooperate.

Doing good deeds for others is another way to share positive social efforts and experiences with your child. Brainstorm with your child about small favors, chores, or thoughtful acts you can do for someone special — a sibling, grandparent, teacher, neighbor, or even a stranger in need.

—ADDITIONAL RESOURCES

Cheltenham Elementary School Kindergartners. *We Are All Alike . . . We Are All Different*. Scholastic, 1991.

Dorros, A. *This Is My House*. Scholastic, 1992.

Drescher, J. *Your Family, My Family*. NY: Walker, 1980.

Klamath County YMCA Preschool. *The Land of Many Colors*. Scholastic, 1991.

Oxenbury, H. *The Great Big Enormous Turnip*. Franklin Watts, 1968.

IX. Project Spectrum Community Resources List

This list was created in 1988. Although outdated, it can serve as a model for discovering resources in your own community.

SCIENCE	Programs Offered
The Arnold Arboretum The Arborway Jamaica Plain, MA 02130 (617) 524-1717	
Boston Children's Museum 300 Congress Street Boston, MA 02210 (617) 426-8855	exhibits, hands-on activities, and special programs
Children's Discovery Museum 177 Main Street Acton, MA 01720 (617) 264-4200	exhibits and hands-on activities
Drumlin Farm Wildlife Sanctuary South Great Road Lincoln, MA 01773 (617) 259-9500	farm animals and group activities
Habitat Institute for the Environment 10 Juniper Road Belmont, MA 02178 (617) 489-5050	guided walks and other nature activities
Harvard University Museums of Natural History 24 Oxford Street Cambridge, MA 02138 (617) 495-1910	
Museum of Science and Charles Hayden Planetarium Science Park Boston, MA 02114 (617) 742-6088	
New England Aquarium Central Wharf Boston, MA 02110 (617) 742-8870	

VISUAL ARTS	Programs Offered
Brookline Arts Center 86 Monmouth Street Brookline, MA 02146 (617) 566-5152	art classes
Children's Workshop 1963 Massachusetts Avenue Cambridge, MA 02140 (617) 354-1633	arts and crafts activities
DeCordova Museum School of Art Sandy Pond Road Lincoln, MA 01773 (617) 259-8355	painting and other art classes
Kendall Center for the Arts 226 Beech Street Belmont, MA 02178 (617) 489-4090	drawing, clayworks
Museum of Fine Arts 465 Huntington Avenue Boston, MA 02115 (617) 267-9377	workshops and family art activities
Newton Art Center P.O. Box 330 61 Washington Park Newton, MA 02161 (617) 964-3424	drawing, painting, crafts

MUSIC

All Newton Music School 321 Chestnut Street West Newton, MA 02165 (617) 527-4553	
Powers Music School 380 Concord Avenue Belmont, MA 02178 (617) 484-4696	Kidsongs, eurythmics
Boston Symphony Orchestra Youth Concerts Symphony Hall 251 Huntington Avenue Boston, MA 02115 (617) 266-1492	

MUSIC (cont.)	Programs Offered
Brookline Music School 115 Greenough Street Brookline, MA 02146 (617) 277-4593	introduction to music
The Family Yamaha Music School 123 Harvard Street Brookline, MA 02146 (617) 232-2778	primary music instruction
Longy School of Music 1 Follen Street Cambridge, MA 02138 (617) 876-0956	Dalcroze eurythmics
Malden School of Music 15 Irving Street Malden, MA 02148 (617) 321-3313	keyboard, recorder
New England Conservatory 290 Huntington Avenue Boston, MA 02115 (617) 262-1120	assorted programs

MOVEMENT

The Ballet Center, Inc. 185 Cory Road Brookline, MA 02146 (617) 277-1139	preballet, body games
Powers Music School 380 Concord Avenue Belmont, MA 02178 (617) 484-4696	eurythmics
Brookline Music School 115 Greenough Street Brookline, MA 02146 (617) 277-4593	eurythmics
Children's Workshop 1963 Massachusetts Avenue Cambridge, MA 02138 (617) 354-1633	creative movement

MOVEMENT (cont.)	Programs Offered
Gymnastics Academy of Boston 177 Charlemont Street Newton, MA 02158 (617)964-0334	tumbling, open gym
MJT Dance Company P.O. Box 108 Watertown, MA 02172 (617) 482-0351	modern dance, rhythm and movement
Room for Children 75 Newbury Street Boston, MA 02116 (617) 437-7997	gymnastics
Williams School of the Dance 614 Main Street Malden, MA 02148 (617) 324-3126	tap, ballet

YMCAs and YWCAs

Cambridge: (617) 661-9622	YMCA, 820 Massachusetts Ave. (swimming, crafts)
Malden: (617) 322-3760	YWCA, 54 Washington (swimming, crafts)
Somerville: (617) 625-5050	YMCA, 101 Highland (swimming)

Skating Rinks

Simoni Rink (operated by the Metropolitan District Commission)	155 Gore Street Cambridge, MA 02138 (617) 354-9523
Flynn Rink (MDC)	Woodland Road & Elm Street Medford, MA 02155 (617) 395-8492
Veterans Memorial Rink (MDC)	581 Somerville Avenue Somerville, MA 02143 (617) 623-3523

THEATERS	Programs Offered
Belmont Children's Theater 226 Beech Street Belmont, MA 02178 (617) 489-4380	performances
Boston Children's Theater, Inc. 652 Hammond Street Chestnut Hill, MA 02167 (617) 277-3277	performances
The Loon and Heron Theater for Children 194 Boylston Street Brookline, MA 02146 (617) 232-1715	performances
Puppet Showplace Theater 32 Station Street Brookline, MA 02146 (617) 731-6400	performances
Wheelock Family Theater 180 The Riverway Boston, MA 02215 (617) 734-5203	performances

LIBRARIES

Cambridge:	North Cambridge, 70 Rindge Avenue (storytelling, movies)	(617) 498-9086
Field Branch:	Cambridge Street (preschool films, storytelling)	(617) 498-9083
	Observatory Hill, 178 Huron Avenue (films, storytelling)	(617) 498-9084
	East Cambridge, 66 Sixth Street (preschool films, storytelling)	(617) 498-9082
Medford:	111 High Street (films, storytelling, arts and crafts)	(617) 395-7950
Somerville:	Main Library, 79 Highland Avenue (films, storytelling, arts and crafts, cooking)	(617) 623-5000
	West Branch, 40 College Avenue (films, storytelling, arts and crafts)	(617) 625-1895
Winchester:	80 Washington Street (storytelling)	(617) 721-7140

APPENDIX H: RELATED ARTICLES

Adams, M .L., & Feldman, D. H. (1993). Project Spectrum: A theory-based approach to early education. In R. Pasnak & M. L. Howe (Eds.), *Emerging themes in cognitive development* (Vol. 2, pp. 53–76). New York: Springer-Verlag.

Chen, J. Q. (1993). *Building on children's strengths: Examination of a Project Spectrum intervention program for students at risk for school failure.* Biennial meeting of the Society for Research in Child Development, New Orleans, LA.

Gardner, H., & Hatch, T. (1989). Multiple intelligences go to school. *Educational Researcher, 18*(8), 4–10.

Gardner, H., & Viens, J. (1990). Multiple intelligences and styles: Partners in effective education. *The Clearinghouse Bulletin: Learning/Teaching Styles and Brain Behavior, 4*(2), 4–5.

Gray, J., & Viens, J. (1994). The theory of multiple intelligences: Understanding cognitive diversity in schools. *National Forum, 74*(1), 22–26.

Hatch, T. & Gardner, H. (1986). From testing intelligence to assessing competences: A pluralistic view of intellect. *The Roeper Review, 8,* 147–150.

Hatch, T., & Gardner, H. (1990). If Binet had looked beyond the classroom: The assessment of multiple intelligences. *International Journal of Educational Research,* 415–429.

Krechevsky, M. (1991). Project Spectrum: An innovative assessment alternative. *Educational Leadership, 48*(5), 43–49.

Krechevsky, M., Hoerr, T., & Gardner, H. (1995). Complementary energies: Multiple Intelligences in the lab and in the field. Paper prepared for J. Oakes & K. H. Quartz (Eds.), *Creating new educational communities: Schools and classrooms where all children can be smart* (pp. 166–186). Chicago: National Society for the Study of Education.

Krechevsky, M., & Gardner, H. (1990). The emergence and nurturance of multiple intelligences. In M. J. A. Howe (Ed.), *Encouraging the development of exceptional abilities and talents* (pp. 222–245). Leicester, UK: The British Psychological Society.

Krechevsky, M., & Malkus, U. (1997). Telling their stories, singing their songs. In J. Flood, S. Brice Heath, and D. Lapp (Eds.), *A handbook for literacy educators: Research on teaching the communicative and visual arts* (pp. 305–313). New York: Macmillian.

Malkus, U., Feldman, D. H., & Gardner, H. (1988). Dimensions of mind in early childhood. In A. D. Pelligrini (Ed.), *Psychological bases of early education* (pp. 26–38). Chichester, UK: Wiley.

Ramos-Ford, V., Feldman, D. H., & Gardner, H. (1988). A new look at intelligence through Project Spectrum. *New Horizons for Learning: On the Beam, 8* (3), 6–7, 15.

Ramos-Ford, V., & Gardner, H. (1991). Giftedness from a multiple intelligences perspective. In N. Colangelo & G. Davis (Eds.), *The handbook of gifted education* (pp. 55–64). Boston: Allyn & Bacon.

Viens, J. (1990). Project Spectrum: A pluralistic approach to intelligence and assessment in early education, Part I. *Teaching Thinking and Problem Solving, 12*(2),1–4.

Viens, J. (1990). Project Spectrum: A pluralistic approach to intelligence and assessment in early education, Part II. *Teaching Thinking and Problem Solving, 12*(3), 6–12.

Wexler-Sherman, C., Gardner, H., & Feldman, D. (1988). A pluralistic view of early assessment: The Project Spectrum approach. *Theory Into Practice, 27*(1), 77–83.

APPENDIX I: OTHER MATERIALS AVAILABLE FROM PROJECT SPECTRUM

(1) PROJECT SPECTRUM: EARLY LEARNING ACTIVITIES

Project Spectrum: Early Learning Activities contains nearly 400 activities in eight domains of knowledge (science, math, music, movement, art, language, mechanical, and social understanding) that can be incorporated into the kindergarten and first grade curriculum. The activities were designed to help children develop key abilities in each domain.

(2) SPECTRUM WORKSHOPS

Researchers from Project Spectrum have prepared a set of presentations and workshops on the Spectrum approach ranging in length from one hour to 2 or 3 days. The workshops provide an introduction to the theory of multiple intelligences and an in-depth exploration of some of the assessment and curriculum activities.

(3) BUILDING ON CHILDREN'S STRENGTHS: THE EXPERIENCE OF PROJECT SPECTRUM

Building on Children's Strengths: The Experience of Project Spectrum details Howard Gardner's and David Feldman's theories in accessible, nontechnical language. It shows how the Spectrum research team put the theories to work in preschool and early elementary classrooms, and how other educators have applied the approach in their own schools.

The following people have generously provided their names as contacts regarding the use of the Spectrum approach in a research or applied context or both. Their areas of expertise are listed below their addresses. These people may charge consulting fees.

Dr. Margaret Adams
Consultant
1604 Quail Court
Roanoke Rapids, NC 27870
(919) 537-3748

> *Design and administration of the Spectrum Field Inventory, a set of preschool assessments in six domains*

Loretta Beecher
Kindergarten Teacher
Centennial School
522 Mason Lane
Nampa, ID 83686
(208) 465-2711

> *Spectrum learning centers*
> *Spectrum assessment activities*

Sheila Callahan-Young (Teacher)
Pamela Card (Teacher)
Julie Carter (Teacher)
Alyce McMenimen (Teacher)
Anna O'Connor (Teacher)
Fuller School
Gloucester, MA 01930
(508) 281-9840

> *Application of Spectrum in kindergarten classrooms*
> *Curriculum development*
> *Integrating special needs children in the classroom*

Dr. Jie-Qi Chen
Professor
Erikson Institute
420 North Wabash Avenue
Chicago, IL 60611
(312) 755-2250

> *All phases of Spectrum research*
> *Multiple intelligences/Spectrum workshops*
> *Staff development*
> *Early childhood assessment*

Ronald Eckel
Principal
Furnace Brook School
Furnace Street
Marshfield, MA 02050
(617)834-5025

> *Application of Spectrum in kindergarten classrooms*
> *Curriculum development*
> *Integrating special needs children in the classroom*

Mara Krechevsky
Project Director, Project Spectrum
Project Zero
Harvard Graduate School of Education
323 Longfellow Hall, Appian Way
Cambridge, MA 02138
(617) 495-4342

> *All phases of Spectrum research*
> *Multiple intelligences/Spectrum workshops*
> *Staff development*
> *Early childhood assessment*

Laurie Leibowitz
Early Childhood Teacher/Consultant
15 Northern Road
Hartsdale, NY 10530
(914) 674-4529

> *Spectrum assessment activities*

Dr. Ulla Makus
Consultant
72 Shade Street
Lexington, MA 02173
(617) 862-5986

> *Staff development*
> *Curriculum development*
> *Early childhood assessment*

Dr. Christine McGrath
Superintendent of Schools
Tewksbury Public Schools
139 Pleasant Street
Tewksbury, MA 01876
(508) 851-7347

> *Benefits to special education*
> *Promotion of inclusion programs*
> *Spectrum assessments used as pre-referral and screening instruments*

Miriam Raider-Roth
Teacher/Consultant
113 Pinehurst Avenue
Albany, NY 12203
(518) 459-2883

Portfolio assessment
Staff development
Curriculum development
Spectrum learning centers

Valerie Ramos-Ford
Consultant
298 N. Post Road
Princeton Junction, NJ 08550
(609) 936-9563

Curriculum development
Staff development

Dr. Hilda Rosselli
Department of Special Education
University of South Florida
Tampa, FL 33620
(813) 974-3410

Implementing Spectrum assessment activities in private and commercial
day care centers and with at-risk students
Ongoing training strategies for day care staff

Joyce Rubin
Director of Gifted Programs
Community School District 18
755 East 100 Street
Brooklyn, NY 11236
(718) 927-5100

Staff development
Curriculum development
Early childhood assessment
Parent workshops and nurturing multiple intelligences at home

Debbie Leibowitz (Early Childhood Specialist)
Pamela Prue (formerly Principal, now Dirctor of Early Childhood Services)
Karen Bulman (Teacher/Trainer, Javitz Grant Program)
Carol Hylton (Teacher Specialist)
Sylvia de la Torre-Spencer (English for Speakers of Other Languages)
Barbara Williams (First-Grade Teacher)

Montgomery County Public Schools
850 Hungerford Drive
Rockville, MD 20850
(301/279) 3000

Montgomery Knolls Elementary School
807 Daleview Drive
Silver Spring, MD 20901
301/ 431-7667

Staff development
Curriculum development
Addressing students who speak English as a second language
Addressing potentially learning-disabled students
Individualizing instruction

Janet Stork
Educational Consultant
39 Prospect Hill Rd.
Lexington, MA 02173
(781) 862-9951

Staff development
Curriculum development

Dr. Wilma Vialle
4 Gilmore Street
West Wollongon
N5W 2500 Australia

Implementing Spectrum assessment activities in private and commercial
day care centers and with at-risk students
Ongoing training strategies for day care staff

Julie Viens
Spectrum Researcher
Project Zero
Harvard Graduate School of Education
323 Longfellow Hall, Appian Way
Cambridge, MA 02138
(617) 495-4342

All phases of Spectrum research
Multiple intelligences/Spectrum workshops
Staff development
Early childhood assessment

APPENDIX K: HANDBOOK EVALUATION FORM

1. What parts of the handbook were most helpful?

2. What questions or concerns do you have that were not addressed?

3. Are there sections or aspects that should be changed if we revise this edition in the future?

4. In what ways, if any, have your classroom practices, policies, or research interests changed as a result of reading this handbook? Please describe any changes you made that worked and any that did not work.

5. Additional questions or comments.

Please send this form to: Project Spectrum, Project Zero; Harvard Graduate School of Education; 323 Longfellow Hall, Appian Way; Cambridge, MA 02138.

THANK YOU.